THE FOUR FACES OF THE UNIVERSE

THE FOUR FACES OF THE UNIVERSE

An Integrated View of the Cosmos

Robert M. Kleinman

Published by:
LOTUS PRESS
P.O. Box 325
Twin Lakes, WI 53181 USA
800 824 6396
email: lotuspress@lotuspress.com
website: www.lotuspress.com

ISBN 13: 978-0-9409-8591-9
ISBN 10: 0-9409-8591-8

Library of Congress Control Number: 2006930242

Printed in the United States of America

Frontispiece: Deogarh, Daśāvatāra Temple, relief on the south wall showing Viṣṇu Anantaśāyin

A DESCRIPTION OF THE FRONTISPIECE

Brahmā, the four-faced Hindu god of creation, who can be taken to represent the universe in all of its aspects, is seated on a lotus blossom above the reclining figure of Viṣṇu. Only three of Brahmā's faces are visible in the illustration since the fourth is looking backward. Viṣṇu, the underlying support of the cosmic manifestation, is sleeping on the coils of the giant serpent, Ananta. Both are drifting blissfully on an eternal ocean of milk, indicating the primeval waters of creation. As Viṣṇu sleeps, he dreams of universes to be born. The milk symbolizes the Divine Mother; she is the creative power that turns his dreams into realities. Normally, the lotus plant is shown blooming from Viṣṇu's navel. But here the lotus, with Brahmā seated upon it, is depicted separately above Viṣṇu. The ocean of milk is also not clearly delineated in this sculptural rendition of the myth. The essential point of the myth is clear, though somewhat obscure in the illustration. Without the Divine Mother, Viṣṇu would remain unmanifested and the drama of the universe could not begin.

DEDICATION

With homage

to

Sri Aurobindo
Without whom this far journey
Could not have begun

Table of Contents

List of Illustrations

Plates

Figures

PREFACE

One hesitates to offer the public a book representing a lifetime of inquiry. Doing so can expose an author's innermost personality to the idle curiosity of strangers. I now believe that the risk should be taken. Writing it seemed like chiseling into a block of hard granite, but the attitude that sustained me is exemplified by a remark attributed to the Zen Master Miura Roshi. When presented with a small wooden statue of Bodhidharma, he said that in olden days the carving of a sacred figure was accompanied by three bows before each cut.

This book addresses readers who have a general interest in cosmology. Many people today are dissatisfied with the scientific approach to the universe, but do not know where to find something better. Modern science, while enlarging our picture of the physical universe, fails to offer insight into its meaning. This is not surprising. Broadly speaking, science is a refinement of everyday common sense relying on logic, mathematics, and controlled experiments. It works exceptionally well within its proper domain, but, like common sense, stumbles when exceeding it. The universe is a good example of this: although the *observable* universe can be studied in detail, there is much beyond it that is inaccessible to science. A more comprehensive approach is needed to encompass the universe *as a whole*. We will adopt an integrated view that examines the major types of cosmology and shows how they can be unified in a total vision of the cosmos. Rather than simply compare different theories, my purpose is to *integrate* them. Integration implies becoming "whole or complete," and involves more than a mere synthesis of ideas. Above all, the integration of cosmologies requires an inner center that can bring them all into a single focus.

Our approach will not be purely mental, because mind is incapable of integrating in the way intended. An attempt to establish everything on the basis of thinking misconstrues mind as God (Divine Judge), but it is a confused mixture of truth and falsehood, and thus cannot be God. Far from being the creator and knower of the world, mind is the *problem*. The more unified our vision of the universe becomes, the greater the delight it awakens. If mind is too assertive, it will drive away this delight. Admittedly, we are transitional mental beings who employ thinking in the pursuit of cosmological knowledge. Nevertheless, mind is a limited instrument that should be used with caution and restraint; otherwise, we invite endless controversy. Mind will never reach the perfection it seeks, which lies beyond its scope. At best it arranges our thoughts about the universe in a way that reflects the unity inherent in the nature of things.

To deepen our awareness of cosmic harmony, we rely on a power other than mind existing in the soul. This is the power of feeling, which reveals itself clearly when restless mental activity ceases. For mind only speculates about the universe, but soul experiences it through feeling. We have retained the word "feeling" throughout because of its close association with the experience of delight. It is also meant to indicate a mode of apprehending truth beyond the intellectual capacity of the mind. "Feeling-knowledge" would be more accurate, but is too awkward to bear frequent repetition. Yet the kind of feeling referred to has an inseparable cognitive aspect. Mind as a thinking instrument is linked with the brain, and limited by the latter's neural structure. Sri Aurobindo speaks of higher mental powers that do not depend upon the brain, though they too are subject to a shadow of ignorance. Feeling, on the other hand, is commonly associated with the heart, since there is an inner relation between heart and soul. Although the heart is close to the seat of vital emotions, our spiritual feelings arise from a source deeper than emotion.

While both speculation and feeling have a place in cosmology, the latter is more effective in the search for wholeness. Mind functions as a coordinator of our experience. It synthesizes the wealth of impressions it receives by creating systems of ideas to organize them, but this is not the kind of integration we seek. Mental systems are founded on the pivotal idea of an inner subject of knowledge, or ego, which becomes the focus of everything going on around it. The ego functions as the center of an objective world, but can never achieve wholeness with it. The appearance of this incomplete and hence false self opens a rift between subject and object. As in the story of Pandora's Box, this rift releases all the ills that plague us. There cannot be complete integration where such a duality prevails. The ego plays an important, though limited, role in human evolution. Yet, when we inquire into the nature of this inner subject, we fail to find anything substantial on which to anchor our search. Given sufficient time, the ego will fade away like frozen ice in the heat of the sun; only soul will remain as the true center of one's being.

The integration we are seeking is founded on *soul,* where spiritual feelings arise, *cosmic consciousness*, in which these feelings open out to embrace the whole universe, and the *World Mother*, who brings all things to fruition in the fullness of time. Our thesis is that soul, which perceives things from the center of one's being, is the most reliable guide to knowledge of the unity of the universe. The will to integrate originates in the soul. Thus feeling is our principal means of penetrating depths inaccessible to the mind.

Soul does not merely transcend the physical body, but also must be distinguished from our vital and mental functions. We discover it as an indefinable awareness existing behind them. It is always there, whether we are aware of it or not. Although difficult to detect, since it is not overtly involved in our ordinary activities, it becomes influential when its presence is clearly recognized. The difficulty is primarily mental, because mind has assumed temporary leadership in our lives and does not want to relinquish it. "Soul" is the name for something that can never be grasped as an object. If fish could think, what would the word "water" convey to them, for they spend their entire lives moving within it? This is only a crude analogy that breaks down because fish can be clearly distinguished from water, whereas the soul we intuit is not really separate from the rest of being. On the contrary, it is a golden thread holding the world together. If a descriptive word is wanted, consciousness is better than most, since there would be no awareness of things without it. To complete the analogy, consciousness is the water and soul an individualized formation of consciousness existing in it.

We cannot grasp the soul by trying to conceptualize it, which is how the mind usually proceeds. But even though the way into it is through feeling, there are some misunderstandings to be avoided. As in the case of consciousness, pure feeling is too subtle to be captured by abstract thought, for it becomes confused with emotions directed toward external objects. Emotions have their source in our vital being, while feeling originates in the soul, where there is no sense of separation between oneself and an external world. From the standpoint of soul, all existence is the manifestation of one indivisible consciousness. Soul aspires for a divine perfection that can only manifest through the descent of higher powers than we now possess. The closest we usually come to such aspiration is in great music and poetry. That is why a chapter on cosmic poetry is included. Poetry is a most powerful expression of the soul's feelings about the universe, but even then feeling is exposed to other influences. It is thus subject to the capacity of the poet to respond to overhead sources of inspiration.

Whereas logic and mathematics are the language of science, poetry is the language of vision. The universe should be experienced as deeply as possible, not merely treated as something to be explained. This requires a vision of it as a whole. We are not concerned exclusively with *explanations*, which can never completely convince. It may turn out that, when clearly seen, what is a mystery to the mind is not really a mystery in itself. Leibniz wondered why there is a universe at all. If we begin with the Vedantic Saccidānanda (Existence-Consciousness-Delight), however, why should there *not* be a universe? Puzzles may arise concerning why it is like this rather than like that, but there would be no mystery about its existence per se. Our emphasis is on the *visions* that underlie a serious consideration of the universe as a whole. The scope of vision extends beyond science—for while science presupposes a general view of the world, the power of vision cannot be reduced to a science.

Furthermore, the function of vision is connected with a more intuitive capacity of mind than discursive thought. Hence poetry is an invaluable resource for the study of cosmology.

Imaginative speculation (as opposed to pure fantasy) plays an important role in cosmology, since the available evidence can be interpreted in different ways. Still, it must be remembered that models of the universe are scientific theories and consequently contain some empirical content. We will employ speculation chiefly to stretch the imagination beyond its customary range. This enables us to sharpen our awareness of the tremendous potential of the Infinite. Readers are invited to embark on *an inner journey* during which several stops will be made to admire the view. But if they remain too long at any stage along the way, they will never arrive at the goal of perceiving the universe from the standpoint of the soul. At the journey's conclusion, readers will have a better understanding of the spiritual value of cosmology. Whether or not one accepts the approach taken here is another matter. This depends to some extent on our personal beliefs about how we are related to the universe.

This book is deeply indebted to the efforts of a number of special people. My wife, Jan, typed the manuscript with careful attention to detail. She was an invaluable source of suggestions and encouragement throughout the process. Rand Hicks, who directs the Integral Knowledge Study Center in Pensacola, Florida, generously undertook the necessary editorial labors. His incisive comments and unfailing patience were indispensable as the work developed. I am grateful to Vicki Hall, Navaja Llope, and Michael Dawson for their unstinting help with figures and images. Their efforts have rendered the book more beautiful. Others close to me supported the progress of the book in various ways. I also offer unreserved gratitude to the many teachers and friends whose wisdom helped illumine my way. Yet one bears sole responsibility for a book that marks the culmination of a long personal journey of discovery. May it reach those readers who will value it.

ACKNOWLEDGMENTS

The author gratefully acknowledges a number of institutions for permission to reproduce their copyrighted images in this book. In order of their appearance, we first thank the Archives of the Theosophical Society in Pasadena for allowing the reproduction of the photograph of Helena Petrovna Blavatsky, taken by Sarony in 1877. The bronze statue titled *The Dancing Shiva* resides in the Museum van Aziatische Kunst, Amsterdam, and a photograph of it is reproduced here by permission. Permission to present the photograph of Albert Einstein, taken by Yousef Karsh in 1948, was granted by Retna Ltd. The Chinese landscape, titled *A Solitary Temple Amid Clearing Peaks (Ch'ing-luan Hsiao-ssu)*, Northern Song Dynasty, is attributed to Li Cheng. Permission to include it was granted by the Nelson-Atkins Museum of Art in Kansas City. Robert Newcombe took the photograph. The Sri Aurobindo Ashram Trust in Pondicherry, India, generously allowed us to reproduce the photographs of Sri Aurobindo (taken in 1950 by Cartier-Bresson) and of The Mother (taken in 1917 by an unnamed photographer). The Trust also permitted reproduction of The Mother's sketch, *Ascent to the Truth,* and Priti Ghosh's painting, *Savitri's Arrival.* We gratefully received the cover design and art from CYP Publishing in Pondicherry.

ACKNOWLEDGMENTS

4 — MANIFESTATION

Four means integrality: the four states of being, mental, psychic, vital, physical.

Words of the Mother
27 December 1933

A NOTE ON GENDER

The use of gender-specific words is a politically sensitive issue for many people. But the metaphysical roots of the problem lie much deeper; they will be examined later in this book. My reliance on the figure of the World Mother will become clearer as we proceed. The all-inclusive wholeness of the universe is most fully expressed in this way. At the same time, it should be recognized that cosmology transcends a literal understanding of human sexual distinctions, since the cosmos is essentially One. Further, occurrences of the term "man" refer to the soul, which is not restricted to gender specificity.

PROLOGUE

Fellow travelers
Crossing a Gobi expanse
Feasting on starlight.

AN INTEGRATED VIEW OF THE COSMOS

> This Vedic imagery throws a clear light on the similar symbolic images of the Puranas, especially on the famous symbol of Vishnu sleeping after the *pralaya* on the folds of the snake Ananta upon the ocean of sweet milk. . . . For they [the poets] have given a name to Vishnu's snake, the name Ananta, and Ananta means the Infinite; therefore they have told us plainly enough that the image is an allegory and that Vishnu, the all-pervading Deity, sleeps in the periods of non-creation on the coils of the Infinite. As for the ocean, the Vedic imagery shows us that it must be the ocean of eternal existence and this ocean of eternal existence is an ocean of absolute sweetness, in other words, of pure Bliss.
>
> Sri Aurobindo, *The Secret of the Veda*[1]

The general plan of this book is suggested by the illustration chosen for its frontispiece. Brahmā, the four-faced god of creation, is sitting on a lotus blossom above the sleeping figure of Vishnu, the all-pervading Deity. We will take the figure of Brahmā to represent the universe in the four aspects referred to in the title as "faces." Universes can be imagined as bubbles emerging from an infinite sea, symbolized in Hindu mythology as an ocean of milk. The bubble we live in is large and richly varied. As indicated by the above quotation from *The Secret of the Veda,* the ocean of sweet milk out of which worlds arise symbolizes pure bliss, the delight that underlies creation.[2] This suggests that the universe is a delightful place to be, though it does not always appear that way. The highest aim of cosmology should be to aid us in recovering the secret delight that is concealed within the universe.[3] But a superficial approach that excludes any of the faces must be avoided; hence we will examine the universe in terms of each one. Afterward, they can all be integrated into a single cosmic picture.

Cosmology is an ongoing search for knowledge of the universe as a whole that has a long history going back to the earliest known civilizations. It is more than simply a science, for it involves the search for a total worldview that will make the universe and our place in it intelligible to us. Today cosmology is widely considered to be a branch of modern physics. But physics is concerned with only one face—the physical. This is the most well-defined face of the universe. Modern science is capable of supplying us with a wealth of useful information about it, but our knowledge of the nature of the physical world is incomplete. We have been conditioned by the scientific culture we share to think of the universe exclusively as a world of stars and galaxies. Yet there are competing theories based on the current laws of physics and none of them can completely satisfy us. They are, after all, only mental attempts to coordinate what we observe through our physical senses.

There are other faces beyond the physical, which are dealt with by different types of cosmology. These include a psychic face, a magical face, and an evolving face. They are not directly perceptible to us.[4] We can observe part of the *physical face,* though much of it still lies beyond our means of detection. Scientific theories attempt to bridge the gap. The *psychic face* appears to us in the form of dreams and visionary experiences.[5] Mythical stories and symbols are employed to express what is revealed in this way. Pictorial images are needed to represent the *magical face,* which is fluid and difficult to fix in strictly logical terms. Finally, metaphysical principles are required for a comprehension of the *evolving face,* the most elusive and far-reaching of them all. Thus a different type of cosmology is necessary for each face.

We survey four types of cosmology and link them to the faces just mentioned. These are *mythical cosmology* (Psychic Face), *scientific cosmology* (Physical Face), *traditional cosmology* (Magical Face), and *evolutionary cosmology* (Evolving Face). Each type describes an aspect of the universe, which as a whole displays various facets of a single complex being. The faces appear to be independent; in reality, however, they are closely interwoven in a grand harmony. Although we are aware of only one universe, it manifests itself in different ways. [6] A single type of cosmology cannot exhaust its manifold nature. Even when all four types are combined, they only offer a glimpse of an indivisible reality that lies hidden from view. For that reality is an intrinsic whole, not a constructed unity that the mind pieces together from sundered parts.

This enlarged approach to cosmology has many advantages, the most important being that it avoids the reductionism implicit in an exclusively physical picture of the universe. Much of modern science is strongly reductionist in character; this has been a great hindrance to those seeking a more holistic conception of the world. But little can be gained by mingling together the different faces of the universe in an indiscriminate fashion. Many people who are opposed to reductionism have chosen this alternative, including physicists who try to see parallels between modern physics and Eastern mysticism. Nevertheless, the worldviews involved in such efforts are literally "worlds" apart. [7] The potential dangers in merging conflicting views were recognized in the seventeenth century by the German philosopher Leibniz. He distinguished carefully between organic and mechanistic modes of thought, yet accepted both of them as complementary ways of viewing the world.

Our approach is similar, in this respect, to that of Leibniz.[8] We will not confuse the various types of cosmology, for there are fundamental differences between them. Each type is considered in its own terms as fairly as possible. This by no means implies that they should be treated as independent of one another. Some of them are more inclusive and reveal deeper layers of reality than others. As will become evident toward the end of this book, I consider the view of an evolving universe presented by Sri Aurobindo to be the deepest and most comprehensive of all. His vision encompasses all of the cosmic faces in its vast scope, illuminating the inner spring of delight and showing us the most effective path leading to it.

We will draw upon the resources of philosophy, science, mythology, religion, and poetry to assist us in finding an appropriate way of relating to the universe. All of them have traditional connections with our deepest cosmological concerns. They may not give us the working knowledge of material systems that modern science affords, but they suggest answers to ultimate questions on which it must remain mute. This kind of science, with its associated technology, caters primarily to our material interests and reduces knowledge to an accumulation of facts and theories.[9] The knowledge we are seeking is an understanding of the universe that will enable us to recapture the delight that underlies its existence. Delight like this cannot be bought and sold in commercial marketplaces. Sometimes, it arises spontaneously within us when we least expect it. Poets have often noted this; for example, it awakened in the English poet Wordsworth a sense of divinity in Nature:

> And I have felt
> A presence that disturbs me with the joy
> Of elevated thoughts; a sense sublime
> Of something far more deeply interfused,
> Whose dwelling is the light of setting suns,
> And the round ocean and the living air,
> And the blue sky, and in the mind of man;
> A motion and a spirit, that impels
> All thinking things, all objects of all thought,
> And rolls through all things.[10]

Later in life, it enabled him to hear "the still, sad music of humanity, nor harsh nor grating," that chastened and subdued his restless spirit.[11]

The order of exposition followed is not primarily historical. After an introductory chapter covering some general ideas presupposed throughout the book, we turn to a consideration of mythical cosmology. This provides an overview of the issues concerning cosmic manifestation. A discussion of scientific cosmology comes next, in which models of the physical universe are examined. The magical three worlds model of traditional cosmology is then contrasted with them. A chapter on evolutionary cosmology completes our survey of the four faces of the universe. Finally, we consider the role of cosmic poetry in cosmology and sum up the conclusions derived from our study.

Chapter I, "Consciousness and the Universe," is concerned with how we become aware of the universe, different theories about its origin, and the importance of cosmic consciousness. The view in this chapter is that the universe is a manifestation of Consciousness. Different modes of consciousness are distinguished within the totality of being. Related themes of harmony and variety are also noted, for they play significant roles throughout the book. We also compare different motivations for studying cosmology and conclude that the primary motive is to experience the universe from the standpoint of cosmic consciousness. This is the unifying thread running through the various types of cosmology presented here. It can offer us a taste of the delight that generated the universe with its manifold beauties. The chapter ends with a consideration of the relation of general worldviews to cosmology, and a thumbnail sketch of the history of Western cosmology from the ancient Greeks to our own time.

The next two chapters deal with the Psychic Face. Chapter II, "Mythical Cosmology," describes the world picture found in early cultures. We compare creation myths with scientific cosmology, and various theories of myth are examined. Brief summaries of Sri Aurobindo's interpretation of the Veda and a discussion of the role of the Great Mother Goddess in creation myth are followed by a few examples to illustrate mythical approaches to the question of cosmic origins. The crucial notion of a boundary between different states of being is introduced here. This concept appears frequently in later chapters. Chapter III, "The Stanzas of Dzyan," is concerned with a widely overlooked creation myth that forms the core of H.P. Blavatsky's neglected masterpiece, *The Secret Doctrine*. Consideration is given to the inner source of creation myths and the importance of transitional states. In addition, the Stanzas of Dzyan are treated in enough detail to bring out the pervasive features of creation myths. For this purpose, a commentary is provided for selected verses from the opening Stanzas on cosmogenesis. The chapter closes with a short analysis of Beethoven's Ninth Symphony viewed from a cosmological perspective.

After myth, we take up the Physical Face. Chapter IV, "Modern Scientific Cosmology," begins with an examination of the expression "laws of nature," summarizes the discovery of the realm of the galaxies by the American astronomer, Edwin Hubble, and discusses Einstein's general theory of relativity. It proceeds with the topic of cosmological models, showing how various kinds of models have been derived from general relativity. Some implications of the singularity that appears at the origin of the universe are also touched upon. In Chapter V, "The Big Bang and Beyond," an overview is given of the foundations of quantum mechanics. This leads into the theory that the universe began as a quantum vacuum fluctuation. The chapter continues with a consideration of a few puzzles associated with the Standard Big Bang Model. We introduce concepts of fine-tuning, the anthropic principle, and multiple universes, after which a short description of inflationary universe models is given. Scientific and religious explanations of fine-tuning are compared, and a resolution of their differences is proposed. Finally, we explore some speculative implications of the recent and still controversial discovery of a runaway universe.

Our attention then shifts to the Magical Face. Chapter VI, "Traditional Cosmology," focuses on the relationship of the macrocosm and the microcosm together with some additional doctrines that are related to it. In this type of cosmology, man as the microcosm is the central image for understanding the universe. This is the essential key to the picture of the magical universe being examined in this chapter. Beginning with roots in Plato's influential cosmological dialogue, the *Timaeus,* it reached its climax in Renaissance Hermeticism. A section follows in which a comparison is made between the traditional three worlds model of the universe and modern scientific models. The chapter ends with the summary of a traditional cosmology developed in ancient China. It provides a contemplative interlude before entering into a discussion of evolutionary cosmology.

The last face of the universe to be examined is the Evolving Face. Chapter VII, "Evolutionary Cosmology," is an introduction to this topic. We present a survey of evolutionary biology along with its connections to Darwinism. Several speculative Western philosophies of evolution are then reviewed. The major emphasis, however, is on Sri Aurobindo's conception of spiritual evolution as expounded in *The Life Divine*. He sees the universe as an evolutionary manifestation of a transcendent reality with soul as the central element in the process. His views are considered on the relation between creation and evolution, the principles of Being, and the way in which spiritual evolution proceeds. This chapter ends with the implications of his vision for the future of the soul in the universe.

In Chapter VIII, "Cosmic Poetry," each type of cosmology is illustrated by a great poem that places the question of human destiny in a broad cosmological context. Poetry is an integral part of our study of cosmology. It is a powerful force for refining and deepening our understanding of the world rather than, as sometimes thought, a mere diversion from more "serious" pursuits. Moreover, our viewpoint is that the universe appears to be more like a great poem than a logic machine or computer. This will be our final clue to the vast consciousness behind it. We must feel our way into the universe and not simply describe it in mathematical terms (though this is also important in cosmology). Several examples illustrate the capacity of cosmic poetry to illumine our relationship with the universe, and each one represents a different type of cosmology. These poems derive with varying degrees of insight from an experience of cosmic consciousness. Each is capable of opening a door to the fuller delight we are seeking.

Some readers might be tempted to omit the chapters that least interest them. That is of course possible, but the book develops progressively and is designed to be read as a continuous whole. All the types of cosmology deserve our attention; each has an intrinsic interest of its own, bringing out certain features of the universe neglected by the others. In this connection, a word of caution is necessary at the outset: we will cross the traditional demarcations among academic disciplines, and many professional scholars might frown upon our temerity. But cosmology is so broad in scope that the only way to see the whole forest without having our vision blocked by the trees is to omit nonessential details wherever possible. Technical difficulties are recognized only where it is necessary to do so. The endnotes often amplify points made in the text, so should not be ignored.

The present book is not exhaustive. Rather, it should encourage readers to regard the universe in a new way. For cosmology does not belong entirely to professionals, be they scientists, philosophers, or theologians. In a complex technological society like our own, we are inclined to believe that experts can solve every problem for us. Even cosmology is delegated to specialists, who are usually reluctant to stray outside the bounds of their chosen disciplines. The universe, however, lies beyond limited academic boundaries. It is the totality that includes us all and upon which our existence as biological organisms depends.

Each person has to establish a basis of spiritual solidarity with it or be resigned to leading a fragmented life in the world. This fragmentation applies to social and religious institutions as well as to individuals; they generally fall short of true universality by underestimating the importance of forging a strong inner bond with the cosmos. Only a concentrated individual effort can accomplish such a task. Nevertheless, a book like this could not be written without relying on the knowledge gained by countless scholars and scientists working in different fields. Yet experts cannot be expected to do it all for us. They can tell us a great deal about the details, but we need not accept their interpretations of the universe *as a whole*. For this, we rely on our own judgment and power of integration.

INTRODUCTION

An elusive Swan
Cleaving the moonbright waters
Leaves only a trace.

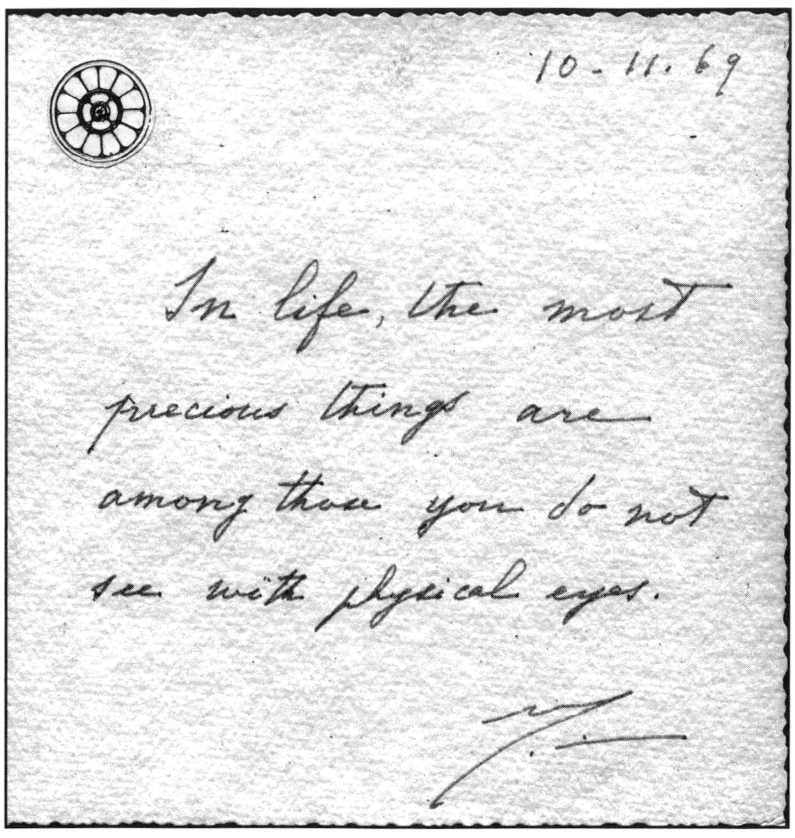

10-11-69

In life, the most precious things are among those you do not see with physical eyes.

Plate I: A Message from the Mother

I

CONSCIOUSNESS AND THE UNIVERSE

Our Awareness of the Universe

When we speak of the universe, we are not always aware of the problems that arise with the mere utterance of the word. For example, are we talking about something that has an objective existence of its own? Is it real, a mere appearance, or only an illusion? Was it created, or is it simply to be accepted as being there in some mysterious way? Is it a form of consciousness, a material substance, or a whirl of pure energy? Does it include other states of being besides the physical? Do we live in an infinite universe or one that is spatially and temporally finite? Is it evolving in any significant way? Can there be more than one universe? Above all, why is there a universe, and why are we a part of it? There is no end to the questions we could ask about the universe. But whatever it may be, it is something that is with us as long as we live (and then what?). For now, I will suggest a way of approaching the universe and review a number of possibilities concerning its origin. Then we can proceed to a more extended treatment of the questions raised.

Consider how we come to know about the world around us. Each person has an awareness of it that is unique. The experienced universe appears in one's own consciousness and is not exactly the same as for others. It includes not only our sensory perceptions but also the biases, beliefs, and personal history that accompany them; therefore, it is a part of ourselves that we carry around everywhere. Too, each person is always at the center of this personal universe. Wherever one happens to be is the central location for that person. Even in heaven, an individual would be the center of the world then being experienced; the same would be true in hell. This implies that, in the deepest sense, *we never really go anywhere*. At least it can be said that there is a center within us remaining unmoved no matter how our relations with things may change. It is not the ego, which moves around with us, but something unseen that observes movement from behind.[1] Later, there will be occasion to consider what it could be. Although at first sight this approach might appear to be very subjective, it is the same for every individual. There are also many similarities among the worlds being experienced by different persons. This could be an indication of a reality in which they all share.[2]

Our worlds intersect one another in a complex web of relations, suggesting that there is something they all have in common. This web represents an objective universe that does not depend on our experiencing it. Otherwise, how could these personal worlds be so closely interwoven with one another? Just as they appear in our consciousness, so the (to us) objective universe may be an appearance in a supreme Consciousness in which we all participate; individual selves would then be points of view within this larger Consciousness. Freeing ourselves from the idiosyncrasies of our particular worlds could make us more responsive to the beautiful harmonies of the objective universe and the vast Consciousness it reveals.[3] What has been said so far, however, may seem remote from familiar modes of thought. Before proceeding further, an example from my personal experience may focus things more clearly, for my own search began with such a perception and launched a lifelong inquiry.

While serving with a field artillery unit in wartime Europe, I was part of a convoy moving from northern France to the battlefront along the Rhine River in Germany. We would be in combat shortly, so all of us were understandably nervous. On the way, we stopped overnight in an open field outside the city of Maastrict in Holland. There was no time to bivouac and, even though it was early March, the ground was still too frozen to pitch tents. We just threw ourselves down fully clothed to catch a few hours of sleep. Lying there, I happened to notice the constellation of Orion setting in the western sky.[4] I had observed this many times in the past, but now suddenly realized that in relation to the universe *there was no difference between my current location and being at home*; it was as if I had not gone anywhere. The experience left me wondering about the mysterious relationship that we seem to have with the world around us. Then I fell asleep. The curious thing is that afterward all of the anxieties accompanying entry into a battle zone disappeared.

I decided that after the war I would go to college and study cosmology, in the hope that this would shed some light on what had really happened. New York University was the only institution with a course in cosmology, so I went there as an undergraduate. When the general requirements were completed, I tackled the subject of cosmology. It had been part of the philosophy curriculum but was no longer being offered. Nevertheless, I was able to take other courses with the professor who had taught it. He was interested in the methodological problems arising out of the developing field of scientific cosmology.[5] After graduation, he encouraged me to concentrate on the philosophy of science at Columbia University. I did. At that time, American philosophy was heavily influenced by logical positivism; needless to say, this contained nothing that could help me understand the universe. It soon became apparent that the path I was following would not take me where I wanted to go. My interest began to branch out into the history of philosophy, classical literature, and world religions. Like Omar Khayyam, I "heard great Argument/ About it and about; but evermore/ Came out by the same Door where in I went."[6] Yet I also learned many things that deepened my understanding of our mysterious relationship with the universe.

Four Views about the Origin of the Universe

Returning to the topic with which we started, what is the universe really like? Is it only matter existing on its own, or is it some form of consciousness that we do not yet understand? Is it the result of a divine creative process, or is its existence an incomprehensible mystery? We will group the possible answers that may be given to these questions under four headings: scientific materialism, creationism, divine manifestation, and inscrutable mystery.

Scientific Materialism

The first view is popularly known as *scientific materialism.*[7] It assumes that the universe is a huge system of unconscious matter and energy. Consciousness is thought to be only an appearance produced by physical processes alone. Although not all scientists are confirmed materialists, the technological successes of science have reinforced a broadly materialistic outlook in modern society. The object of science is to discover the laws governing the material world, and perhaps to explain how it came into being. At present, the universe is viewed as the result of a single event—the so-called "Big Bang"—that brought it into existence about fifteen billion years ago. The Big Bang produced space, time, and matter, but despite a number of tentative proposals, there is still a lack of scientific consensus as to what, if anything, may have preceded it. This has led many people to adopt a religious answer to the question concerning the origin of the universe, explaining it in terms of creation by God.

Creationism

Creationism in cosmology is the belief that the universe was created as a free act of the Divine Will. This is usually interpreted as creation *ex nihilo* ("out of nothing"), though it could also mean the shaping of the universe out of some previously existing material. In either case, to speak of "creation" suggests that there is an external cause for the existence of the physical universe. Three major religions (Judaism, Christianity, and Islam) accept creationism as a dogma based upon divine revelation. In spite of their differences, however, the creationist view is best represented by the opening chapters of the Book of Genesis. This account, as interpreted by most theologians, shares the common scientific assumption that the universe is made of matter and energy existing independent of consciousness—only here it is supposed to have been created by God. Although creationism complements and, in a way, completes the scientific picture, it suffers from the drawback that we do not know how to understand creation (or causality) when it is extended beyond our experience. How can we possibly conceive God to be the creator of the universe out of absolute nothingness, when we have no experience of this? Even if some kind of matter different from God existed prior to creation, there would still be a problem. For unless God himself were in some sense material, how could he act upon matter to produce an ordered world?

Divine Manifestation

This less familiar approach accepts God as the only reality, but holds that a distinction arises within God when he chooses to manifest himself. It denies a real difference between God and the universe. Instead of referring to an external cause, the focus is on the internal process by which God transforms himself into the universe. To emphasize the inner nature of this process, we will take the word "cosmogenesis" to be more appropriate than creation. The underlying problem of the two views we have just discussed is that everything around us eventually decays and perishes, which suggests that nothing is really permanent about the world. Even its most elementary constituents, whether conceived as particles or strings, may be insubstantial. It does not mean, however, that the universe as a whole is completely valueless, since it can still be viewed as a *divine manifestation.*

Seeing the universe as a divine manifestation implies that it is the result of God becoming conscious of himself as an object. Instead of assuming that the universe has a reality outside God, it is understood to be a manifestation of God's power to know himself. Some kind of causality may be operating here, but it is neither creation *ex nihilo* nor creation out of some pre-existing form of matter. The situation is comparable to awakening from deep sleep, where we gradually become aware of the world around us. When this happens, we also become conscious of ourselves perceiving it. But, as already pointed out, this perceived world is part of the universe existing in one's own consciousness. The universe *as we experience it* has no reality outside of personal consciousness. We are always at its center experiencing ourselves as objects.

Similarly, with respect to God, when the objective universe appears, he becomes conscious of himself as its perceiver. Just as the universe that we experience individually has no existence separate from our consciousness of it, the objective universe would have no existence separate from God. We could say that God has made himself the object of his own self-regard; he is then perceiving himself as the universe. God becomes the universe in order to manifest his inner potentialities and thus to know himself fully as God. But there remains a question concerning what happens within the divine being that brings about its manifestation as the universe. In other words, what is the nature of the creative process (cosmogenesis) itself? Neither scientific materialism nor dogmatic religion can help us to understand it, because both assume that the universe has a substantial existence of its own; they differ only with respect to whether or not it was created by God. We will see in the next chapter that some creation myths, when interpreted symbolically, can suggest how cosmogenesis may take place.

Before proceeding further, let us understand how we will use the word "God." The term originally referred to an object (or objects) of religious worship. In monotheistic religions, God is conceived as the Supreme Being who is creator and ruler of the universe. Its meaning depends on how deeply we see into the nature of God. Obviously, this will vary from person to person and from culture to culture. God is usually conceptualized as personal, transcendent, and masculine ("our Father in heaven"). This view has several limitations. For example, it is becoming more and more evident that God has a feminine nature as well, represented traditionally as the "Great Mother," or Goddess. Another disadvantage of the conventional idea of God is that for many people it implies an absolute distinction between God and the universe (as in Creator and creature). The universe is thus construed to be different from and existing outside God. But if God is infinite and one, how can there be anything outside God?

The closest approach the philosophical mind can make to the vast, mysterious Presence behind everything we do and experience is to identify it as Infinite Consciousness. In a sense, this can be misleading, because we tend to oppose consciousness to matter. Nevertheless, there is no such opposition within Infinite Consciousness, because it possesses the power to become all worlds. When this Consciousness is conceived as God, there is a problem in relating the world to him. As the Creator, he stands above and beyond it, more or less unreachable. The result is that the world is seen as different from God, and consequently lacks divinity. Such a world is in constant danger of losing its direction and purpose. Hence the fascination with saviors in many religions.

In order to create, Infinite Consciousness becomes its own object, since there is no object other than itself. As object, it is the Goddess, who encompasses the whole world down to the darkest recesses of matter. It follows, in a strange overlap of divine images, that the Goddess is also God; he knows himself as her. She is the Divine Mother, who brings the universe out of herself, thus establishing its divinity. In some formulations, this is rendered as God giving birth to himself, but the inadequacy of such a notion is obvious. The Divine Mother plays the role of Creatrix, and it is she who appears throughout time in many forms and guises to guide all creatures, who are really herself.

Some mystics have rejected the conventional view; God is seen by them as Absolute Being encompassing the whole of reality. In their eyes, God is everything and there is nothing outside God. A reality like this transcends all mental categories and is consequently indescribable. It is so different from the ordinary understanding of God that the term "Godhead" (the inner nature or essence of divinity) is sometimes employed. "Being-Consciousness" is also possible, because consciousness is experienced being, and being that is beyond consciousness is too abstract for us to fully comprehend. Even this fails to capture the essential quality of divine existence, which is pure bliss or delight.[8] "The Divine" covers all of these meanings and is the term preferred in this book. We will continue to use the word God where appropriate because of its personal associations. Our approach recognizes the existence of a transcendent principle and strives to develop an awareness of its many aspects.

Inscrutable Mystery

Another alternative, the most radical of all, must be mentioned since it denies that there is anything besides pure consciousness. The universe is considered to be an *inscrutable mystery*, God himself being only an appearance in consciousness. From this point of view, there is nothing that could have *caused* the universe to exist; therefore, its creation never happened. The existence of the universe is thus accepted, but a creative process is denied. The appearance of a world outside consciousness is traced to our ignorance of its true nature, for the universe has no inherent reality of its own. It shares the nature of consciousness, rather than being a self-existing system of matter and energy. One way of expressing this is to say that the universe is *unreal* when perceived to be separate from consciousness and *real* as an appearance in it. Thus, the problem of creation is bogus: there is no reason *why* the world exists. We must simply recognize it as an *inscrutable mystery* and act accordingly. It is claimed that both the universe and the perceiving self can eventually be dissolved into pure undifferentiated consciousness. This might require a long process of spiritual discipline, but we are told that it is the ultimate solution to the mystery of the cosmos.[9]

There is much to be said for this absolutist view; some traditions hold it to be the highest truth. If so, cosmology is a misguided endeavor. What enduring value could there be in studying a universe that lacks inherent reality and cannot be transformed into something supremely perfect in its own right? This has been compared with the attempt to straighten a dog's tail, which always returns to its natural curve. Although distinguished by its razor-sharp logic supported by centuries of past experience, a nagging suspicion remains that this view neglects a fundamental aspect of reality. The universe, in spite of its incomprehensible harshness, is too beautiful and precisely adapted to our presence in it to be given up entirely for lost. We can imagine many kinds of worlds that would not be at all conducive to the pursuit of higher spiritual goals. Why is this one so well suited to such a purpose? It is possible that the universe has a destiny far greater than anything we can yet imagine; our presence in it could also be intimately bound up with the eventual fulfillment of that destiny. There may be a mode of consciousness that can account for the kind of world we live in. If so, it would be important to know what it is before ending our cosmological inquiry too abruptly.

This is not to say that the views discussed so far are completely false, since all are rooted to some extent in perception. Each grasps a single aspect of reality, but fails to achieve full comprehension. Readers will adhere to the one which seems most plausible to them. Still, it should be kept in mind that another view, which seems implausible right now, might become more compelling later on. Worldviews have a way of changing with spiritual growth; their value lies in how effective they are in leading us to deeper and more universal levels of perception. The best approach is to assume that we do not know enough about the nature of the universe at this point to rule out any of them. So without denying indiscriminately any claims to legitimacy on their behalf, we will seek a way of understanding the universe that can make its study a profitable one. This does not involve a return to either the scientific or the dogmatic religious standpoints mentioned previously. They are useful only if it is maintained that the universe has a substantial reality independent of consciousness.[10] This assumption is too limited. If it is relinquished, a world of marvelous coherence and unsurpassed beauty can reveal itself. To see this, a deeper basis must be found for cosmology. The way chosen should enable us to retain the essential unity of consciousness in terms of a larger understanding of its functions and powers.

Three Modes of Consciousness

Our primary affirmation will be that the universe is a manifestation of Consciousness, which is self-revealing and divine. Everything is a form of consciousness and nothing that we know of exists beyond it.[11] Being is infinite and eternal; whatever else it may possibly be, it must be conscious, since the universe is its object. Although there are other methods of analyzing this, they would not provide an adequate basis for our suggested approach to cosmology.[12] Many types of analysis fail to support a serious consideration of the point of view being proposed here, since they imply a fundamental duality between the knower and the known. To understand consciousness, we have to avoid thinking of it as a blank, undifferentiated, and ultimately impotent reality. Countless nuances are present within it, for there is at least as much variety and complexity in consciousness as in matter.

Although science has discovered numerous facts about the material world, there are also discoveries that can be made through a systematic examination of the nature of consciousness. Since our position is that the universe cannot be divorced from consciousness, what is learned about the nature of consciousness will have a decided impact on our understanding of the universe. But our inquiry will differ from other methods that are usually employed. We will not be concerned with the techniques of dream analysis favored by many modern psychologists, nor shall we enter the domain of the philosophical phenomenologists. Speculations about the connection between consciousness and the phenomena of subatomic physics, which are popular in some interpretations of quantum mechanics, will also be bypassed. All of these approaches have a value of their own; nonetheless, they would only be diversions from this book's path, for they do not probe deeply enough into the nature of consciousness.

The kind of exploration we will pursue is suggested in the writings of Sri Aurobindo, who went farther in this direction than most people are aware. Only a few salient features of his analysis of consciousness will be mentioned here, since they bear directly upon our present concerns. Sri Aurobindo distinguishes between different modes or statuses of one indivisible consciousness. There are three major modes that must be identified at this stage of our inquiry: the transcendent, the cosmic, and the individual. All are divine, yet each expresses the divine consciousness in a different way:

> The Transcendent, the Universal, the Individual are three powers overarching, underlying and penetrating the whole manifestation; this is the first of the Trinities. In the unfolding of consciousness also, these are the three fundamental terms and none of them can be neglected if we would have the experience of the whole Truth of existence. Out of the individual we wake into a vaster freer cosmic consciousness; but out of the universal too with its complex of forms and powers we must emerge by a still greater self-exceeding into a consciousness without limits that is founded on the Absolute. And yet in this ascension we do not really abolish but take up and transfigure what we seem to leave; for there is a height where the three live eternally in each other, on that height they are blissfully joined in a nodus of their harmonised oneness.[13]

This summary statement has a number of strands that need to be carefully unraveled.

Transcendent Consciousness is the all-embracing timeless reality supporting the other modes. It is the Supreme Self (Paramātman) and much more, the imperishable foundation of the world. This mode is beyond our mental grasp and cannot be fully described. Many mystics who have caught a glimpse of it were absorbed into the eternal silence forever. Nevertheless, this is not the culmination that we are seeking here. For, as suggested by the above quotation, there are other possibilities as well; their ultimate fulfillment rests on realization of the Self, but this should be sought in the world rather than beyond it. Sri Aurobindo maintains that there is a height on which all three modes exist in perfect harmony. The goal of spiritual life would then be to experience this harmony here on earth. Later, in our discussion of evolutionary cosmology, we will see that an attainment of such magnitude could only be achieved by the soul in conjunction with a higher power of Knowledge. In this book, we are especially concerned with cosmic consciousness, but it must be treated in relation to the other modes. While contacts with cosmic consciousness are more common than might be supposed, it requires a deeper centering to establish them firmly as parts of one's being and awareness.

Cosmic Consciousness is a term that has been rendered almost vacuous by its indiscriminate usage in mystical writings. It means a consciousness of the cosmos, or the universe as a unified whole. For Sri Aurobindo, it refers to an extraordinary awareness of the infinite extension of divine consciousness in the manifested universe. In one of his letters, he writes:

> The cosmic consciousness is that of the universe, of the cosmic spirit and cosmic Nature with all the beings and forces within it. All that is as much conscious as a whole as the individual separately is, though in a different way. The consciousness of the individual is part of this, but a part feeling itself as a separate being. Yet all the time most of what he is comes into him from the cosmic consciousness. . . . The soul comes from beyond this nature of mind, life and body. It belongs to the transcendent and because of it we can open to the higher Nature beyond.[14]

This kind of consciousness, divine in origin, can be experienced by the soul on many levels. Sometimes, even a casual glance at the night sky, or seeing an early sunrise over still waters, can be an occasion for it. There is an uncanny sense of infinitude, like that felt when viewing the horizon from a solitary mountain peak. Although its first awakening may be on the physical plane, we can easily be misled into thinking that this is all there is to it and proceed no further. On any level of awareness, however, cosmic consciousness is accompanied by certain spiritual feelings that, if strong enough, can inspire a person to build an entire life upon it.

An early attempt to analyze cosmic consciousness from a psychological point of view was made by the Canadian psychologist Richard Maurice Bucke.[15] He was a personal friend of the American poet Walt Whitman and became one of Whitman's literary executors after the poet had passed away. Bucke's book, *Cosmic Consciousness*, has become a classic in its field, though seriously flawed by his lack of metaphysical insight into the subject. Bucke was led to this study by an experience he had while riding home late one night in a hansom cab. He was suddenly wrapped in a flame-colored cloud and simultaneously became assured of eternal life and the immortality of the soul:

> . . . he saw and knew that the Cosmos is not dead matter but a living Presence, that the soul of man is immortal, that the universe is so built and ordered that without any peradventure all things work together for the good of each and all, that the foundation principle of the world is what we call love and that the happiness of every one is in the long run absolutely certain.[16]

Bucke believed that his experience had already been anticipated in Whitman's poetry, and this belief led him to venerate the poet for the rest of his life.

Whitman had occasional glimpses of cosmic consciousness that seem to have deepened as he grew older, but they were primarily physical and vital yearnings. They are revealed in many passages scattered throughout his masterpiece, *Leaves of Grass*. A few brief examples will illustrate this:

> O vast Rondure, swimming in space,
> Cover'd all over with visible power and beauty,
> Alternate light and day and the teeming spiritual darkness,
> Unspeakable high processions of sun and moon and countless stars
>   above,
> Below, the manifold grass and waters, animals, mountains, trees,
> With inscrutable purpose, some hidden prophetic intention,
> Now first it seems my thought begins to span thee.[17]
>
> . . . .
>
> O Thou transcendent,
> Nameless, the fibre and the breath,
> Light of the light, shedding forth universes, thou centre of them,
> Thou mightier centre of the true, the good, the loving,
> Thou moral, spiritual fountain—affection's source—thou reservoir
>
> . . . .
>
> Thou pulse—thou motive of the stars, suns, systems,
> That, circling, move in order, safe, harmonious,
> Athwart the shapeless vastnesses of space,

> How should I think, how breathe a single breath, how speak, if, out of myself,
> I could not launch, to those, superior universes?[18]

In another poem, Whitman is alone on the beach at night:

> As the old mother sways her to and fro singing her husky song,
> As I watch the bright stars shining, I think a thought of the clef of the
> universes and of the future.
> A vast similitude interlocks all,
> . . . .
> This vast similitude spans them, and always has spann'd,
> And shall forever span them and compactly hold and enclose them.[19]

Bucke was impressed by Whitman the man as much as by Whitman the poet. This led him to believe that the man exemplified a higher stage in the development of human consciousness. Some of the most inspired passages in *Cosmic Consciousness* are connected with this belief. For instance, Bucke predicts that, in the future, cosmic consciousness will be established as the norm of life on earth:

> In contact with the flux of cosmic consciousness all religions known and named today will be melted down. The human soul will be revolutionized. Religion will absolutely dominate the race. It will not depend on tradition. It will not be believed and disbelieved. It will not be a part of life, belonging to certain hours, times, occasions. It will not be in sacred books nor in the mouths of priests. It will not dwell in churches and meetings and forms and days. Its life will not be in prayers, hymns nor discourses. It will not depend on special revelations, on the words of gods who came down to teach, nor on any bible or bibles. It will have no mission to save men from their sins or to secure them entrance to heaven. It will not teach a future immortality nor future glories, for immortality and all glory will exist in the here and now. The evidence of immortality will live in every heart as sight in every eye. Doubt of God and of eternal life will be as impossible as is now doubt of existence; the evidence of each will be the same. Religion will govern every minute of every day of all life. Churches, priests, forms, creeds, prayers, all agents, all intermediaries between the individual man and God will be permanently replaced by direct unmistakable intercourse. Sin will

> no longer exist nor will salvation be desired. Men will not worry about death or a future, about the kingdom of heaven, about what may come with and after the cessation of the life of the present body. Each soul will feel and know itself to be immortal, will feel and know that the entire universe with all its good and with all its beauty is for it and belongs to it forever. The world peopled by men [and women] possessing cosmic consciousness will be as far removed from the world of today as this is from the world as it was before the advent of self consciousness.[20]

At the end of his book, he predicts that "this new race is in act of being born from us, and in the near future it will occupy and possess the earth."[21] He could not have foreseen the deeper implications of this insight. Toward the close of the present work, we will see that a more powerful Reality than Bucke conceived would be necessary to make possible a transformation like this.

Whatever the truth may be, it is evident from what has been said that cosmic consciousness needs to be taken seriously in the study of cosmology. Contemplation of any of the four faces of the universe can be a means of experiencing it. Although varying in power and life-transforming effect, it is always a vast impersonal mode of consciousness in which the sense of a personal self is almost non-existent. Our awareness widens into the limitless expanses of space and time; everything is perceived to exist within the unity of the universe as a whole. Ordinary consciousness of separation and antagonism between things dissolves into pure harmony. Later, it will be seen that this harmony embraces the so-called "laws of nature" that the mind formulates in an attempt to comprehend it. The universe appears as a shoreless ocean teeming with an inexhaustible abundance of beautiful forms. One feels an identity with all of them, though bound by none. A Cosmic Self embraces all things and experiences the freedom and delight of universal existence. Both a grand pervasive harmony and a marvelous variety of forms are seen to be inseparable features of the world. Together, they direct our gaze beyond the cosmic toward the transcendent consciousness that permeates and contains it. For *harmony* reflects the supreme Wisdom behind the universe, and *variety* attests to its Power to manifest in infinitely many ways.

Cosmic Consciousness is an expansion of *Individual Consciousness*, which is the third mode mentioned by Sri Aurobindo. An Individual Self (Jivātman) is the central being of each person; it cannot be obliterated even though personal egoism may disappear. Poised beyond space and time, Sri Aurobindo maintains that the central being (the true individual) is immutable and never becomes separated from transcendent consciousness, but it appears partially in the universe as the psychic being (Caitya Puruṣa).[22] The psychic being is not the same as what is normally called "soul," for it lies at a deeper level than the personality we are familiar with.[23] Its unique cosmic role is to evolve into a fully manifested divinity on earth. Although a spark of the divine flame burning within the heart, it is obscured at present by outer vehicles of mind, life, and body. Nevertheless, just as fire can be viewed either as one continuous flame or as a multiplicity of sparks, consciousness is a universal self-awareness that is also a multitude of souls. More will be said about this in Chapter VII, where evolutionary cosmology is discussed further.

Realization of the soul is necessary for a safe and wholesome entry into cosmic consciousness. Otherwise, there is danger of falling prey to a dry, uncaring indifference to all particular forms of existence, or a bloating of the ego, for the latter subverts all attempts to bring about a real transformation of our nature. One also begins to feel the cumulative shock of the world's experiences, which can be overwhelming when it first appears.[24] As Sri Aurobindo cautions:

> The thing one has to be on guard against in the cosmic consciousness is the play of a magnified ego, the vaster attacks of the hostile forces—for they too are part of the cosmic consciousness—and the attempt of the cosmic Illusion (Ignorance, *Avidyā*) to prevent the growth of the soul into the cosmic Truth. These are things that one has to learn from experience; mental teaching or explanation is quite insufficient. To enter safely into the cosmic consciousness and to pass safely through it, it is necessary to have a strong central unegoistic sincerity and to have the psychic being, with its divination of truth and unfaltering orientation towards the Divine, already in front in the nature.[25]

Still, complete transformation can come only when the power of transcendent consciousness becomes fully operative in the world. This topic will be pursued in later chapters.[26]

MOTIVATIONS FOR THE STUDY OF COSMOLOGY

But what has this to do with the study of cosmology? Scientific cosmology is the type most widely practiced today. Its motivation is disinterested curiosity about the origin, extent, and contents of the physical universe in space and time. For scientific cosmologists the universe is just another, though larger, field for the application of the methods and theories that comprise the subject matter of physics, astronomy and, to a lesser extent, other sciences. It presents a set of puzzles to be solved by employing the standard procedures of science. But modern science fails to provide satisfying answers to our deepest cosmological questions. Although the spatial and temporal boundaries of the physical universe are constantly being stretched, its existence remains as mysterious as ever. While scientists today have diverse answers to questions concerning the beginning of the universe, its possible end, and whether there are many universes or only one, they are all more or less speculative. In short, scientific cosmology advances our ideas about the universe considerably, but does not explain convincingly *why* it exists and has one form rather than another.

The satisfaction of intellectual curiosity should not be the sole, or even the primary, motivation for the study of cosmology. No matter what answers we arrive at on the scientific level, there will always be more questions to ask. Cosmology may begin with curiosity, but we need a deeper motivation as well to satisfy our interest in the universe. This can be found in the opportunity that cosmology affords for developing a sense of cosmic consciousness. Not just scientists, but philosophers, poets and mystics have written on cosmological themes. Many of them suggest that this mode of consciousness was involved in their efforts to understand the universe. References to the perception of cosmic harmony and beauty, free from the divisive egoism that mars so much of our personal lives, abound in their works. To have a mere taste of cosmic consciousness on any level of experience is enough to justify a serious study of cosmology.

The life of the Italian Renaissance philosopher Giordano Bruno offers a dramatic example of how cosmic consciousness can affect an individual and the society in which he lives. He was a Dominican monk in Naples, but a powerful impulse led him out of his monastery to wander throughout Europe, proclaiming a new vision of the universe. This came at a time when European culture was beginning to change its cosmology from the "closed world" of the Middle Ages to an infinite universe of stars.[27] Bruno foresaw the tremendous effects this change would have, for he was the first philosopher to grasp its deeper cosmological implications. He expressed his discovery of cosmic consciousness in a poem describing the freedom and delight he felt in escaping from the medieval system of crystalline spheres:

> Escaped from the narrow murky prison
> Where for so many years error held me straitly,
> Here I leave the chain that bound me
> And the shadow of my fiercely malicious foe
> Who can force me no longer to the gloomy dusk of night.
> For he [Apollo] who hath overcome the great Python
> With whose blood he hath dyed the waters of the sea
> Hath put to flight the Fury that pursued me.
> To thee I turn, I soar, O my sustaining Voice;
> I render thanks to thee, my Sun, my divine Light,
> For thou hast summoned me from that horrible torture,
> Thou hast led me to a goodlier tabernacle;
> Thou hast brought healing to my bruised heart.
>
> Thou art my delight and the warmth of my heart;
> Thou makest me without fear of Fate or of Death;
> Thou breakest the chains and bars
> Whence few come forth free.
> Seasons, years, months, days, and hours—
> The children and weapons of Time—and that Court
> Where neither steel nor treasure avail
> Have secured me from the fury [of the foe].
> *Henceforth I spread confident wings to space;*
> *I fear no barrier of crystal or of glass;*

I cleave the heavens and soar to the infinite.
And while I rise from my own globe to others
And penetrate ever further through the eternal field,
That which others saw from afar, I leave far behind me
[italics added].[28]

Throughout his life Bruno had great difficulty in assimilating cosmic consciousness. It seems to have come upon him more or less by chance, occasioned, perhaps, by a childhood impression of the vastness of the universe. While still a boy in Nola, he climbed nearby Mount Cicala to observe the stars and noticed how dark and gloomy Mount Vesuvius looked in the distance. But when he stood on the slopes of Vesuvius itself, he found it lush and fruitful, and far-off Cicala then appeared dim and indistinct. This led him to believe that the universe at large must be the same everywhere. Sameness could be found amid the shifting horizons of the experienced world. It suggested a pervasive unity manifested in an infinitely varied universe that lacked a unique center. Any place within it was roughly equivalent to any other. Only distance made the stars look so small when seen from the earth; if the latter were viewed from a star, the relative sizes would be reversed.

Thus, Bruno arrived at a conception of the universe that was later formulated as the *cosmological principle.* This experience must have left a deep impression upon him, since he still referred to it much later in life. It was reinforced by his reading of the Roman poet Lucretius' then recently rediscovered poem on ancient atomism, *De Rerum Natura*, in conjunction with the new Copernican ideas in astronomy that were just beginning to sweep across Europe.[29]

Bruno attempted to assimilate his experience of cosmic consciousness by working out an elaborate philosophical system. He saw the universe as a *divine manifestation* in which God could be found everywhere. Declaring this publicly required courage, as it drew a harsh reaction from the Catholic Church. Returning to Italy after years of wandering, he was imprisoned and subsequently burned at the stake as a dangerous heretic.[30] Toward the end of his long imprisonment in the dungeons of the

Inquisition, after some initial hesitation, he firmly refused to recant his cosmological beliefs. One can see this as a result of his success in finally coming to terms with cosmic consciousness. In any event, he seems to have attained complete peace within himself by the time of the last ordeal at the hands of his tormentors. Bruno's vision of an infinite universe containing innumerable worlds was the real beginning of modern Western cosmology.[31]

Worldviews and Cosmology

Before embarking on a survey of the different types of cosmology, something must be said about worldviews. Loosely, a worldview can be called a "cosmology," but this can be confusing. Cosmology *involves* worldviews, which are general ways of regarding the nature of the world and our place in it. Some of them are unsympathetic to a purely scientific approach to the universe. There are also many kinds of worldviews, such as materialism and theism, that are insufficient for our integrative purposes. Each one of the four types of cosmology that we have distinguished is associated with a particular conception of the universe as a whole. Yet, at the same time, the four are interrelated with one another. For example, the worldview underlying mythical cosmology implies the reality of a psychic universe. This need not exclude the physical world, however, which is the subject matter of scientific cosmology.[32] The physical world in this case may be thought of as derived in some way from a deeper psychic reality. Similar considerations apply to the other types as well. Worldviews are expressed symbolically in creation myths and logically in philosophical systems. Most people assimilate them unconsciously, or acquire them through social conditioning. Several worldviews may exist side by side in a complex society, but one is usually predominant. They can change from one historical era to another, though some of the features of earlier views may reappear in later ones. No person or society lacks a worldview, regardless of how vague it might be, for having one is a mark of being human.

Worldviews play an important role in cosmology, but they should be distinguished from specific scientific models of the universe. This distinction is roughly parallel to the German *Weltanshauung* (total view of reality) and *Weltbild* (unified theory of the physical world). An extensive treatment of the relation between these terms can be found in Gerhard Sonnert, *Einstein and Culture,* especially Chapter III (see Bibliography). The scientific study of the universe is always undertaken in the context of a larger set of assumptions about the nature of things. A worldview is not in itself scientific, since it cannot be deduced from science alone, nor is it subject to scientific verification and refutation; rather, it is a precondition for any cosmological inquiry. In the history of Western cosmology, there were several competing traditions based on different assumptions about the nature of the universe. These assumptions determined the kinds of scientific theories that were appropriate in a given tradition and the methods to be used for their confirmation. It could even be maintained that there were different conceptions of science operating in each tradition. All of them were based on assumptions that involved specific goals, though these were not always clearly attainable. But rationality depends as much on the nature of the goals being sought as on their actual achievement. The great successes of modern science blind us to the fact that it is not the only reasonable way of doing cosmology. It follows that the universe can be studied and explained in alternative ways, each depending upon the kind of worldview that is involved. Nevertheless, this does not imply that all worldviews are equally valid, since this would make cosmology an exercise in relativism rather than a serious search for truth.

The various conceptions of the universe in Western cosmology were based upon analogies found in human experience. Ancient Greek cosmology, for example, was heavily indebted to the view of an *organic universe* based upon the observed properties of living organisms. Consequently, Greek cosmologists (with a few notable exceptions) sought to explain the universe in terms of growth, potentiality, and purpose. The organic view culminated in Aristotle's conception of final causes, which continued to dominate much of medieval natural philosophy. Another tradition, employing the idea of a *magical universe*, came into vogue during the Renaissance. The key analogy in this tradition was a correspondence between the macrocosm (great world) and the microcosm (little world), the latter being identified with man. Renaissance cosmologists tried to understand the universe in terms of the operation of mysterious forces revealed in sympathies and antipathies between its various parts. For example, astrological correspondences between the heavens and the earth were deemed to be fundamental. By the seventeenth century, a third cosmological tradition began to appear. At that time, the universe was conceived to be analogous to a machine. Consequently, the idea of a *mechanistic universe* eventually replaced the organic and magical world views. Scientists concentrated on those aspects of nature that were most easily explained in mechanical terms. This view of the universe, with several important modifications, became the basis of Newtonian physics and led to the unprecedented developments of twentieth century scientific cosmology.

These traditions were not completely distinct and often operated simultaneously in early modern Europe, influencing one another in significant ways. All of them offered reasonable conceptions of the universe, but only the mechanistic worldview managed to gain widespread acceptance. It now dominates the contemporary scene, although in a drastically revised form. Scientific cosmology today is a restatement of mechanism in the light of radical innovations in theoretical physics.[33] The successes of relativity theory and quantum mechanics have led to the replacement of the older idea of a mechanistic universe (based on the machine analogy) by a new concept of an *energetic universe* obeying precise mathematical laws. This does not constitute a complete break with earlier mechanistic ideas; nevertheless, the emphasis is now placed on the mathematical properties of particles and their associated fields rather than on crude mechanical analogies. The energetic universe is now the reigning worldview in scientific cosmology, even though physicists cannot tell us what energy is, where it comes from, or why it exists.

Four Types of Cosmology

In the next two chapters, we are going to discuss *mythical cosmology*, which is the earliest type of cosmology on record. It is concerned above all with cosmogenesis, or the transition from absolute consciousness to the physical universe. Despite its antiquity, it still has many valuable things to tell us about this process. We will then proceed in turn to an examination of *scientific cosmology*, *traditional cosmology*, and *evolutionary cosmology*. Taken together, they give a complete picture of the universe as a whole. In itself, each type of cosmology is based on a general worldview that determines the kinds of principles and models that can be used to give an account of the universe. Although they have been regarded as antagonistic to one another, our position is that they are really complementary. Each calls attention to aspects of the universe ignored by the others. Thus, it reinforces the image of a complex universe that is not exhausted by any one type. This way of approaching cosmology enables us to see more deeply into the Consciousness that is manifested in all things.

THE PSYCHIC FACE

Leaning supinely
Dreaming of worlds yet unborn
He drifts in silence.

Plate II. Helena Petrovna Blavatsky

II
MYTHICAL COSMOLOGY

ANCIENT SCIENCE

Mythical cosmology appears in creation myths that express symbolically the worldviews of ancient cultures. Their general function is to relate people harmoniously to the world in which they live. This type of myth binds together human groups by showing them a purpose for existence beyond the mere struggle for survival. Although they still play a role in modern societies, creation myths have roots in the past, where they were more prominent than they are today. We must not assume, however, that the ancients relied on mythical thought as the only source of their ideas about the universe. Until recently, scholars considered early societies to be prescientific and assumed that their explanations were based entirely on naïve beliefs about the world. But this view has changed radically through the work of an intrepid band of inquirers in the new discipline of *archaeoastronomy,* which is the study of the practice of astronomy in preliterate cultures. Drawing on the discovery of astronomical alignments in prehistoric monuments (e.g., at Stonehenge and other sites around the world), as well as on available written records, archaeoastronomers have uncovered a wealth of information about the scientific knowledge of early peoples.[1]

Their technology was simple compared to modern standards, and they were restricted to naked eye observations in astronomy. Nonetheless, they were capable of making accurate measurements when it suited their purposes. Despite a limited experience of the surrounding physical world, they produced a science that was quite adequate for their needs. There is no reason to assume that they were less gifted than modern scientists, though their thinking may not have been the same as ours. They thought about the world in symbolic rather than logical terms, since it was deemed a sacred place inhabited by mysterious powers. This did not prevent them from developing intricate cosmologies involving both science and myth. These cosmologies played an indispensable role in their lives, even extending to the design of cities and the building of temples for the worship of their gods.

In what follows, we will focus on the general picture of the universe that emerges from these ancient cultures. Although varying in details, this picture seems to hold everywhere in the ancient world and was taken for granted in most creation myths. Mythical cosmology considers the earth to be a cosmic principle coequal with the sky. There is an important truth contained in this idea that is obscured by the scientific treatment of the earth as a planet circling the sun. Mankind lives on the surface of the earth, which was viewed as a flat disc with a rim representing the horizon. The subterranean caverns of the earth extended downward into the mysterious nether regions below. These regions were identified with dark waters; they became the location of the various hells of ancient religions. Above the sky, which was visualized as a vast dome covering the earth, were mostly unknown regions imagined as bright waters.[2] The dome of the sky represented the separation of the triple world of earth, atmosphere (or "mid-region"), and sky from the spiritual worlds beyond, the home of the higher gods. These upper worlds represented the heavens of ancient religions. Obviously, this picture of the universe, while partially based on observation, goes far beyond what could be observed with the physical senses. Creation myths deal with it symbolically, though a question still remains concerning the inner resources that mythical poets drew upon. This question will be pursued in the next chapter, but first we should examine a view of ancient astronomy that is emerging from recent studies of the subject.

MYTHICAL ASTRONOMY

One important, though generally misunderstood, aspect of early societies is the cultural role played by the sun, the moon, and the stars. There was then a "mythical astronomy" antedating both astronomy and astrology as they were shaped by the subsequent development of mathematics. Mythical astronomy predates even ancient Babylonian culture. It was based on a general belief in the correspondence between sky phenomena and events on earth. In ancient times, the heavens were observed more for practical and spiritual guidance than to satisfy curiosity.[3] It is known that detailed and accurate astronomical observations were kept. The celestial bodies were watched and their motions calculated; sometimes their cycles were marked with buildings, alignments, and stone monuments. Much of our knowledge of ancient astronomy is admittedly speculative, but archaeoastronomy, supplemented by anthropological studies of existing tribal groups, lends support to a belief in the existence of an extensive body of astronomical knowledge in preliterate societies. According to one view discussed below, this knowledge was encoded in the language of myth to preserve it for future generations.[4]

A central concern of ancient societies was that of orientation in the physical world. In many myths, for example, creation is allocated to specific spatial directions. Directions in Native American cultures were determined by observation of the rising and setting sun at the time of the solstices. They were treated as zones of the land presided over by special cosmic powers. In creation myths, the four directions were marked out first, after which the sky above and the regions below could come into being. This process was not confined to myths alone, since the marking out of directions was intentionally imposed on the physical organization of ancient cultures. Cities, provinces, and countries were appointed directions, and quarters were assigned to various forces and qualities. Tribes, castes, and activities of all sorts were arrayed around the central hub. Human culture was located at the center of a living cosmos ordered and peopled by conscious powers.

The directional ordering of society was thus rooted in creation myth, rather than the other way around. Furthermore, when space is defined according to the four directions, with the sky above and the underworld below, the earth and mankind constitute a region existing between sky and underworld in a multileveled universe that includes these three different worlds. And these worlds were bound together by an *Axis Mundi,* or World Axis, around which the sky turns.[5] The Axis was widely symbolized as a tree, such as the Scandinavian World Tree (Yggdrasil), or a mountain like the Hindu Mount Meru, but could also be represented by a vertical pole connecting earth and sky wherever it happened to be placed.

There seems to be an astronomical basis for this mythical picture of the universe. Among ancient peoples, it was crucially important to establish a calendar as a means of ordering their temporal experience of the changing seasons. The important transitional points in the annual agricultural cycle were the winter and summer solstices, as well as the spring and autumnal equinoxes. Observing the sun's position relative to known markers on the horizon—for example, a certain tree or mountain peak—identified these cardinal points. Noting which stars appear on the eastern horizon just prior to sunrise (heliacal rising) would also have sufficed. A controversial attempt to link mythical cosmology to ancient astronomy was made by Giorgio de Santillana and Hertha von Dechend in their book *Hamlet's Mill.* They interpreted the Mill as an image of the revolving universe and proposed that all mythology was derived from astronomy.

According to these authors, the "earth" referred to in myth was not the actual earth on which we live. Instead, it represented an ideal plane defined by the *ecliptic* (apparent path of the sun), or the *celestial equator* that divides the "dry land" from the "waters below." Directions were defined in terms of a picture of the earth as a plane going through the celestial equator. The ecliptic is divided into two halves. The *northern half* (reaching from the spring to the autumnal equinox) represents dry land, and the *southern half* (extending in the opposite direction) the deep waters. In this picture, the four corners of the world are the equinoxes and the solstices, which are located in the zodiacal constellations rising heliacally with them. Hence the ancient idea of a flat earth may have an astronomical reference that is unrelated to the shape of the actual earth. If so, their conception is more subtle and sophisticated than we have imagined. The central frame of the cosmos is established by the World Axis passing through the three worlds. But this is surely only one of several ways in which the ancients may have understood mythical cosmology. It has been said that there is more than one key for unlocking the mysteries of mythology. Even so, there may have been an underlying parallelism of all the interpretations that were given to the myths, for all of them were valid in their eyes.

Another claim made by the authors of *Hamlet's Mill* is that myth was connected with the *precession of the equinoxes*. They believed that this was observed, and later forgotten, long before its rediscovery by the Greek astronomer Hipparchus in the second century B.C.E. In their quest for harmony, the ancients looked for perfect order in the heavens. Any irregularity, such as eclipses or the appearance of comets, was looked upon as inauspicious and threatening. The precession of the equinoxes, if they were aware of it, would have been disturbing indeed. An apparent daily rotation of the stars around the earth from east to west, and the observed eastward passage of the sun, moon, and planets throughout the year, were familiar to them. Precession is a third movement in which the equinoxes seem to drift slowly along the ecliptic in a direction opposite to the course of the sun. An entire circuit around the ecliptic takes approximately 26,000 years. The annual change is so small that it is almost imperceptible. According to conventional history of science, such a slow shift would not have been noticed prior to the time of Hipparchus. But there is no empirical reason for rejecting the possibility that ancient priest-astronomers before Hipparchus could have recognized it from systematic observations passed down over several generations.[6]

Furthermore, the authors suggested that precession was used to define the great ages of the world, which were marked out by the apparent passage of the equinoxes through the signs of the zodiac. There are a number of myths about monstrous deeds inflicted by celestial beings on their fellows that may have been connected with the universe. The story of Cronus castrating his father Uranus, for example, can represent the separation between the Earth and the Sky. In many ancient civilizations, the inclination of the sun's path with respect to the celestial equator was taken as evidence of some earlier cosmic disaster. Precessional changes of the equinoctial points from one constellation to the next (which take approximately 2,160 years to complete) could also have been regarded as major alterations, each heralding a new age for mankind. The end of each age in the precessional cycle was believed to be have been preceded by cataclysmic floods and fires. Past cultures belonging to different equinoctial periods were thought to display a corresponding shift of emphasis from the motif of the *Cosmic Twins* (Age of Gemini) to the *Bull* (Age of Taurus), the *Ram* (Age of Aries), and the *Fish* (Age of Pisces). In each age, a new imagery seems to have been created for ancient beliefs. The next equinoctial constellation will be *Aquarius* (the Water Bearer), but no one knows when the "Aquarian Age" will begin.

It is possible that myth could be connected with prolonged observation of the positions of the heavenly bodies. This is especially true with respect to the precession of the equinoxes. Creation myths are primarily concerned with what came before the beginning of the whole precessional cycle, but they could also deal with the "re-creations" that occur as the equinoxes move through the zodiac.

The entire picture presented in *Hamlet's Mill* remains speculative, though the authors have collected an impressive amount of evidence for it that deserves careful attention. Still, the astronomical interpretation of myth has only secondary importance for our approach. Our view of creation myths is that they originally derive from a deeper source than astronomy and deal with the state of things *prior to* the appearance of a physical world.

Creation Myths and Modern Scientific Cosmology

Creation myths are symbolic narratives about how the universe began. There are a wide variety of creation stories to be found throughout the world (not all of them genuine *myths*), and anthropologists have collected thousands of them. They are variously classified, differing in quality and complexity from simple folk tales to profound metaphysical poetry. But the myths we possess today are much later than the originals, having been adapted to suit the conditions of societies that succeeded the earlier ones in time. No one really knows when or where the first creation myths appeared. They were transmitted orally from the distant past, antedating our oldest surviving records. Scholars are unable to establish a reliable date for either their origin or the traditions they represent. Myths have always been around, in one form or another, as permanent parts of human culture. Besides presenting a view of the beginning of the universe, many creation myths incorporate legends of supernatural beings, elements of cultural history, a succession of world ages, and sometimes even a conception of the end of the world.

Myths take the form of stories because narrative is an indispensable ordering principle when dealing with events connected with the psychic world. But myths are not mere fictions or fantasies without any basis in reality. Although not literally true, they tell us a great deal about things that transcend our sensory experience. They are usually found in a religious context, but this is not always essential. Most religions contain an inner pivot that persists despite their burden of rituals and doctrinal interpretations. This is why myths are composed, churches and temples built, and hymns sung. The forms they are given are human attempts to preserve and transmit past realizations that might otherwise have been lost. Anyone can make up stories about how the world began: it is the symbolism that turns a story into a genuine myth.[7] Psychologists assert that myths, like dreams, come from the so-called "unconscious mind." There is a grain of truth in this, as long as we remember that the term refers to what *we* are normally unconscious of, rather than to the unconscious as a fixed ontological category.

Creation myths begin as stories about the origin of the universe, but as they become more elaborate they may also include a description of the birth of gods and of mankind as well.[8] They are, therefore, part of the subject of *cosmogony,* which deals with hypotheses concerning the origin and evolution of the universe. Any speculative view of this kind can be called a cosmogony, whether it is an ancient myth or a recent scientific model; in either case, it is assumed that the universe had a unique beginning. Creation myths are not, however, causal explanations of how it came into being. They are primarily ways of teaching certain truths about the universe that cannot be expressed entirely in logical or scientific terms. This accounts for the existence of "non-creation" myths denying that there was a unique cosmic beginning, for they also reveal something important about the universe. Genuine creation myths employ symbols that point to a psychic realm of being transcending the physical world. They describe the universe emerging out of this realm and have the capacity to enlarge our comprehension of the possibilities of cosmic existence. These myths deal primarily with the *psychic face of the universe* that lies beyond the physical.[9]

Cosmology today is pursued as a physical science employing a host of sophisticated instruments for exploring the universe. The relevance of myth is far from clear to those scientists who are engaged in this kind of research. But every ancient culture had a view of the cosmos enshrined in creation myths that were composed long before physics and astronomy became exact sciences. Although the stories vary widely in content and quality, there is a consistency in their basic themes. Creation myths were more than pre-scientific accounts of the origin of the universe, since they also dealt with the history of the world, the origin of man, and the development of human society. The emergence of the universe was traced to a divine precosmic source; in addition, the mythical cosmos was believed to be a purposive one. These myths were deeply concerned with questions about human destiny and emphasized the importance of man as an integral part of the universe. A unified vision of the world empowered human beings to lead meaningful lives within it. To accomplish this, symbolic images were employed to awaken appropriate feelings about humanity's relationship to the cosmos. In these ways, creation myths revealed aspects of the universe that are essential to a complete understanding of cosmology.

This depth of understanding cannot be gained without recourse to myth, since the universe *as a whole* is not open to direct inspection. Conceiving it as a single object, rather than as a loose association of distinct things, requires a sustained effort of imagination. To be honest with ourselves, we should recognize that the universe ultimately defies an exclusively scientific explanation. The contemporary Big Bang model, for instance, cannot escape from mythic language because of problems related to the singularity at the beginning of things. This theory describes the origin of the universe as an explosion of elementary particles occurring spontaneously out of a virtual vacuum. The formation of atoms, stars, and galaxies is subject to thermodynamic cooling as the universe expands. For science, life is an accidental combination of molecules on a suitably disposed planet, and human existence is without a cosmic purpose. The value of life is reduced to a successful adaptation of individuals or groups in the instinctive struggle to survive. In the end, it is assumed that the universe is doomed to a final heat death from which nothing can escape. The entire process is viewed as the interaction of blind physical forces against a background of spatial emptiness.

Views like this are widely accepted today, leading one to wonder how long a culture can maintain itself on the basis of such a "creation story." Nor can it be claimed that science has proven all of this to be true. Modern science fails to account for its own assumptions, since it neglects to assign a credible role to myth in its prevailing worldview. It cannot provide a real myth for people because it lacks the sense of a transcendent purpose beyond the requirements of human survival.

The situation is becoming more critical as science moves closer to confirmation of the Big Bang theory. Regardless of the final form this theory takes, it is difficult to ignore the mounting evidence that the physical universe as we know it did not always exist. The idea of a cosmic origin is taken for granted in creation myths. For many myths, it has no more importance than any other beginning in the course of time. The mythical significance of origins lies in the suggestion that everything is derived from a transcendent source preceding the appearance of the present world. Connections between this source and the subsequent organization of the cosmos are worked out differently in various myths but, in the end, the object is to place man within a meaningful cosmic framework. Many myths begin with a primordial chaos out of which the cosmos springs forth as the result of the pressure of forces active within it. In some of them, chaos itself is accounted for in terms of deeper principles. Even though it has no discernible form of its own, chaos acts like a great womb, or matrix, containing the seeds of all things. At some point in the story, gods may be born to overcome the reactionary forces of chaos and establish the order of the universe. The implication in myth is that human beings should strive to unite themselves with the gods and share in the fruits of a final divine victory.

Theories of Myth

The modern science of mythology began in the nineteenth century, when Western scholars first took a serious interest in the large variety of myths found in different cultures around the world. The myths ranged from the simple tales of primal societies, both past and present, to those of more highly developed cultures that were still in touch with their ancient traditions. Early mythologists were primarily interested in the origins of myth, which they tried to understand on the basis of an evolutionary model derived from the increasingly popular views of Darwin in biology. They saw myths as the obsolete remnants of primitive man's attempts to explain the world around him. Scholars like Max Müller and Sir James Frazer developed elaborate theories along these lines. Their method was comparative, since they hoped to find a universal key for understanding myths. Connections among myth, ritual, and magic were explored and elaborate theories constructed to explain what had been discovered. These scholars were completely unaware of the cultural presuppositions and prejudices that they were unconsciously introducing into their work. Still, their views have merit when suitably integrated into a comprehensive picture of myth.

In the twentieth century, mythologists moved away from a literary interest in the origin of myths to inquire into the way that myths were meant to function in society. This necessitated a great deal of fieldwork in which anthropologists went out to live in surviving traditional societies that they wished to study. They criticized earlier scholars for only speculating about myths on the basis of reading rather than making an empirical study of their living environment. The result was a strongly anthropological bias in the academic study of myth. In addition, it engendered a host of new theories about the structure and purpose of myths, many of them sharply conflicting with one another. There is now a wide variety of theories, including *sociological* interpretations (Durkheim), *psychological* theories (Freud and Jung), *non-psychological* theories like "structuralism" (Lévi-Strauss) and the "history of religions" approach (Eliade). Regardless of their sophistication, these theories have not captured the essence of creation myth as a form of cosmological thought. This may be due to their lack of familiarity (perhaps mixed with disdain) with cosmic consciousness, which would certainly be foreign to the methods employed in their studies. But it is just here that the key to an understanding of creation myths may lie.

The problem inherent in mythological scholarship is that it is largely an external study of myth. Scholars have recorded a large number of myths, but the sheer wealth of this material makes it difficult to find a unifying thread to bring order into the subject as a whole. It is useful to catalogue myths according to different motifs (as is done, for example, in Stith Thompson's magisterial compilation, *Motif-Index of Folk Literature*), or to classify creation myths into general types that disregard their diverse cultural contexts. All of this work is invaluable for the use of academic scholars, but it is of little value to nonprofessionals who lack the interest and training to make much out of it. This is unfortunate, since myth was historically meant to have a direct and powerful impact on the way people actually live. The scientific study of myth cannot fill this role, because the assumptions governing such a study are primarily intellectual, not mythical. Until recently, the only voice decrying this inadequacy in the scholarly study of myth was that of Joseph Campbell.

By most accounts, Campbell's was an extraordinary life that is aptly characterized as a "Hero's Journey."[10] It illustrated the advice he gave others to "follow your bliss." After devoting years to the study of medieval and Romantic literature, both in America and abroad, he decided not to pursue a doctorate. Instead, he launched into a personal intellectual odyssey that eventually led him to a teaching position at Sarah Lawrence College in New York. He remained there for the next thirty-eight years until his retirement. During this time, he introduced a popular course in comparative mythology in which myths were used as models for understanding the world. In addition to writing many books of his own, he edited the lecture notes of the distinguished scholar of Indian thought, Heinrich Zimmer, who had died without completing them for publication. Campbell stated that he was deeply indebted to Zimmer for his method of freely interpreting the symbols of myth in order to bring meaning into personal life. Campbell saw myths as life-affirming images that encouraged a positive outlook on the world and surrounded everyday life with an aura of transcendence. He went his own way in the face of mounting academic criticism, awakening a widespread interest in mythology through his numerous books, television appearances, and seminars.

In his book, *Myths to Live By*, Campbell stated succinctly his view of the nature of myths:

> They are telling us in picture language of powers of the psyche to be recognized and integrated in our lives, powers that have been common to the human spirit forever, and which represent that wisdom of the species by which man has weathered the millenniums. Thus they have not been, and can never be, displaced by the findings of science, which relate rather to the outside world than to the depths that we enter in sleep.[11]

As can be seen, he takes a basically psychological approach to myth. Although not a strict disciple of the Swiss psychologist Carl Jung, his orientation is Jungian. Jung assumed the existence of a "collective unconscious" that is common to all human beings regardless of their culture. He claimed that the collective unconscious contains certain patterns, called "archetypes," that appear in dreams and myth. These archetypes can influence a person's behavior when they rise to the surface of consciousness. But this is not the only way of interpreting myth, and Campbell never concludes that it is. Rather, his stance seems to have been that it is the most adequate way available for interpreting myth, so why not use it.

A more serious criticism is that Campbell wavers between two different approaches to myth. In one approach, he interprets myth to be *psychological*, merely functioning as a means of adjusting one's inner life to the demands of the surrounding world in which we live. In the other, which is *metaphysical*, he sees myth as the reflection of a psychic reality transcending the physical world.[12] He is somewhat remiss with regard to the latter, preferring to stress the purely psychological interpretation in the bulk of his work. But a wider view of mythical cosmology suggests that a sharp differentiation between the psychological and the metaphysical interpretations of myth is unnecessary. For if we accept Consciousness as the essential reality, the two interpretations will merge into one.

Two general issues, reflected but by no means resolved in Campbell's writings, bear upon our present concerns. One relates to the difference between a universalist and a relativist point of view, and the other to the merits of a symbolic versus a literal interpretation of myth. Campbell was a universalist with regard to myth, stressing similarities found in myths rather than their differences. But studies in the distribution of myths suggest that there is no universal myth that is found in all cultures. Hence most anthropologists who study myths are confirmed cultural relativists. They claim that the differences among myths outweigh in importance the similarities that universalists are prone to find in them. Parallels exist, however, among myths (especially creation myths) that allow them to be classified into general types. Even though these types differ from one another, they suggest that there are some similarities among myths, at least within a given class.

Those who support universalist theories must explain why the same myths fail to appear in all cultures. Two prominent theories about this are diffusion and psychic unity. In the *diffusion* theory, it is claimed that myths originated in a few centers of high civilization and then spread from one culture to another, always retaining certain essential features. An extension of this idea is that the core myths, such as creation myths, are different versions of an ancient doctrine that became corrupted in the course of time. Nevertheless, diffusion does not explain how myths originated in the first place. The theory of *psychic unity* traces the similarities found in myths to something inherent in the human psyche (e.g., the collective unconscious), or else to the universal psychic structure of reality.

The other issue concerning us is whether a literal or a symbolic approach to myths is the correct way to understand them. This raises the question of how myths are to be interpreted. Should we look for a rational explanation of the available texts, or is an intuitive and mystical view more appropriate? If the psychological theory of archetypes is correct, then a mystical and symbolic interpretation is preferable, for the archetypes belong to the collective unconscious. According to Jung, they can never be made fully conscious, and thus cannot be subjects for rational analysis.[13] On the other hand, there are treatments of myth claiming that it is both literal and susceptible to rational explanation. Bronislaw Malinowski, a pioneering anthropologist, rejected the idea that myth is symbolic. He thought it to be a literal explanation of social customs and practices.[14] Mircea Eliade, a scholar in the history of religions, went further in asserting that myth represents "sacred history;" in this sense, it should also be taken literally. He believed that myth is a permanent part of human consciousness reflecting a reality that transcends the mundane (or "profane") world. The institutions, morality, and culture of a society are thus dependent on a shared sacred history and cannot be understood apart from it.[15] Here again, without committing ourselves wholly to either Jung's theory of archetypes or Eliade's understanding of sacred history, we will take the position that myth refers to a transcendent psychic world best described in terms of symbolic images. This is illustrated by Sri Aurobindo's interpretation of the Veda.

Sri Aurobindo's Interpretation of the Veda

A profound conception of myth is found in Sri Aurobindo's approach to the *Ṛg Veda* of ancient India.[16] This Veda is a collection of over a thousand hymns addressed to various gods and goddesses. They were composed to accompany a fire sacrifice, which was the central ritual of ancient Vedic religion. Some scholars trace the hymns back to about 1500 B.C.E., but others believe that they stem from a much earlier period. Although Sri Aurobindo is mainly concerned with the Veda as the source of Indian culture, he notes that it is representative of developments elsewhere:

> Now, in ancient Europe the schools of intellectual philosophy were preceded by the secret doctrines of the mystics; Orphic and Eleusinian mysteries prepared the rich soil of mentality out of which sprang Pythagoras and Plato. A similar starting-point is at least probable for the later march of thought in India. Much indeed of the forms and symbols of thought which we find in the Upanishads, much of the substance of the Brahmanas supposes a period in India in which thought took the form or the veil of secret teachings such as those of the Greek mysteries.[17]

It is still not known how far back in time the Vedic period extends. The standard explanation of an Aryan invasion that occurred around 1500 B.C.E., subjugating the native Dravidian peoples, is increasingly improbable in the light of recent archaeological evidence. There is a strong possibility that the *Ṛg Veda* represents a high civilization existing in northern India in prehistoric times; the Aryans may actually have been an indigenous culture dwelling side by side with the other elements of society.[18] This view would accord more with the preeminent status given to the spiritual wisdom of the Vedic tradition than with the theory that the hymns were composed by invading nomadic tribes with a primitive religion of nature worship.

In the nineteenth century, European scholars began to take a critical interest in the Veda. They interpreted the hymns as products of a superstitious worship of the phenomena of nature (such as the sun, rain, thunder, and dawn), personified as gods by a primitive people. Traditional Indian scholarship, represented by the Vedic commentator Sayana, did not fare much better. Sayana understood the Veda from the standpoint of sacrificial rites. He tried to discover the nature of the Vedic sacrifice and give a full account of the ceremonies performed in it. But neither of these views explains the supreme status ascribed to the Veda as the foundation of Indian culture. For Sri Aurobindo, though, the Veda ("Knowledge") is the expression of spiritual realizations, reporting knowledge of the ultimate Truth experienced by the ancient seer-poets (Rishis or Kavis). He claimed that a careful psychological examination of the hymns would reveal the inner "secret of the Veda," which had been concealed from the profane:

> The hypothesis I propose is that the Rig-veda is itself the one considerable document that remains to us from the early period of human thought of which the historic Eleusinian and Orphic mysteries were the failing remnants, when the spiritual and psychological knowledge of the race was concealed, for reasons now difficult to determine, in a veil of concrete and material figures and symbols which protected the sense from the profane and revealed it to the initiated.[19]

This hypothesis of a double meaning in the Veda is the basis of his approach to the hymns.

Sri Aurobindo's view is the result of a close examination of the language of the hymns with an open mind unhampered by previous scholarly theories, of which he was well aware. This was supplemented by the instincts of a great poet and seer. He maintains that:

> One of the leading principles of the mystics was the sacredness and secrecy of self-knowledge and the true knowledge of the Gods. This wisdom was, they thought, unfit, perhaps even dangerous to the ordinary human mind or in any case liable to perversion and misuse and loss of virtue if revealed to vulgar and unpurified spirits. Hence they favoured the existence of an outer worship, effective but imperfect, for the profane, an inner discipline for the initiate, and clothed their language in words and images which had, equally, a spiritual sense for the elect, a concrete sense for the mass of ordinary worshippers.[20]

A modern student of the Veda must therefore try to discover the "sense of Vedic symbols and the psychological functions of the Gods."[21] In this case, the Vedic sacrifice becomes a vehicle for spiritual growth presided over by the gods. Man by his self-offering actualizes the divine qualities within himself, acquiring in this way the means for living a more opulent life on earth. The sacrificial ritual was understood by the Seers to be the outer symbol of a deep psychological process. Its core meaning was that of *an inner journey* to the home of the gods in which the performer of the sacrifice offers himself, along with his works and attainments, in order to gain a greater truth and delight of existence. In Sri Aurobindo's words:

> The work of the Aryan is a sacrifice which is at once a battle and an ascent and a journey, a battle against the powers of darkness, an ascent to the highest peaks of the mountain beyond earth and heaven into Swar [the luminous heaven of divine Truth], a journey to the other shore of the rivers and the ocean into the farthest Infinity of things. . . . The higher existence is the divine, the infinite of which the shining Cow, the infinite Mother, Aditi, is the symbol; the lower is subject to her dark form Diti. The *object* of the sacrifice is to win the higher or divine being and possess with it and make subject to its law and truth the lower or human existence.[22]

According to this interpretation, the gods of the Veda are the powers and personalities of one ultimate Reality that manifests itself in the universe in multifarious forms. In the famous "Hymn of Creation" (*Ṛg Veda*, 10. 129), for example, "That One" (*Tad Ekam*) brings itself into cosmic existence by a massive concentration of spiritual force (*Tapas*); the energies released in this process result in the appearance of an ordered world. The essential feature of the manifested universe is the *Ṛta* (Ritam), which Sri Aurobindo refers to as "almost the key-word of any psychological or spiritual interpretation" of the Veda.[23] *Ṛta* is the Right, the vast Truth of being, on which the whole cosmos is based. It is the objective aspect of cosmic consciousness and can thus be rendered as the Cosmic Order, or Cosmic Harmony; as Eternal Law, it regulates right activity in the world.[24] The later Hindu concepts of *karma* (action) and *dharma* (law) represent its main aspects. *Ṛta* also governs the Vedic sacrifice, supporting the proper reciprocal relations between the gods and man. Sri Aurobindo's interpretation of the Veda is thus at once psychological and metaphysical; it provides the key not only to the secret of the Veda but to a deeper understanding of creation myths. For creation can be regarded as a *Supreme Sacrifice* by which the One becomes fragmented into the Many, without losing its essential unity. In so doing, it can have the delight of multiple existence in a universe manifested by its own nature. But one further aspect of myth, found in the Veda and elsewhere, deserves emphasis—the role of the Great Mother in the creative process.

The Great Mother and Creation Myth

The earliest myths may belong to prehistoric cultures that worshipped a Goddess as the original source of all things. She was identified with Nature in general and the Earth in particular. Every culture in the ancient world recognized her in one form or another. As the Great Mother, she gave birth to the universe or to lesser gods who then went on to fashion it; she embraces all beings as her children and nurtures them to maturity. In the Vedas she appears as *Aditi,* the infinite Mother of the Gods, who in later Hinduism became *Mahādevī* (Great Goddess), the divine feminine manifested in a thousand goddess-forms. She is Śakti (Divine Force), who saves the world again and again when called upon to subdue the dark powers that threaten it. The Greeks knew her in many guises. Among the earliest were *Gaia* (Earth) and *Rhea* (the Flow), since she was associated with the waters of creation. This theme is also found in early Near Eastern creation myths, where the waters appear as *Tiamat* in Mesopotamia and *Nun* in Egypt, both signifying a primordial ocean from which the world arose. Later, she took the forms of *Isis* in Egypt, *Inanna* in Sumeria, *Astarte* in Phoenicia, and *Ishtar* in Babylon, but men did not understand her ways and demeaned her in their rites. In ancient Persia she was known as *Anahita* (the Pure) and associated with the primeval cosmic waters. To the Romans she was *Cybele,* the Magna Mater, whose ancestry can be traced back to the wild Mountain Goddess of ancient Anatolia. The Gnostics called her *Sophia* (Wisdom), and the Kabbalists *Shekhinah* (Indwelling Glory); in Christianity, she appears as *Mary,* the Mother of God. Mahayana Buddhism sees her as *Prajñāpāramitā* (the Perfection of Wisdom) and *Tārā,* the Divine Savioress. China venerates her as *Kwan Yin,* the Goddess of Mercy. Philosophically, she is Universal Nature, *Natura naturans* (Nature begetting), and the immanent cause of all things (Spinoza).

An extensive literature is available on the Goddess and her cultural roots.[25] Her worship is very old; according to one theory, it preceded the appearance of warlike nomadic tribes that founded the patriarchal societies of the Iron Age. These societies were responsible for reworking the earlier myths of the Goddess to reflect their own veneration of a male war god associated with the sky. Many of the subordinate goddesses who were included in their pantheons were originally aspects of the one Goddess, or Great Mother. In the nineteenth century, the Swiss scholar Johann Jacob Bachofen developed the theory of an early stage of matriarchal culture existing prior to the patriarchal reorganization of society; this was followed by a gradual decline of Goddess worship.[26] His theory was recently revived and considerably elaborated, by feminist writers who see in it a justification of their struggle for women's rights. Regardless of the social and political issues involved in this conflict, it is obvious that the status of the Goddess has suffered from the exclusively masculine conception of God so prevalent in monotheistic religions.

Evidence supporting belief in the Goddess in "Old Europe" was gathered by the noted archaeologist, Marija Gimbutas, whose works were seminal to a revival of interest in the subject. They are crammed with a wealth of archaeological detail, which is interpreted in terms of her theory of Kurgan invasions from the steppes of Asia.[27] The material uncovered in her researches supports the view of a prehistoric egalitarian society that once existed in Europe, but it is still not conclusive and has many critics in academic circles. Despite being denigrated by many, partly due to the prominent role it assigns to the feminine in creation, worship of the Goddess is alive and growing today. Because tangible evidence is scarce, experts differ in their appraisal of Gimbutas's interpretation of the centrality of the Goddess in ancient cultures. Before the advent of writing, myths were transmitted orally for many millenniums. By the time that written records were kept, their original form may have long since disappeared. Yet there are hints of the Great Mother in the creation myths that we now possess, for she appears in disguised form in many of them. This will become evident in the next section where some typical creation myths are examined.

TYPES OF CREATION MYTHS

Creation myths can be classed and categorized in different ways. Each classification has merits, but we are not concerned with an exhaustive typology. Instead, a few myths are chosen to illustrate a variety of views on creation that have been influential in mythical cosmology. We will, moreover, concentrate on that part of the story describing how the universe initially comes into existence. This process is entirely psychic, but it also implies that the ultimate result will be the appearance of the physical world. It is not essential that the universe actually had a beginning in time, since mythical time (which can be cyclic or spiral) is not the same as physical time, which is usually linear. Under the appropriate conditions, it is even conceivable that time could vanish back into the precosmic condition from which it arose. Myth, though couched in temporal terms, seems to be saying something about an "Origin" transcending time altogether. The Origin toward which our attention is directed is eternal and hence present at all times. Where science fails to uncover it, myth reveals its enduring presence in the universe. Different symbols are employed that display a remarkable resemblance, suggesting the possibility of a universal key for understanding creation myths. This key, however, is elusive.[28]

We will treat four types of creation myth: creation by God, divine withdrawal, emergence from chaos, and cosmic cycles. Each type is illustrated by a myth taken from a major cultural tradition. They represent different ways of regarding the psychic beginnings of the universe. Bear in mind that the creative process is prior to physical time. Although the narrative form of the myth usually begins at a definite instant, this need not mean that creation (or manifestation) is restricted to that instant, since it may extend over the entire range of time (see Chapter VII).

Creation by God

> In the beginning God created the heavens and the earth. (2) The earth was without form and void, and darkness was upon the face of

> the deep; and the Spirit of God was moving over the face of the waters. (3) And God said, "Let there be light"; and there was light. (4) And God saw that the light was good; and God separated the light from the darkness. (5) God called the light Day, and darkness he called Night. And there was evening and there was morning, one day. (6) And God said, "Let there be a firmament in the midst of the waters, and let it separate the waters from the waters." (7) And God made the firmament and separated the waters which were under the firmament from the waters which were above the firmament. And it was so. (8) And God called the firmament Heaven. And there was evening and there was morning, a second day.[29]

Because of its widespread familiarity, our first example is taken from the biblical story in Genesis 1-2:3. Many scholars believe that it was inserted into the Bible after the return of the Israelites from their captivity in Babylon. They generally distinguish it from the more anthropomorphic account in Genesis 2:4-23. In that older version, God (*Yahweh*) seems to be derived from the male sky god worshipped by ancient warrior tribes. He walks on earth and converses with Adam, the first man, whom he formed "of dust from the ground." According to this story, woman was created later than man, and almost as an afterthought. The later version, where God (*Elohim*) is more remote and impersonal, is the most elaborate creation myth in the Bible. Calling Genesis a myth may seem odd, since it has been incorporated into an extensive theological framework that treats it literally as a divinely revealed truth. But it is studded with the influence of mythological traditions from Mesopotamia and elsewhere.

The story in Genesis 1-2:3 is more intellectual than others, suggesting that earlier mythic materials were worked over by priests and scribes. In particular, it contains traces of Babylonian ideas of the world emerging out of a watery chaos. Although theologians have interpreted Genesis to mean that God created the universe *ex nihilo,* references to "the deep" and "the waters" (1:2) seem to point to something preceding creation. In the first verse, we are told that "God created the heavens and the earth", but creation of the waters is not mentioned. Water is a fundamental mythological symbol traceable back to the worship of the Great Mother as the primary creatrix of the world. The primeval waters of myth were generally associated with feminine qualities, possibly because of a perceived relation with the amniotic fluids of birth. In Hindu mythology, they were said to consist of milk—another connection to the imagery of the Great Mother.

A puzzling feature of the Genesis story is that light is created before the sun and the stars (1:3). This is difficult to understand, unless it refers to a psychic process that occurred prior to the coming into being of the physical universe. That process, which we have called cosmogenesis, is the core of many creation myths. Genesis 1:4-5 develops the imagery further, for it is said that "God separated the light from the darkness" and called the light "Day" and the darkness "Night." This symbolism is similar to that of other myths where the phenomena of night and day, darkness and light, play an essential role in the story, but they are relative terms that can be understood in different ways. For mystics, darkness signifies light on a higher level of existence and, conversely, light on our level is viewed as darkness.[30] In these verses, darkness may refer to the unmanifested being of God that remains hidden from us; light would then represent the first manifestation of the psychic cosmos from which the physical world is derived. The suggestion of a separation, or boundary, between opposites is also important in many other creation myths. It reappears in Genesis 1:6-8 as the firmament (or sky), which divides the waters above from the waters below.

The rest of the story is taken up with God shaping the earth, filling the heavens with "lights," bringing forth living creatures, and creating man in his own image.[31] From a cosmological standpoint, these are secondary details; in many myths they are left to the work of lesser gods. There are other ways of interpreting Genesis, of course, but it clearly can be treated as a myth. One advantage of doing so is that we can then see parallels with other creation myths. In spite of the differences among cultures, there are remarkable similarities in their patterns of thought about creation. Images of the primeval waters, night and day, darkness and light, are common among them. The myths that will be considered next, however, contrast sharply with Genesis. The first provides a deeper insight into the Biblical outlook, the second offers a view of emergence from chaos, and the third presents the conception of cosmic cycles.

Divine Withdrawal

> At the beginning of creation, when Ein Sof withdrew its presence all around in every direction, it left a vacuum in the middle, surrounded on all sides by the light of Ein Sof, empty precisely in the middle. . . . Descending into the vacuum, it transformed into an amorphous mass, surrounded in every direction by the light of Ein Sof. Out of this mass emanated the four worlds: emanation, creation, formation, and actualization. For in its simple desire to realize its intention, the emanator relumined the mass with a ray of the light withdrawn at first—not all of the light, because if it had all returned, the original state would have been restored, which was not the intention.[32]

An esoteric version of Genesis can be found in Kabbalistic speculations concerning the relationship between God and the world he created. For example, the sixteenth century Safed mystic, Isaac Luria, developed the idea of an intentional contraction (*tsimtsum*) of the Infinite (*Ein Sof*) into itself. This "God beyond God" is an absolute abyss, the limitless, unfathomable reality both beyond and within all things. Therefore, without limiting its own infinity, nothing else could have come into existence. Only some kind of self-limitation could restrict the Infinite. Contraction, in this myth, is not understood as concentration at a single point, but as withdrawal or retreat *from* a point. Room was thus left for the universe to come into being. It was necessary that a primordial space (*tehiru*), or "vacuum," be established in which creation could proceed. This space is not the "nothing" of Biblical theology, which is outside God, but a place created *within* Ein Sof where the universe could be brought into existence. It is not completely empty, for an "aroma" of the Divine remains in it.

Divine withdrawal was followed by the emanation of a single ray of light into space, where it became the "amorphous mass" mentioned in the above quotation. The dual activity of withdrawal and emanation is comparable to the inhalation and exhalation of breath. It is the dynamism underlying all cosmic processes. The first being to emerge out of the divine light is *Adam Kadmon,* the Primordial Man, who encompasses all humanity. He is the androgynous human archetype, a macrocosmic (and microcosmic) principle, embodying the ten *sefirot,* or divine emanations. The sefirot are associated with the various names and attributes of God. They can be visualized as separate globes of light connected by a network of lines or "paths." Originally contained within the initial ray, they subsequently became arranged into the shape of Adam Kadmon. As creation proceeds, they are further differentiated and acquire translucent vessels of their own. At this early stage, however, they are simply concentrations of light that do not need special vessels to contain them.

Four worlds emanated from the central mass, now identified with Adam Kadmon: *Atzilut* (Emanation), *Beriah* (Creation), *Yetzirah* (Formation), and *Asiyyah* (Actualization). They are sometimes imagined as concentric spheres defining the structure of the Kabbalistic universe. Atzilut is the most spiritual of the four, being closest to the source of light. Beriah is next, containing the mental forms that organize the phenomena of the lower worlds. In Yetzirah, the creative energies become fluid vital forces seeking embodiment in the fourth world of material things (Asiyyah). Even here there is a guiding light, the *Shekhinah,* or indwelling presence of the Divine Mother in this fallen world. All of these worlds are filled with beings of their own kind, such as angels, archangels, and so forth. Thus the physical universe is only a part of an extensive network of worlds, psychic in nature, which penetrate and interact with one another. As they descend from Atzilut, differentiation increases and there is a coarsening of their substance.

The sefirot appear in all of the worlds, their strength diminishing in each succeeding one; in their purest state they reside in the world of Atzilut. *Keter* (Crown), *Hokhmah*

(Wisdom), and *Binah* (Understanding) are the highest sefirot. All being is united in Keter, also called "nothingness" (*ayin*) because its nature is unknowable. It is commonly depicted as the "rootless root" of the cosmic Tree of Life, composed of the original sefirot. Like the *Aśvattha* tree in the *Bhagavad Gītā,* it grows downward through the worlds. Hokhmah is the primordial point or seed of creation (hence the Father) that proceeds from Keter. It gave rise to Binah, the Kabbalistic version of the Great Mother, for "Understanding" conceives and brings forth the seven lower sefirot that complete the spiritual body of Adam Kadmon. The three higher sefirot are said to represent his head. After this beginning, the rest of creation becomes more complex.

In the ensuing process of emanation, light poured out in all directions from the eyes, mouth, ears, and nose of Adam Kadmon, streaming in a more concentrated form from his eyes. Although this stream of light was easily contained by the first three sefirot, its excessive intensity shattered the weaker vessels of the remaining ones. This cataclysm is called *shevirah,* the breaking of the vessels, which scattered sparks in all directions. Many of the sparks were trapped by falling shards, which are likened to dark shells (*kelippot*). These shells are demonic powers that had descended into the deepest abyss of the universe. They generally oppose the divine intention of creation. Everything was thrown into confusion by this apparent flaw in the cosmic process; some Kabbalists find it difficult to explain why it occurred. The intention of Ein Sof was to illuminate the whole world with its light, but now only a few portions were brightened by sparks leaving the rest of the universe in darkness. Therefore, it had to be freed from the polluting influence of the demonic kelippot.

When the vessels shattered, most of the light flowed back to its source. This enabled the demonic powers, with their imprisoned sparks, to upset the harmony of the lower worlds. A new light then burst forth from the forehead of Adam Kadmon in an effort to control the damage. The broken vessels were reconstituted in Atzilut and once more rendered capable of holding the divine light. It was the beginning of the work of restoration, or repair (*tikkun*), by which the scattered sparks are to be reunited. This work was made more difficult because the breaking of the vessels implies that Adam Kadmon, through unrestrained self-will, had disrupted the divine unity. Since he is the archetype of humanity, all human souls shared in the catastrophe. Hence the disunity following the breaking of the vessels became more severe and can only be mended with the help of a spiritually regenerated mankind. Many Kabbalists believe that this is part of the purpose of Ein Sof in creating the world.[33]

There are several important aspects of this myth that deserve emphasis. The intention of Ein Sof was to manifest the divine light in an infinitely varied universe, in order to behold itself objectively from countless individual centers. The breaking of the vessels, far from being a defeat of this intention, was instrumental to the appearance of greater multiplicity in the world. But further action is required to repair the rupture that it caused, with humanity playing a key role in the renewal of cosmic harmony. The three stages of creative unfoldment (contraction, breaking of the vessels, and restoration) can be viewed as phases of a comprehensive plan for divine manifestation. Although the internal transitions are not easy to follow, the overall framework remains intact. A related consideration is that the lower worlds are no longer found in their proper places after the breaking of the vessels, each world being displaced to a lower level than before. The world of Asiyyah, for example, is now mixed with the demonic realm of the kelippot, where the densest matter is located. An important part of the work of restoration is to raise it to the next higher level, now occupied by Yetzirah. If this happens, a more subtle physical world composed of a finer grade of matter could replace the present one.

There are other implications of this myth that are being taken seriously in some quarters today. Many scholars see parallels between it and ideas in modern scientific cosmology, particularly the big bang theory. The image of the universe exploding into stars and galaxies brings to mind the scattering of sparks when the vessels of light shattered. Suggestive as this may be, it must be remembered that the Kabbalistic view of creation is fundamentally psychic and reaches far beyond the physical universe. The latter is only the final result of a series of complicated events occurring prior to its coming into existence. According to the Kabbalah, therefore, the psychic worlds are vaster and more potent than we can yet imagine.

Emergence from Chaos

> In the beginning this [universe] was non-existent. It became existent. It grew. It turned into an egg. The egg lay for the period of a year. Then it broke open. Of the two halves of the egg-shell, one half was of silver, the other of gold. That which was of silver became the earth; that which was of gold, heaven. What was the thick membrane [of the white] became the mountains; the thin membrane [of the yolk], the mist and the clouds. The veins became the rivers; the fluid in the bladder, the ocean. And what was born of it was yonder *Aditya*, the sun. When it was born shouts of "Hurrah!" arose, together with all beings and all objects of desire. Therefore at its rise and its every return shouts of "Hurrah!" together with all beings and all objects of desire arise.[34]

There are many creation myths that tell of the emergence of the universe out of *chaos*. The original meaning of the Greek word chaos (as it appears, for instance, at the beginning of Hesiod's *Theogony*) was "gap" or "chasm," and did not imply the later idea of a confused mixture of elements. What it seems to represent is a formless, undifferentiated state of existence that prevailed before a cosmos came into being. Appearing at the beginning of a creation myth, chaos is best understood as the potentiality for becoming a universe that has not yet been manifested.[35] It suggests that something, no matter how indefinite, already existed; thus even in the state of chaos there is the possibility of a cosmos. Chaos almost never signifies a condition of absolute nothingness. In ancient Near Eastern myths, it was symbolized by the primeval waters out of which the gods were born; they then proceeded to shape the world. Hesiod's myth describes Mother Earth (Gaia) as emerging from Chaos and producing Father Sky

(Uranus), implying the primacy of the feminine principle in creation.

An interesting version of this theme occurs in one of the Upanishads (see the above quotation).[36] It describes a world egg appearing out of the non-existent. Non-existence does not imply *absolute nothingness*, because the universe could not have come out of nothing at all. Here it refers to the formless state of chaos prior to the coming into being of a cosmos. Other Hindu myths represent it as a primeval ocean of milk. After a year, the egg is said to have broken open to become the universe. The year mentioned is most likely symbolic, since Hindu tradition incorporates a complex system of calendric calculations in which human years are replaced by divine years of much longer duration. These calculations are based on the idea of cosmic cycles, which will be discussed at greater length in the next section. The myth we are now considering goes on to say that the sun (*Āditya*) was born from the egg when it hatched, but the reference may be to the birth of the first God (*Brahmā?*), who became the progenitor of the cosmos.

Imagery associated with the world egg is common in creation myths and often appears together with that of chaos. This is not a crude attempt at a biological account of the origin of the physical universe, for the egg represents a formation that lies wholly within the psychic world; its various parts stand for psychic principles rather than physical things. Further details about this will be considered in the next chapter on the *Stanzas of Dzyan*. The egg is a universal symbol of the original unity of the cosmos and its potential for life. Obviously, this is another aspect of the feminine creative principle associated with the Great Mother. A world egg also occurs in the ancient Orphic myth about Phanes, the firstborn God. In the beginning, Time (a symbol for chaos?) is said to have created a silver egg out of which Phanes was born. He was an androgynous being who bore within himself the seeds of the gods and other creatures. As can be seen, parallels with the Hindu myth are striking. Even though in both myths the egg comes into existence without the intervention of a supreme deity, a God who appears after it hatches brings forth the universe. The relationship between this God and the "non-existent" prior to creation will be explored further in the next section on cosmic cycles.

Cosmic Cycles

> In the night of Brahma, Nature is inert, and cannot dance till Shiva wills it: He rises from His rapture, and dancing sends through inert matter pulsing waves of awakening sound, and lo! matter also dances appearing as a glory round about Him. Dancing, He sustains its manifold phenomena. In the fulness of time, still dancing, he destroys all forms and names by fire and gives new rest.[37]

A fourth type of creation myth, more characteristic of later Hindu thought, portrays a universe that is being created and destroyed in a cycle that repeats itself throughout infinite time; thus, like an ever-turning wheel, it has neither beginning nor end. This implies a distinction between *linear time* and *cyclic time*. The former goes on forever (though it may have had a beginning), but the latter renews itself again and again. In Hindu myth, there are cycles within cycles, built upon a basic one consisting of four "ages" (*yuga*). A cycle of four ages represents the steady decline from a perfect state at the beginning to the *kali yuga,* which ends in widespread devastation; this scheme is incorporated into larger ones up to the cycle of the universe itself. The period of four ages (*mahāyuga*) amounts to 4,320,000 human years. A thousand *mahāyuga* is known as a *kalpa,* or "Day of *Brahmā*." This is matched by a "Night of *Brahmā,*" in which the universe lies inert in a state of dissolution (*pralaya*). There is an even larger cycle of one hundred *Brahmā* years (over 300 trillion human years) that is not reflected in the above quotation. The creator God (here called Śiva) re-emerges after each pralaya to start the entire process anew. The exact figures given are not important, but the vast time scales involved are very impressive.[38]

Cyclic time is illustrated by the well-known figure of the Dancing Shiva (Plate III). The universe is viewed as a recurring manifestation of Śiva's power. As *Naṭarāja* (Lord of the Dance), he dances blissfully within a flaming halo that symbolizes the Cosmic Fire consuming the worlds. This Fire represents his Śakti (divine feminine energy in Hinduism). The drum in one of his hands sounds the cosmic beat that paces the succession of cycles, while in another he holds the fire that destroys, or renders non-manifest, each world at the end of its cycle. In this way, the figure portrays the creative and destructive forces that drive the universe onward. It is implied that the initial source of these forces is Shiva, whose entranced expression signifies his inner poise.

There is a timeless background of this process, called Brahman (the Absolute) in Hindu metaphysics.[39] Brahman is not another god besides Śiva but the One Reality behind and within all manifestation (including Śiva). Thus, Brahman is eternal Being, while Śiva creates and destroys worlds in innumerable cycles. In the rendition of the myth given here, however, time does not appear to be continuous over successive cycles. The "night of *Brahmā*" (*pralaya*) refers to a period of inactivity between the kalpas; Śiva subsides into the complete silence of Brahman ("His rapture"). Time would also disappear, since nothing exists to mark its passing. When the next world begins it would have a new time. What this seems to imply is that time is discontinuous from one cycle to the next. Each cycle would be a new universe with a unique beginning, rather than a recycling of the same one.

According to this myth, a new world does not appear out of nothing, because even during *pralaya* there is eternal Being (Brahman). But the relation between time and eternity remains mysterious. There are several reasons for rejecting the idea of a continuously recurring universe in time, one being that, from a physical perspective, increasing entropy in successive cycles would limit them to a finite number.[40] Another reason is that it implies a monotonous "eternal return," the same universe repeating itself over and over again. The view of a discontinuity in time seems preferable to this, despite the difficulty of conceiving it.

Plate III. The Dancing Shiva

Still, if there is no continuity at all between successive cycles, why postulate more than one world, since we could never know of the others? But in the present myth, there is an eternal background from which Śiva arises to dance new worlds into existence. Something must therefore carry over from one cycle to the next, suggesting a continuity of some sort between them. The following chapter contains a hint that throws some light on this mystery, at least in symbolic terms. For the Stanzas of Dzyan state that before this universe came into being, time "lay asleep in the infinite bosom of duration" (Stanza I.2). Duration signifies eternal time, which is always "now." The time of our experience, on the other hand, is conceived as a living entity that grows from one universe to the next, with periods of inactivity between them. It is implied that, instead of being completely annihilated at the end of a cosmic cycle, time temporarily ceases to be active.[41]

Even if it is conceded that other universes have existed prior to our present one, we may be inclined to wonder whether any will succeed it. Must it always be necessary for a universe to end in a *pralaya?* There is a curious reference to this in the *Collected Works of the Mother*. She remarks that:

> Traditions say that a universe is created, then withdrawn in the *pralaya,* then a new one comes and so on; and according to them we should be the seventh universe, and being the seventh universe, we are that which will not return into *pralaya* but progress constantly without going back.[42]

The Mother does not identify the traditions she is referring to, but her remark could be a significant insight into the future.[43] At first glance, it is difficult to imagine constant progress in a world ruled by the law of entropy, since everything would be doomed to eventual dissolution (*pralaya*).[44] Still, there is evidence that increasingly complex organization has occurred in the universe. The only way that progress could continue to occur would be for another kind of matter to become operative in the world, possibly a more subtle form of it than now exists. This would depend on an inner psychic process rather than physical means. Subtle matter could also obey new laws transcending those now operating in the physical world. Regarding such a possibility, we should note that in the Hindu theory of five elements, or substantial principles, the primary one is *Ākāsha* (Ether). This element is more subtle and fluid than the others, and differs from the obsolete mechanical ether of classical physics.[45] *Ākāsha* fills space everywhere; if some part of it were to condense into definite forms, they might become permanent features of the universe that are not subject to entropic decay. For the time being, however, this possibility is locked away in the depths of the psychic world, which is the primary subject of creation myths.

III
THE STANZAS OF DZYAN

THE SECRET DOCTRINE

The Stanzas of Dzyan, though rarely noticed in the academic world, are an excellent example of a creation myth. Many scholars overlook them because of their ambiguous origins, wide-ranging eclecticism, and difficulty of interpretation. They appeared in a massive two-volume work, *The Secret Doctrine*, written by the charismatic and much maligned Russian occultist, Madame Helena Petrovna Blavatsky. Her early life remains sketchy, but she herself claimed to have been everywhere and done just about everything. By her own account, her childhood in Russia was filled with paranormal experiences. After a brief and unhappy marriage, she traveled extensively in North America, Egypt, and Tibet (where she claimed to have studied the secrets of the universe with learned sages). After living in the United States for a short period, she met Colonel Henry S. Olcott, who became her collaborator in founding the Theosophical Society. They traveled together to India, where she became a center of controversy. She eventually left India in the face of venomous criticism, spending the last part of her life in Europe. Her masterpiece was finished in England just before she passed away at the age of fifty-nine.[1]

Madame Blavatsky did not claim to be the primary author of her books. Nevertheless, her dominant personality is invariably reflected in them. She railed against the scientific materialism of her age, strongly disapproving of nineteenth century Spiritualism and dogmatic Christianity. A sworn enemy of sham and hypocrisy, she scorned all forms of authority over the freedom of the inquiring spirit.

Her considerable gifts, and occasional failings, are all reflected in *The Secret Doctrine*. The book is an extended commentary on the Stanzas of Dzyan, which constitute the core of its teaching. Madame Blavatsky presented them as part of a lost ancient text accessible only through psychic mediumship, a claim confounding easy proof. They may have actually issued from her fertile imagination, though she insisted that she merely transcribed them. We can ignore these alternative positions: the Stanzas are able to stand on their own merits, independent of their origin. They bear all the marks of an authentic creation myth, and in a genuine search for insight into the nature of the universe, we are free to make use of them.When dealing with a subject as vast as the universe *as a whole*, they enable us to gain a better sense of its psychic roots. In this respect, it is remarkable that a physicist of Einstein's stature was reading *The Secret Doctrine* shortly before he passed away. A copy of the book was found open on his desk after his death. This could indicate a growing awareness on his part of the deep connection between the physical and psychic areas of experience.

The Secret Doctrine was published in 1888. It consists of two volumes that claim to set forth the primordial wisdom from which religion, philosophy, and science have all derived. The first volume (*Cosmogenesis*) contains seven Stanzas dealing with the origin of the universe, and the second volume (*Anthropogenesis*) describes the evolution of the earth and mankind through a succession of "root-races," each inhabiting a different continent. We will focus upon a few verses taken from the first three Stanzas on cosmogenesis. The Stanzas of Dzyan are less attached to specific religious and cultural forms than other myths, and are thus more universal. They are Madame Blavatsky's attempt to translate the original text as best she could from an archaic language (*Senzar*), unknown to scholars, in which they were supposedly written. For this purpose, she used terms from Sanskrit, Tibetan, Chinese and other scriptural sources unfamiliar to most people. This has caused endless confusion, so we will avoid as much of it as possible when discussing the Stanzas.

We must distinguish the tradition of the "Secret Doctrine" from the book that bears its name. The first is ageless, the latter seeks to capture its essence. The "Secret Doctrine" was never deliberately withheld from those who were prepared to receive it. On the contrary, it points to an innate wisdom that everyone possesses but only a few utilize. As the yogi Sri Krishna Prem points out, it cannot be adequately known or explained in words:

> It is the eternal Wisdom underlying the teachings of all religions, the actual facts, of which we can never have more than interpretations unless we ourselves gain experience of them. For this reason it is secret.[2]

According to Madame Blavatsky, her book represents a minute part of this wisdom from which the world's religions have sprung. Her purpose in writing *The Secret Doctrine* is stated in the Preface to the book:

> The aim of this work may be thus stated: to show that Nature is not "a fortuitous concurrence of atoms," and to assign to man his rightful place in the scheme of the Universe; to rescue from degradation the archaic truths which are the basis of all religions; and to uncover, to some extent, the fundamental unity from which they all spring; finally, to show that the occult side of Nature has never been approached by the Science of modern civilization.[3]

To accomplish these ends, she drew upon the Stanzas of Dzyan.

The Stanzas are based upon three general propositions: (1) the existence of one boundless Reality which is the infinite and eternal cause of the cosmos, (2) the appearance and disappearance of numberless universes in an endless succession of cycles, and (3) the identity of all souls in the Absolute and their pilgrimage through the "cycle of incarnation" in accordance with karmic law.[4] While Madame Blavatsky offers but a small selection of material culled from a larger, now lost work, it amply illustrates these propositions. The Stanzas suggest the existence of a psychic realm of invisible worlds and forces that is somehow connected with the universe we perceive. It consists of different grades of matter that are subtler than the physical senses can detect. These constitute a series of cosmic levels or planes on which various kinds of beings are said to exist.

Madame Blavatsky tells us that the Stanzas of Dzyan are primarily concerned with our solar system rather than the entire universe. Knowledge about the latter was available, but temporarily held back from an unready humanity.[5] The cosmic picture presented in the first volume of *The Secret Doctrine* is a complex system of worlds made up of planetary chains with globes existing on different psychic levels. Generally, there are seven planetary chains in a solar system, each possessing seven interpenetrating globes. All but one of the globes in each chain lie in the psychic world and are thus invisible to us. The fourth, or most material, globe is the only one that can be seen. In our planetary chain, the physical earth is the visible exemplar of the others. Life waves traverse these globes in descending and ascending evolutionary arcs. As they pass from one globe to another, the globes become active or dormant in turn. When a life wave finishes its rounds in one chain, it moves on to another in a seemingly endless progression. The commentary goes into great detail about the development of life on earth, which experiences seven rounds or cycles of evolution. Increasing materialization continues until the fourth round on the visible earth. At the present time, human evolution is said to have just passed the middle point of the fourth round, when the life wave begins its ascent toward higher forms of being. The second volume, on anthropogenesis, continues the story of the earth's history, focusing upon the evolution of human races as they appear in successive ages.

Our concern is with the Stanzas as creation myth, not with a wealth of detail which can confuse and distract us from the essential cosmological principles. The account also goes far beyond what can be established by modern science. Trained psychics claim to have verified parts of it using introspective methods, but these methods are rarely accessible and depend on the interpretive abilities of the investigator. One need not accept everything presented in *The Secret Doctrine* in order to benefit from its picture of cosmic evolution. At the time the book was written, cosmology was bogged down in a mass of inadequately supported scientific speculations. Even today, when the advance of science has drawn our attention beyond the solar system to the vast realm of the galaxies, it is worthwhile to keep in mind the possible significance of our existence on earth. The sense of a greater destiny for mankind can easily be lost in the overwhelming astronomical panorama that is being unfolded before us. Cosmological knowledge seems to progress in cycles, and after each period of increase, we must return to our terrestrial roots to regain a human perspective. The knowledge of the extent of the physical universe that is now being acquired needs to be assimilated. In this task, the Stanzas of Dzyan are invaluable. For instance, the use of analogy in myth can be a powerful tool for extending the scope of inquiry beyond the range to which these verses were originally restricted. This becomes apparent from an examination of the earlier Stanzas, which are just as applicable to the entire universe as to the solar system.

We will draw upon *Man, the Measure of All Things*, a superb commentary on the Stanzas about cosmogenesis, to guide our interpretation. Its principal author, Sri Krishna Prem, had an exceptional grasp of the psychic face of the universe. The introduction to his book is a penetrating analysis of the nature and purpose of creation myths.[6]

Sri Krishna Prem was an Englishman (Ronald Nixon) who had served in the Royal Air Force as a fighter pilot during the First World War. After the war, he earned an M.A. at Cambridge University and in 1920 went to India to seek out the wisdom of the East. He taught English literature there for many years at the University of Lucknow, leaving only to follow his guru to a remote ashram in the foothills of the Himalayas. After her passing, he was left in charge of the ashram, where he presided until his death.[7] In addition to his work on the Stanzas of Dzyan, he wrote insightful commentaries on the *Bhagavad Gītā* and the *Kaṭha Upaniṣad.* In *Man, the Measure of All Things,* he summarizes his approach to the Stanzas in the following passage:

> The reader will find no astronomy and geology, no planets, nebulae and rocks, none of the apparatus of a 'real' cosmogony. We repeat that this commentary is dealing with cosmogenesis *from a psychic point of view.* We are considering the universe as a tissue of psychic experience; our categories are psychic ones, and with their help we

> have attempted to show that the process of cosmic manifestation is entirely a movement within the unity of conscious being towards the achievement of self-conscious experience [italics added].[8]

This raises a question concerning the inner source of creation myths in general; according to Sri Krishna Prem, their authors were mystics and seers. Before proceeding to interpret the Stanzas, we should consider the psychological resources from which these authors may have drawn.

THE INNER SOURCE OF CREATION MYTHS

These Stanzas assuredly came from a deeper layer of consciousness than is normally accessible. In ancient societies, the authors of such myths were set apart from other people by their superior wisdom and magical powers. There were profound mystics among them who were capable of expressing their attainments in great deeds, poetry, and music. One thinks of legendary figures like Orpheus, Merlin, Hermes Trismegistus, and Krishna. Legends of their prowess persist into our own times. They remind us of "the unacknowledged legislators of the world" proclaimed by Shelley in his essay, "A Defence of Poetry."[9] We do not know if these names refer to historical persons, but they are associated with traditions famed for possessing a secret knowledge of divine things. Mystical centers that preserved and transmitted knowledge of this kind existed in the ancient world. They included the Greek Mysteries, Druid schools in Celtic lands, ancient Egyptian temple teachings, and Vedic academies in Aryan India. Their sacred knowledge was available only to initiates who had undergone a rigorous psychological and spiritual training to attain it. If we are looking for the source of creation myths, we would do well to search for it in places like these. Creation myths vary in sophistication, depending upon the capacities of the early tribal shamans who composed them. Profounder myths derived from ancient cultures where more accomplished mystics and seers were able to flourish.

But if creation myths are the work of advanced Seer-Poets, how can we understand them? Assuming that they went deep into the so-called "Unconscious" using the methods they had mastered, we can best view the myths as accounts of their inner experiences. They treated the universe from a psychic point of view and weren't primarily concerned with the outer world of the senses. To read creation myths as naïve prescientific explanations of the physical world is to miss the point altogether. The starting place of the Seers was within themselves, and they used the inner discoveries made there as analogues of the whole cosmos.

If we want to understand creation myths, therefore, we have to search for their meaning within ourselves. Creation myths are symbolic links between the inner and outer worlds of experience; both worlds are viewed as having a similar psychic structure. This is the central insight of the ancient doctrine of the correspondence between the macrocosm and the microcosm, in which the universe and one of its parts are treated as mirror images of one another. In the more developed myths, the microcosm is identified with man, but it can be applied to other things as well. Man is viewed as a reflection in miniature of all the levels of the macrocosm, though full realization of them is uncommon. While the macrocosm is commonly taken to be the physical universe of which we are all parts, it can also refer to one great Cosmos, the levels of which correspond subjectively to each person, or microcosm.

A suggestive illustration of this idea can be found in the familiar diagram of a yogi sitting in the so-called "lotus" posture (Figure 1). Variations of the symbolism depicted in this diagram have been discovered all over the world from the Ancient Near East to Native American cultures, but they reached their fullest expression in India.[10] We use it here as a means of deepening our understanding of creation myths. The seated yogi has several noteworthy features. The figure is a visual depiction of the subtle,

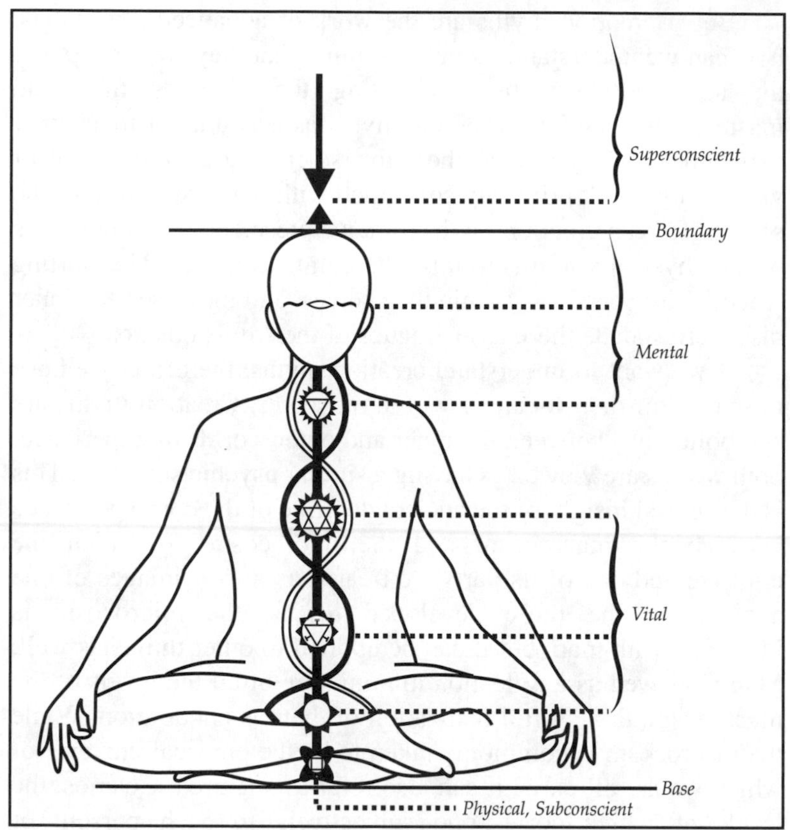

Figure 1. A Seated Yogi

not the physical, body. A number of centers called *cakras* (symbolized as "lotuses") are located along the spinal column in the diagram. They refer to loci within the subtle body that have relations with the cosmic levels in the universe. We are not aware of these centers (or grades of experience) because they are normally inactive, but when stimulated they provide access to previously unsuspected inner worlds. This process is related to the circulation of vital energy (*prāṇa*), which originates in the psychic world.

Drawing upon received traditions, the Poets identified the principles of the universe in terms of the structures they discovered within themselves. In the diagram, the lowest level is the physical, though a subconscient region is also linked with it. At the top of the head, there is a boundary between the mental layers and the superconscient, or transcendent, regions above. This boundary takes a variety of forms in many creation myths, including the Stanzas of Dzyan. In mythical cosmology, the lower limit of the physical came to be correlated with the earth and the upper boundary of the mental region with the sky. Thus, we could say that the Seer touches the sky with his head while remaining seated firmly on the earth. The levels between these two limits are identified as mental and vital, corresponding to regions of the cosmos. Each level in the microcosm has its counterpart in the macrocosm, or great universe.[11]

The Importance of Transitional States

Before proceeding to an analysis of the Stanzas themselves, a word must be said about transitional states. The symbolism suggests a transition between different states of being. Reality is not sharply polarized into opposites like darkness and light, night and day, sleeping and waking, for there is a gradual transition from one state to the other. The transitional states between the opposites are places where both of them are present, yet neither one in its fullness. In Stanza II.2, for example, we are told of a state in which "there was neither silence nor sound."[12] The title of Stanza II, "The Idea of Differentiation," suggests that even before a complete differentiation of opposites has occurred, the preparation for it had already begun. These transitions are called intermediate states (*bardos*) in Tibetan Buddhism, and are believed to possess profound spiritual significance; they are valued as auspicious times for practicing meditation. In these periods, the gods are said to walk the earth. In the Stanzas of Dzyan, various images are used to represent the different stages of cosmic manifestation. They can be classified as follows:

Stanza I: *Unmanifested*:	Night	Darkness	Sleeping
Stanza II: *Intermediate*:	Pre-Dawn	Twilight	Dreaming
Stanza III: *Manifested*:	Day	Light	Waking

There is a constant interplay between these images, each parallel set being superimposed upon the others to bring out subtle shades of meaning that may have been neglected.

In the transition from Night to Day, for instance, there is a brief period before Dawn when an almost indiscernible glimmer of light begins to brighten the hushed darkness. This Pre-Dawn period is an intermediate state filled with anticipation of the coming day. To illustrate this, Sri Aurobindo began his great epic poem, *Savitri: A Legend and a Symbol,* at such a time, referring to it as "the hour before the Gods awake."[13] It is a time of introspection preceding the first light of Dawn. What better symbolism could there be for that mysterious passage from the unmanifested condition preceding creation to the manifestation of a cosmos? Another symbolic rendering, conveying a more subjective quality, is the play on Sleeping and Waking. The magical moment between sleeping and waking is unseizable by our conscious minds. There may be a brief flutter of dream before waking, yet at some point we cross an invisible barrier from one state of being to the other. When we wake up, we are completely unaware of how it happened.

Both images are examples of the ubiquitous boundary that appears frequently in creation myths, which can be represented either as the horizon over which the sun rises or as the mysterious transition between sleeping and waking. The boundary is the frontier between the manifested universe and its unmanifested source. It is the place where a transition occurs from one state of being (or consciousness) to another. There is a notable reference to it in the Vedic "Hymn of Creation":

> The seers of Truth discovered the building of being in non-being by will in the heart and by the thought; *their ray was extended horizontally;* but what was there below, what was there above?

> There were Casters of the seed, there were Greatnesses; there was self-law below, there was Will above [italics added].[14]

A transition across the boundary can take place in either direction, depending upon the context, but cosmologically it represents the descent of consciousness into manifestation. The boundary has many applications, and appears everywhere in world mythology as doors, veils, thresholds, walls of fire, and so on. Several boundaries are mentioned in the Stanzas of Dzyan, where the most inclusive term is the *Ring 'Pass-Not'*. Boundaries always indicate a limit beyond which beings on a given cosmic level normally cannot pass. Many myths, however, suggest the possibility of a mystical passage across a boundary. With regard to cosmology, the boundary should tell us that instead of looking for prior *physical causes* to explain the origin of the universe, we ought to be considering the possibility of a transition between different states of being. For the manifestation of the universe may actually be a *psychic transformation* from one state to another. This is as mysterious as the subtle transition from sleeping to waking, which also eludes our mental grasp. Some insight into it can be gained through the mythical symbols in the Stanzas of Dzyan. The cosmological symbolism of the cross can also enrich this insight.

The image of the cross is essentially a representation of a transition between different states of being. The cross is a universal symbol stemming from remote antiquity, suggesting "crossing over" a boundary from one side to the other. Cosmologically, it is the sign of the macrocosm, as also of the microcosm, because it has the form of a man with his arms outstretched. Most people are familiar with its use in Christianity, but may not be aware of the underlying cosmological significance. Christianity stresses the crucifixion, or suffering upon the cross, but the cross is a far older symbol that has many variations. The primordial figure is simply the crossing of two lines, one vertical and the other horizontal. Lying flat, they define the four spatial directions on the surface of the earth; placed like this, they symbolize the whole earth or, more generally, *matter.*

When raised to an upright position, the vertical line becomes the path of descent and ascent across the boundary (horizontal line) between spirit and matter. The center of intersection has immense significance, since it is the locus through which spirit passes in either direction. Spirit descends through it into manifestation and must pass through it again if it wishes to return to its source.

Taken as a whole, the cross signifies the unity of spirit and matter. In a cosmological sense, the horizontal line represents the mysterious boundary between the unmanifested above and the manifested universe below. This boundary is crossed during cosmogenesis, as the cosmos begins to appear in all its glory. The vertical line indicates the actual transition or "crossing over" from one state of being to another. But what crosses the boundary to become the manifested universe? Something exists in an unmanifested state that reveals itself in the creative process. The Stanzas of Dzyan, as we will see, can suggest what this is, though they do not offer a complete answer. Still, why should there be a boundary at all, and if there is one must it always be there? The resolution of these enigmas must wait until we take up evolutionary cosmology.

The Stanzas on Cosmogenesis

In the Stanzas of Dzyan, the principal powers active in bringing forth the cosmos are presented in symbolic terms. They represent the psychic movements that preceded the appearance of the physical universe. The Stanzas are packed with symbolism, one symbol being superimposed upon another in order to bring out the many layers of meaning concealed within them. Despite this complex symbolism, we require only a few principles to understand the creation myth. Symbols are employed to evoke feelings appropriate to what Sri Krishna Prem has called "the great theme of the universe."[15] They should be read as one would read a poem, not a scientific or philosophical treatise. Although there are seven Stanzas on cosmogenesis, we are principally concerned with the first three, for these describe the gradual emergence of the transcendent principles responsible for the manifestation of a cosmos. A brief summary of these Stanzas follows.

In the first Stanza, an attempt is made to suggest the state of one boundless Being in *Pralaya,* "before the first flutter of re-awakening manifestation."[16] In contrast, the period of cosmic manifestation is called a *Manvantara.* Obviously, the unmanifested state is impossible to describe directly, so only negative terms are used to indicate what is latent within it. This device also serves to identify the principles that will become important later on in the process of cosmogenesis. The unmanifested state of Being is symbolized as Cosmic Night, or Sleep. Stanza II hints that something is beginning to happen in the primordial darkness by pointing to signs of stirring, recalling what happens in the transition between sleeping and waking. In Stanza III, the awakening of Cosmos at the start of a new cycle is depicted. It describes the birth of Universal Mind containing the entire universe which is to be manifested. This is symbolized as the Cosmic Dawn, the beginning of a new *Manvantara.* Later Stanzas go on to develop what is implicit in the general principles outlined in the first three.

Stanza IV is concerned with the differentiation of the Universal Mind into the conscious powers that are empowered to shape and govern the universe. They are the builders of the various worlds, entering into them as preservers of the cosmic order. These powers embody in themselves the so-called "laws of nature" that are different aspects of one all-encompassing Cosmic Harmony. Stanza V elaborates on the process by which worlds are formed. The work of Fohat, the Fiery Whirlwind, is presented here in great detail. In Stanza VI, the establishment of planetary chains and globes is described. The globes provide environments for the evolution of successive life waves. Stanza VII traces the descent of life down to the birth of man, who is the culmination of the process described in the preceding Stanzas. For ultimately "these Stanzas are about us, our origins, our development, our conscious selves and our bodily forms."[17] Man is the microcosm in whom the universe is reflected; he is the "measure of all things"—not in the subjective Protagorean sense, but as an image of the whole Cosmos in which he appears.

The Night of the Universe

Stanza I

> The Eternal Parent [Space], wrapped in her ever invisible robes, had slumbered once again for seven eternities." (2) Time was not, for it lay asleep in the infinite bosom of duration. (3) Universal mind was not, for there were no Ah-hi [celestial beings] to contain [hence to manifest] it . . . (5) Darkness alone filled the boundless all, for father, mother and son were once more one, and the son had not awakened yet for the new wheel, and his pilgrimage thereon. . . . (7) The causes of existence had been done away with; the visible that was, and the invisible that is, rested in eternal non-being—the one being. (8) Alone the one form of existence stretched boundless, infinite, causeless, in dreamless sleep; and life pulsated unconscious in universal space, throughout that All-Presence which is sensed by the opened eye of the Dangma [a purified soul].

Stanza II

> (2). . . . Where was silence? Where the ears to sense it? No, there was neither silence nor sound; naught save ceaseless eternal breath [Motion] which knows itself not.[18]

The above verses refer to the state of things prior to the manifestation of a cosmos. At first, the powers that will bring it into being are still undifferentiated and can only be described indirectly. Cosmogenesis must be viewed symbolically, since our ordinary notions of causality do not apply in the psychic world. According to the Seers, mythical images are revealed in higher states of consciousness; they are not merely products of human imagination. Note the reference in the first verse to previous periods of activity ("once again"), which suggests that prior universes have existed. The details are left vague.

Even though the basic powers are unmanifested in the beginning, they must not be thought of as unreal or nothing at all. They are still there in potentiality, just like ourselves when we are fast asleep. Stanza I opens with the unmanifested condition of "the boundless all" (I.5), which signifies infinite, causeless, and eternal Being. The identification of Being with Consciousness is also presupposed in the Stanzas. Being is present everywhere, and everything is a form of it. Thus, if there is to be a universe, it must be a manifestation of Being. But how does manifestation take place? Nothing can act on Being from the outside, since there is no "outside" of Being; the universe must therefore come from within it. This can happen only through an internal differentiation into opposites that then proceed to interact in the formation of a cosmos.

The fundamental role that opposites play in the description of the creative process has already been examined.[19] There must be some kind of differentiation at the beginning, which the Stanzas present in symbolic terms. Being is said to rest in "dreamless sleep," but even in this state "life pulsated unconscious in universal space."[20] Universal space is related to the "Eternal Parent" of verse one and should not be confused with physical space, though there is a connection between them; it signifies the pure extension of Consciousness. If we try to imagine this "subjective" space, we can only think of it as a dimensional object because it is too subtle to be grasped directly by the mind.[21]

Parenthetically, a good example of this ambiguity is afforded by competing views of space in modern physics. The two most successful physical theories are *general relativity,* dealing with gravity on a cosmic scale, and *quantum mechanics,* describing the phenomena of the subatomic world. Each is incomplete as it now stands, since neither includes the subject matter of the other. In relativity, a metric is imposed on a preexisting amorphous expanse (see note 21). Spacetime takes shape as a curved four-dimensional continuum, though many forms are possible. On the other hand, some versions of quantum mechanics favor a space composed of innumerable points whose mutual relations account for the metric.

General relativity has been repeatedly confirmed by cosmological observations, as has quantum mechanics in the detailed experiments of particle physics. Yet each seems to be based on a different philosophy of space. The problem is that it is intuitively unsatisfactory to think of the universe being governed by two incompatible sets of laws, one for the macrocosm and the other for the microcosm.

Today, a unified theory is being sought in terms of a quantized form of gravity ("quantum gravity"), but the mathematics involved is extremely complicated and no experimental confirmation is as yet forthcoming. The two leading candidates are superstring theory and "loop quantum gravity." String theory assumes that dimensionality preexists in a continuous spatial medium filled with tiny vibrating filaments of energy (much smaller than elementary particles). In this sense, it resembles general relativity, though including more dimensions than four. Loop quantum gravity builds space out of discrete geometrical loops, thereby accounting for its large-scale properties in terms of more fundamental elements. As can be seen, alternative views of space underlie the new theories.

Historically, these different spatial conceptions go back at least as far as the controversy between Newton and Leibniz concerning absolute versus relative space and time.[22] Both views seem to recur in ever more subtle forms as physics progresses, and may represent complementary ways of understanding the physical universe. It might be impossible for the mind to decide between them. If so, this failure could be due to the nature of reality itself, the insufficiency of mind as an instrument for understanding the universe, or a combination of both (see Chapters IV and V for further discussion of this topic).

When visualized, space becomes the primeval ocean of myth, where emphasis is placed on its tidal dynamism. The rhythmic pulsation filling space is compared with breathing.[23] Elsewhere in *The Secret Doctrine,* it is called the "Great Breath." It is present even during the period of non-manifestation, like the hum of an idling dynamo. Cosmogenesis begins when the pulsation reaches a critical amplitude and the dormant powers begin to awaken.[24]

The process of differentiation, which develops under the influence of the gradually intensifying breath, is described in symbolic terms. In I.1, we are told of a slumbering Eternal Parent who will awaken to initiate a new cosmos. This is a reference to the Great Mother of ancient cultures. As the inherent Force of the Absolute, she bears the universe within herself and without her no manifestation can take place. Madame Blavatsky describes the Eternal Parent as the "Root of Matter" (not Matter itself), which includes potentially the objective content of Being. She is also called the "Great Waters," since they are the substantial basis of the cosmos that is to be.[25] All the possibilities for existence rest in her, as well as the creative energies that will bring them forth. Behind her lies Being itself, without which she could not exist. Together they form one reality, but must be distinguished from one another once she becomes active. What remains behind, sanctioning and supporting her work, is left undefined. It is referred to as "Spirit," and sometimes called "Father," because we can only describe cosmogenesis in dualistic terms.[26]

Several additional terms used in the opening Stanzas require a brief notice. "Invisible robes" in I.1 is best understood as a reference to Being. As previously pointed out, Being is beyond all description; it cannot be known as an object, for all dualities are merged in it. We can know Being only by realizing our identity with it. "Seven eternities" is also symbolic, as time does not begin to function until the universe comes into being. It can be thought of as an indefinite period of non-manifestation corresponding to a *Manvantara,* because time is not completely annihilated during *Pralaya*. Even though contrasted with timeless duration, its root remains in the Great Breath that never ceases. Time is said to "lay asleep in the infinite bosom of duration."[27] No succession of events between universes is discernible, since nothing exists to measure time and there is no one to feel its passing. Nevertheless, time is somehow there, which supports the reference to seven eternities. We gain some insight into this by returning to the analogy of sleep. When we are asleep, we are unaware of the passing of time. There is no time for us subjectively, because we are unconscious of ourselves or of the world around us. And yet breathing continues, though we are unaware of it. If it did not, we would never wake up to become aware of time again. Thus, there is a continuum of consciousness. It could be argued, of course, that while we are sleeping, objective cosmic time is still going on. But it does not exist *for us* while we are sleeping, nor would it exist for absolute Being before the manifestation of a cosmos. This underscores the correspondence between the individual and the universe.

We should also consider the cryptic reference in I.5 to father, mother, and son being "once more one."[28] Family relationships are frequently employed in creation myths to designate cosmic principles. They refer to *universal* qualities that are only reflected in the relations of human parents and children.[29] This can be summarized in a simple diagram (Figure 2); the circular form suggests that everything is contained within Being. This can be misleading, because in reality Being has no boundary. It would be better represented as an infinite plane, which of course cannot be drawn.[30] We have already identified the Mother and the Father. What principle is to be designated as the Son? He is their *androgynous* child, later called "Father-Mother" because of his role in the ongoing creative process. In I.3, he is called the Universal Mind, though it is also said that at first there were no Ah-hi (celestial beings) to contain it.[31] This is the Son, who "had not awakened yet for the new wheel, and his pilgrimage thereon."[32] The Son is born of the Mother, and contains the whole universe within himself:

> The Universal Mind is the first manifested principle, the farthest shore of the Cosmos. In Vedic times it was symbolised as the god Varuna, the over-arching sky which embraces all that is. It is the Store Consciousness (*Ālaya Vijñāna*) of the Yogāchāra Buddhists, the Universal Intelligence ('Agl-i-kull') of the Sufis, and also the Noëtic World, the Spiritual Cosmos of Plotinus. . . . In any case, it is a unitary and all-embracing consciousness which has as content the Divine Archetypes, the so-called Divine Ideas of Plato, from participation in which arise all the concrete forms within the cosmos.[33]

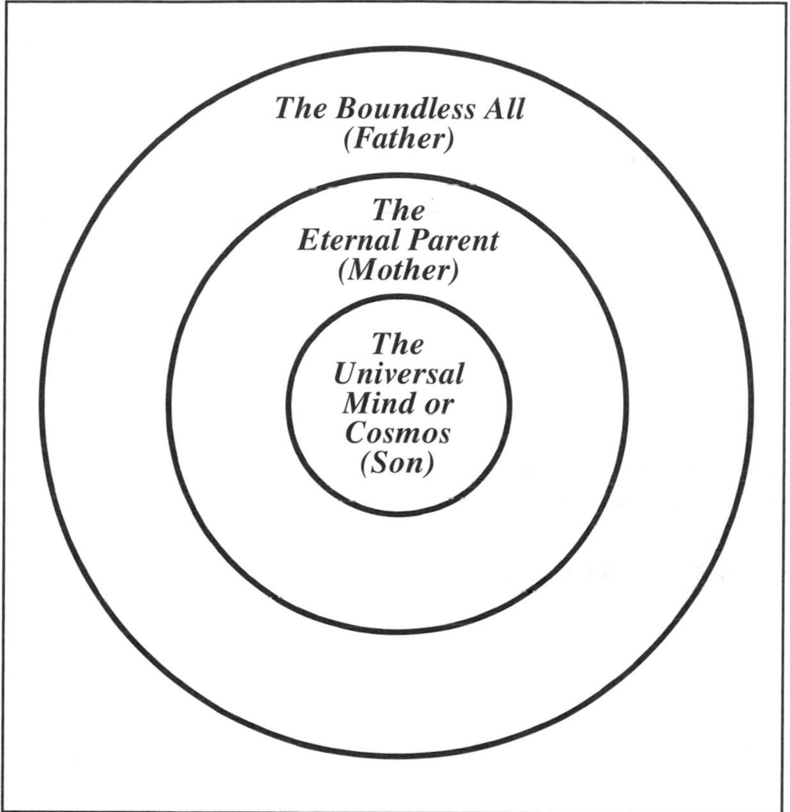

Figure 2. The Cosmic Principles

Universal Mind is the power of "seeing" the truth of ideas (intellectual intuition) and should not be understood as an organ of "thinking" (discursive thought). This is comparable to the Neoplatonic term *Nous*, or Intellect. As such, it is both itself and the contents of its own intellection (Archetypal Ideas). In the Stanzas, Universal Mind is the mighty being out of which the cosmos will emerge. Many traditions have identified it as the God of the universe. In later Hinduism he was known as *Brahmā,* the four-faced creator God who is born from the world egg, referred to in the Stanzas as "the germ that dwelleth in darkness."[34]

Beyond the Son are the still unmanifested principles (Mother and Father) that gave him birth. He is not the whole of Being but its cosmic representative. Universal Mind could not be manifested until there were vehicles to contain it. These are identified as the Ah-hi (celestial beings) of I.3. As Madame Blavatsky says, "They are the Intelligent Forces that give to and enact in Nature her 'laws,' while themselves acting according to laws imposed upon them in a similar manner by still higher Powers; but they are not 'the personifications' of the powers of Nature, as erroneously thought."[35] The Son is the highest of these beings and includes them all as parts of himself. His birth may be compared to the climax of a great symphony, say Beethoven's Ninth, which begins with the tentative search for a theme and ends with a triumphant hymn of joy once it has been discovered. In this symphony, Beethoven displayed more insight into the creative process than can usually be found in the writings of scientists and theologians.[36]

The Awakening of Cosmos

Stanza III

The last vibration of the seventh eternity thrills through infinitude. The mother swells, expanding from within without, like the bud of the lotus. (2) The vibration sweeps along, touching with its swift wing [*simultaneously*] the whole universe, and the germ that dwelleth in darkness: the darkness that breathes [*moves*] over the slumbering waters of life. . . . (7) Behold, oh Lanoo [disciple]! the radiant Child of the two, the unparalleled refulgent Glory: Bright Space Son of Dark Space, which emerges from the depths of the great Dark Waters. . . . He shines forth as the Sun; he is the blazing Divine Dragon of Wisdom. . . . Behold him lifting the Veil and unfurling it from East to West. He shuts out the above, and leaves the below to be seen as the great Illusion. He marks the places for the Shining Ones, and turns the upper into a shoreless Sea of Fire, and the One manifested into the Great Waters. . . . (10) Father-Mother spin a web whose upper end is fastened to Spirit—the light of the one Darkness—and the lower one to its [*the Spirit's*] shadowy end, Matter; and this web is the Universe spun out of the two substances made in one, which is Svabhavat [the "Self-Becoming"]. (11) It [*the Web*] expands when the breath of fire [*the*

> *Father*] is upon it; it contracts when the breath of the mother [*the root of Matter*] touches it. Then the sons dissociate and scatter, to return into their mother's bosom at the end of the great day, and re-become one with her; when it [*the Web*] is cooling it becomes radiant, and the sons expand and contract through their own selves and hearts; they embrace infinitude. (12) Then Svabhavat sends Fohat [the Fiery Whirlwind] to harden the atoms. Each [*of these*] is a part of the web [*Universe*]. Reflecting the "Self-Existent Lord" [*Primeval Light*] like a mirror, each becomes in turn a world.[37]

Stanza III begins with a reference to the "vibration" that brings the Son to birth. This vibration corresponds to the creative Word (*Logos*) of several religious traditions.[38] It transforms the pure bliss of Being into the thrill of delight that fills the universe when it begins to manifest. This auspicious moment is depicted by Sri Aurobindo in his epic poem *Savitri:*

> The persistent thrill of a transfiguring touch
> Persuaded the inert black quietude
> And beauty and wonder disturbed the fields of God.[39]

The triumphant climax of the Stanzas occurs in III.7, with the birth of the Son (Universal Mind) who is the glory of the Cosmos:

> This is the birth of that which the Greeks called Cosmos or the adorned one, and worshipped as a God. This is the Shining Wonder, a mere glimpse of which has made such seers as have been fortunate enough to attain this vision drunk with the wine of utter God intoxication. . . . All strength, all beauty and all truth have their abode within its light. Its symbol is the shining vault of heaven, containing sun, moon, and stars, all linked in interpenetrative harmony. The content of this Mind is a living content; the gleaming Archetypal Images are a hierarchy of living spiritual powers, each with its being mingled with that of all the rest, for, above all, this is a plane of harmonious unity, the music of the spheres.[40]

All of the cosmic levels are contained within him; thus, he is referred to as "Cosmos." This is a term widely used as a synonym for the universe, but with an emphasis on order, harmony, and beauty. The Greek word *kosmos* also meant "adornment"—one is led to wonder what or whom the universe was thought to adorn. It can be taken in the context of the Stanzas to imply that the universe is the adornment of the Son, or Universal Mind, though it may have other associations as well. We will use "cosmos" as a more inclusive term than "universe," which is now generally restricted to the physical world. According to ancient testimony, Pythagoras was the first person to call the universe a cosmos. The Pythagorean School may have been the earliest group of Greek thinkers to formulate models of the universe. This school exercised a strong influence on the subsequent history of cosmology. They were famous for their doctrine of "the Music of the Spheres" and other innovative cosmological ideas. The number "four" was important to them, since it played a key role in the structure of the sacred *Tetraktys:* it signified completion in their speculative numerical theories. Neo-Pythagorean philosophers in the Hellenistic period also considered the universe to be the expression of a Divine Mind.

The appearance of the Son is heralded by a succession of splendid epithets: "radiant Child of the two," "refulgent Glory," "Bright Space, Son of Dark Space," "the Sun," and "the blazing Divine Dragon of Wisdom." He unfurls the Veil of Day that causes the Powers of Night to fade from view, though they are still there in the darkness beyond the Sun's light. This Veil is another version of the "boundary" discussed previously, for it conceals the dark Source of things that remains hidden above.[41] Below is the "great Illusion" of the world—an illusion only because it is mistakenly perceived to exist independently of its unmanifested root, for nothing can exist outside the boundless all (absolute Being). When this is forgotten, we fall prey to illusion. The Son assigns functions to the "Shining Ones" (Devas) who are parts of himself. They are great impersonal beings who supervise the various aspects of the cosmic order. A new boundary is then formed: what is above becomes "a shoreless Sea of Fire," while below it flow the "Great Waters" from which the universe will emerge.[42] But manifestation is not finished with the appearance of the Son, since the other levels of the cosmos have yet to come into being.

Succeeding verses of Stanza III describe the subsequent shaping of the universe. This is supervised by the Son, now called

"Father-Mother" because he contains within himself the features of both parents; he is thus able to continue the course of cosmic manifestation. He is also called "Svabhavat" (literally, the "Self-becoming"), but the term can also refer to the Father, or "Self-Existent Lord" (III.12). We are told in III.10 that he spins a web, fastened at one end to Spirit (Primeval Light) and at the other to Matter (the Great Waters). The web is identified as the Universe, which is an aspect of the Son himself. In III.11, it is said to expand and contract when touched by the breaths of the Father and the Mother. This hearkens back to the original "ceaseless, eternal breath" that is inherent in absolute Being and is the ultimate source of the pulsation of the web.[43] Even the "sons" (the "atoms" of III.12) share in its dynamism. They disperse to enter the "great day" of the new universe and return again to the Mother at its end. Those who are familiar with scientific models of expanding and contracting universes might be tempted to see a connection here, but we are still describing events in the psychic world prior to the appearance of the physical universe.

The web represents the subtle field of forces binding all things together, both psychic and physical, into a total unity. In modern physics, it appears as the speculative ideal of a unified field that would make the physical universe comprehensible. This web is the subtle embodiment of Cosmic Harmony, which is the basis for the so-called "laws of nature." Elsewhere in *The Secret Doctrine,* it is explained in terms of *karma* (action).[44] In the following passage, Madame Blavatsky equates Karmic Law with the maintenance of universal harmony:

> This Law [Karma]—whether Conscious or Unconscious—predestines nothing and no one. It exists from and in Eternity, truly, for it is ETERNITY itself; and as such, since no act can be co-equal with eternity, it cannot be said to act, for it is ACTION itself. . . . Karma creates nothing, nor does it design. It is man [or Nature] who plans and creates causes, and Karmic law adjusts the effects; which adjustment is not an act, but *universal harmony,* tending ever to resume its original position, like a bough, which, bent down too forcibly, rebounds with corresponding vigour. . . . KARMA is an Absolute and Eternal law in the World of manifestation; and as there can only be one Absolute, as One eternal ever present Cause,

> believers in Karma cannot be regarded as Atheists or materialists—still less as fatalists: for Karma is one with the Unknowable, of which it is an aspect in its effects in the phenomenal world [italics added].[45]

Hence Karma is not an *act* in itself, but the *principle* of universal harmony. It pervades the entire cosmos and connects particular causes and effects. "Causal" laws usually refer to specific connections among things, as perceived and formulated by the mind.[46] The ultimate bond of causality in the universe, however, is the tension between Spirit and Matter. This tension holds the web in place and enables the cause-effect relation to operate.

In III.12, we are taken a step further when Fohat (the "Fiery Whirlwind") is employed to harden the atoms. Fohat can be thought of as the energy of the Mother focused through the Son. He is sent forth to prepare souls for their destined pilgrimage in the universe.[47] What are the "atoms" and where do they come from? They are not physical particles, though perhaps related to them in some way, but centers (or "points of view") for experiencing the cosmos. In this sense, the atoms are similar to the monads of the German philosopher Leibniz, except that they are not "windowless" but connected by the invisible threads (tensions) of the cosmic web.[48] Another difference is that whereas Leibniz's monads are created *substances,* these "atoms" are not substances at all but individualized forms of one Consciousness. They represent souls, or perhaps their essential Selves, though the distinction is unexplored. Each one is said to reflect the "Self-Existent Lord" like a mirror (or microcosm). In the Stanzas, the "Self-Existent Lord" refers to the Father (Spirit or Primeval Light) who is the one Self in all beings; the atoms are thus multiple aspects of this Self. "Hardening" particularizes them, accounting for their apparent distinctness from one another. An image that captures the whole concept is "Indra's net," as it is employed in one school of Chinese Buddhism.[49] Indra's net consists of innumerable jewels covering the celestial palace of the Vedic god Indra. The jewels mirror one another in such a way that the whole network is reflected within each one, ad infinitum.

Hence the net is a metaphor that illustrates the interpenetrating unity of what are here called "atoms."

Conclusion of the Stanzas

At this point, the physical universe remains unformed in the shadowy depths below. The transcendent powers of the Mother and the Father are still cloaked in darkness, apparently to remain so until the end of the *Manvantara*.[50] In the succeeding Stanzas on cosmogenesis, the work of the cosmic powers in building the framework of the universe is described, but the actual transition from the psychic to the physical remains obscure. Their efforts culminate in the birth of man. Following this, the Stanzas on anthropogenesis trace the occult history of the earth and mankind down to the present era.[51] They take us beyond the scope of the present study. But one point that these Stanzas raise should be mentioned, because it is in sharp contrast with Darwinian ideas about the evolution of man.

According to *The Secret Doctrine,* man is destined to evolve into a planetary god. In order to achieve this, it is necessary to pass through the human stage, which is seen as a transitional phase. The present planetary gods were once human, having earned their places through the proper use of their humanity in another planetary chain. They are said to help human evolution in various ways. Theosophists assert that these gods assisted in the production of new bodily forms in the course of evolution. According to this doctrine, the first human beings appeared on earth when *Lunar Pitris* (Lunar Fathers) produced subtle physical bodies for souls to inhabit. At each critical stage in the evolutionary process, assistance is provided by beings from a higher level of the psychic world. Consequently, human evolution involves more than a process of natural selection. Further, the *Secret Doctrine* maintains that Man appeared *prior* to animals in the order of evolution. This is conceivable, if Man began as an all-inclusive archetype in the Universal Mind from which animal forms were later derived.

We leave aside the complex symbolism of the later Stanzas. Madame Blavatsky seems to have taken myth to be true as literal history revealing the ancient past of humanity on earth. She believed that it involves deeply buried memories of the previous existence of dragons, giants, and lost continents. Man in her view evolved from the first "boneless," not yet completely physical, beings through a succession of more fully developed forms leading up to the present Fifth Root-Race. The time scale of such changes is enormous in length, involving long ages reminiscent of the Hindu conception of a *mahāyuga*. She even tried to project human evolution into the future, since the Stanzas speak of Sixth and Seventh Root-Races in which mankind becomes more spiritualized. By this stage in her writing, her health was deteriorating rapidly and her powers of inspiration were beginning to fail.

It is not easy to reconcile all of this with what is presently known about the human past. The origin of humanity, despite all that modern science has been able to discover, remains a mystery. When man appeared on earth, an important link was established between the psychic and the physical worlds, for he represents a new power (mind) in the physical universe. It has not been convincingly explained how this connection originated. Creation is an ongoing psychic process continuing throughout the whole course of evolution—even after the appearance of concrete physical forms. As stated in *The Secret Doctrine:*

> Evolution is *an eternal cycle of becoming, . . .* and nature never leaves an atom unused. Moreover, from the beginning of the Round, all in Nature tends to become Man. All the impulses of the dual, centripetal and centrifugal Force are directed towards one point—MAN.[52]

Man, as the microcosm, reflects within himself the entire universe, including the capacity to evolve. But the greater significance of this will not become clear until we discuss the evolving universe in Chapter VII. For now, we will simply stress that cosmic manifestation must take place within absolute Being, or Consciousness, for this is as far as the mind can take us.

Our view of creation, put succinctly, is this: the psychic state precedes the physical, which is derived from and interacts with it. The origin of the physical universe is analogous to the transition from sleeping to waking. It lies in a change of the state of being rather than a linear succession of physical causes that could easily lead to an infinite regress. Mere speculation will not help us here. Even if the universe started with a "bang," the mind is never satisfied with a flat *ex nihilo* statement. It always seeks for further explanation.

BEETHOVEN'S NINTH SYMPHONY: A BRIEF ANALYSIS

The following outline provides an interpretation of Beethoven's Ninth Symphony from a cosmological point of view. Obviously, this is not the only way it can be appreciated. There has always been controversy concerning the introduction of choral music into the final movement of the symphony. Was this a gigantic blunder on Beethoven's part, or the only acceptable resolution of the issues raised in the first three movements? Are there in fact any issues that need to be resolved in the earlier movements, which may simply be pure music without any program at all? An advantage of the analysis we offer is that when the symphony is viewed as a progressive unfoldment of the stages of the creative process, the choral finale becomes an indispensable climax to the whole work. Here again, the four movements signify integrality:

FIRST MOVEMENT (Allegro): Dark primeval waters heaving and swelling in response to the creative urge within.

SECOND MOVEMENT (Scherzo): The play of wild Dionysian energies in the throes of creation.

THIRD MOVEMENT (Adagio): Serene Apollonian reflection on what has been accomplished, followed by a disturbing sense that something is still lacking.

> FOURTH MOVEMENT (Chorale): The triumphant joy (delight) of creation fulfilled, in which humanity embraces the whole universe in its exultation.

The last movement is essential, for it suggests that an artist's creative work is not complete until it has been shared with others. Should we expect anything less from the manifestation of a Cosmos?

THE PHYSICAL FACE

In slumbering skies
Stars burnish the gloom of night
With soft evenglow.

Plate IV. Albert Einstein

IV

MODERN SCIENTIFIC COSMOLOGY

INTRODUCTION

Moving from mythical to scientific cosmology, the psychic face of the universe fades into the background and is replaced by a seemingly limitless expanse of stars and galaxies spread out in space and time. We have descended below the boundary that separates the unmanifested powers from the manifested universe. With this shift of focus, the Universal Mind and the inner cosmos derived from it disappear from view. In modern science, the connection between the physical universe and its hidden sources is severed. The actual transition from psychic consciousness to a physical world remains a mystery that mythical cosmology does not clarify. In fact, a psychic cosmos could just as well have existed without any physical manifestation at all. Alternatively, the physical world could simply be a tissue of psychic events without any function or purpose of their own. This last view has been adopted as final in some traditions. Still, scientific cosmologists would like to have a more detailed account of the physical universe in which we live.

Each type of cosmology treats the existence of the universe in a different way. Scientists accept the physical world as given in experience, and proceed to study how it works by constructing theoretical models to represent what they observe. They describe measurable features of the universe, but do not account for how consciousness arises and flourishes within it.

Our view regards soul as an ever-present reality inherent in the universe. When the soul awakens and becomes self-conscious in its long evolutionary march, it discovers the physical world. At first it tries to account for this by relying on its limited but developing mental powers.[1] Matter is soon taken to be the substantial basis of everything. Physics reigns supreme, since it is a systematic way of dealing with matter and energy.

Consciousness is diminished to a mere by-product of the nervous system and brain as they have evolved on earth. Whatever appears to be otherwise is reduced to a material basis, and even the existence of the soul is questioned. This is not the end of the story, but reflects a limited grasp of the deep perplexities of cosmic existence. (Vide Chapter VII.)

For scientific cosmologists, though, the universe contains everything that exists in space and time. This is hardly a precise definition of the universe. We do not understand what space and time really are, nor do we know how many different kinds of things exist. Attention is focused on the astronomical universe, because its overall structure provides the physical context for whatever appears within it. Scientists assume it to be an ordered whole rather than a mere aggregate, but cannot explain why this is so. Nevertheless, the assumption of cosmic order requires justification by appealing either to eternal laws of nature or to a superior power capable of establishing it. Many scientists, who believe that the laws of physics are sufficient to explain things, reject an appeal to a superior power. If such a power is assumed, however, a deeper question arises: Why do the laws of physics so effectively conceal it? Sri Aurobindo's approach offers a fulfilling answer to this question, but we need some familiarity with other cosmological views before it can be appreciated.

Logically, there can be only one universe, since by definition it contains everything. However, some scientific cosmologists are now using the plural form of the word. When a system of physically interacting things is sufficiently extensive (or on the way to becoming so), and is effectively isolated from other systems, it can be called a universe. Its isolation might be in space, time, or a combination of the two. If other universes exist, ours could be part of a larger "Multiverse" containing an unlimited number of them. An additional feature of these universes, which has come to the forefront in recent discussions among physicists, is that they can have different laws. We will take this up in the next chapter. The singular term "Universe" may be retained, if preferred. It would then consist of many large, isolated domains in a vast superspace. Whichever course we choose, cosmology is still concerned with the nature of the universe *as a whole,* including all of its faces, contents, and laws. It was once considered to be a part of speculative philosophy dealing with the broadest features of the universe, such as time, space, and causality. But since the appearance of Einstein's general theory of relativity, cosmology is considered a branch of physics. As we have begun to see, this ignores the other types of cosmology that are being considered in this book.

Laws of Nature

The philosophical basis of modern science is the idea of "laws of nature." The empirical discovery of such laws reveals the physical forces operating in the "real" world to produce the phenomena we observe. These laws, then, play a key role in the formulation of scientific models of the universe. But the concept of a law of nature is an abstraction based on a particular worldview and is by no means an indisputable fact. It is part of a broadly materialistic approach to nature that sharply distinguishes between the world "out there" and the perceiving subject, thus reducing consciousness to a mere by-product of matter. The universe is conceived as an impersonal mathematical machine in which there is no place for life and humanity as higher orders of existence. This view is thought to be the only means of making sense out of things. Yet despite its scientific usefulness, it is an unsupported presupposition about the nature of the universe.

The success of physics rests on the discovery of general regularities in the behavior of things, which are then called laws of nature. Testable predictions can be derived from them concerning the state of the world at any given time. Physicists have no generally accepted ideas about where these laws come from or why they have a specific form. The laws are the foundation of scientific cosmology, and to question their origin and form goes beyond the practice of physics as a science. From a positivist point of view, this can only give rise to fruitless speculations. Yet, as many physicists have come to realize, metaphysical issues cannot be avoided altogether if we wish to understand the implications of scientific discoveries. It is obvious that not every general statement about the world merits the title of a "law of nature." Although the conception of nature as lawful can be traced back to a very early period, the expression only became widespread in the seventeenth century as a result of the triumph of Newtonian mechanics.[2] Newton's law of universal gravitation was taken as a paradigm case for the mechanical view of nature. It led people to think of the universe as a huge machine obeying the eternal laws of God, just as subjects obey the civil laws of a king. This view is not common in science today, but the conception of laws of nature still plays a fundamental role.

The central feature of a law is its universality; thus laws of nature are sometimes described as universal generalizations based on experience. Philosophers disagree as to what these laws really represent. The major difference lies between two general views about them. Those who subscribe to one view, associated with the Scottish philosopher David Hume, maintain that laws of nature are only generalizations that describe the observed relations between physical objects. They express the regularities that physicists have discovered in the natural world around us; as such, they would be more accurately called the "laws of physics." Furthermore, according to this view, they are contingent statements that do not express any causal necessity. The other traditionally held view is that genuine laws of nature express necessary relations among things. This idea of laws differs radically from the former, since it presumes a metaphysical insight into the nature of reality.

Philosophers of science have modified both conceptions, but we will not pursue the details farther. Rather, we accept the latter view as more fruitful for cosmology and support it by interpreting laws of nature as partial aspects of the Cosmic Harmony that embraces the entire universe. While they express necessary relations of some kind, these laws can be superseded by others in the course of time. In modern physics, for example, conservation laws exhibit the pervasive character of forces now operating in the universe. They assert that certain key quantities remain constant everywhere in space and time. But the nature of the forces at work is not pursued beyond the physical world. From the standpoint of mythical cosmology, these forces are viewed as different forms of one universal consciousness. This suggests that laws are expressions of inflexible cosmic wills. But it is possible that the constancy so indicated may be replaced by higher-level laws as the universe evolves, which would be required by harmonies still latent in the present stage of cosmic development. The requirements can change, though they tend to remain stable over vast stretches of time. In periods of stability, harmony is expressed in customary ways that we can call laws of nature, as long as we are aware of the metaphorical character of this expression.[3]

A basic concept in physics today is that of the *field*, which is a dematerialized version of the mechanical ether of classical physics.[4] Rather than being a material substance filling all space, the field is identified with space (or spacetime) itself. Field relations are expressed in mathematical terms, since theoretical physics is more concerned with the abstract formal structure of nature than with its material contents. The relationship between spacetime and matter is represented by field equations first formulated by Einstein that describe the properties of the gravitational field. These properties seem to hold everywhere throughout the universe, and even to shape its overall structure. Einstein did not derive his equations directly from experience, but claimed that they were an imaginative creation of the mind. They are a genuine, if limited, mathematical rendition of one aspect of cosmic harmony. Gravity, though, is also a massive force of destruction in the universe. This is apparent in violent phenomena like exploding stars and black holes. Something is operating here that opposes the expansive tendencies in nature.[5] Gravity need not be taken to be an eternal law imposed by either God or Nature, for it may be part of the fabric of a universe that is itself changing over time. Nevertheless, the gravitational field equations, sometimes referred to as "Einstein's equation," successfully describe how gravity works. The field equations subsequently became the basis for the development of comprehensive cosmological models, which will be considered later in this chapter.

The Realm of the Galaxies

Before considering the theoretical bases of scientific cosmology, we turn to look briefly at the observed universe of modern science. By the early twentieth century, astronomy had progressed from a world of stars and planets to the realm of the galaxies. New discoveries followed upon the introduction of great reflecting telescopes capable of gathering light from increasingly distant regions of space. But astronomers at first failed to realize the full significance of what they were observing. At a meeting of the National Academy of Sciences in 1920, a "Great Debate" was held between astronomers representing opposite points of view.[6] One side argued that the Milky Way Galaxy, to which our solar system belongs, contains all the stars in the universe. Observations being made of what were at that time called spiral nebulae indicated to its supporters that these mysterious objects were parts of our own Galaxy, beyond which there was only infinite empty space. The other side maintained that the nebulae were stellar systems in their own right, called "island universes," existing far beyond the confines of the Milky Way.

The issue was resolved conclusively in favor of the latter view when the American astronomer Edwin Hubble demonstrated, around 1925, that the Andromeda Galaxy was an independent system existing outside the Milky Way. This had the additional advantage of eliminating the idea of a vast empty region beyond the stars, for galaxies were now found to exist everywhere (Plate V).

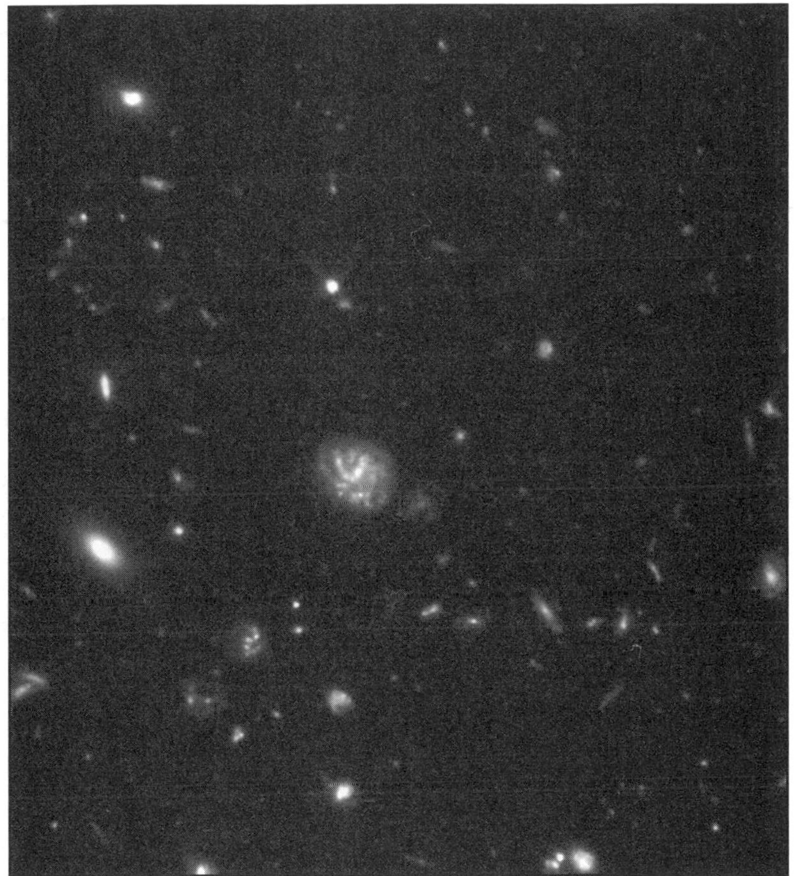

Plate V. The Realm of the Galaxies

Enlarging our picture of the universe was only the first step for Hubble. By 1929, using advanced spectroscopic methods, he found that most of the galaxies exhibited a shift of spectral lines toward the red end of the spectrum. Red shifts are interpreted as motions away from an observer (Doppler Effect), so Hubble treated what he observed as a general recession of the galaxies away from one another. This has become known as the "expanding universe." Hubble also discovered a linear relationship, known as "Hubble's Law," stating that the speed of recession increases with the distance of the galaxy from the observer.[7] This does not mean that the rest of the universe is moving away from *us*, but that all of the galaxies (including our own) are receding from one other. The situation is summed up by the *cosmological principle*, which asserts that on a large enough scale the universe looks the same from every place within it.

A convenient illustration of the expanding universe is that of an inflating soap bubble with specks of dust adhering to its surface. As the bubble inflates, the distances and recessional velocities of the specks, as seen from any one of them, increase according to the same mathematical relationship expressed by Hubble's Law. In this illustration, the dust specks represent the galaxies and the surface of the soap bubble serves as the expanding space containing them. The analogy is not exact, because a bubble has a boundary that is moving outward into the surrounding space, whereas the actual universe does not have such a boundary. An understanding of this involves a comparison of different geometries, which we consider in more detail in the section on general relativity. The situation is more complicated today, because galaxies are now known to form into gigantic clusters and superclusters, but the cosmological principle is still believed to hold on a large enough scale. Ever since Hubble's discovery of the expansion of the universe, our cosmological picture has not been the same as in previous centuries. The universe is now considered to be dynamically expanding rather than static. Obviously, this called for new theories to account for it. They were already available, even before Hubble's discoveries, in the new mathematical models developing on the basis of general relativity.

The General Theory of Relativity

Before addressing scientific theories, we must review the function of a theory in science. Theories are systematic attempts to explain the world. Among the many kinds possible, modern scientific theories have precise meanings of their own. They are useful when investigating certain features of the universe. For many nonscientists, a theory is little more than an unproven idea, or mere speculation. In science, however, this is usually called a hypothesis. Theories may begin as hypotheses, but they require additional input to become scientifically established. A scientific hypothesis becomes a full-fledged *theory* only when it has been tested experimentally. Philosophical criteria, such as causal completeness, are also employed by a few theorists to distinguish between hypotheses and theories. But, generally speaking, hypotheses that are repeatedly confirmed eventually become accepted as theories. When a hypothesis fails a test, it may be rejected or subsequently included in a more complete theory. A scientific theory, like any other, is never final. Nevertheless, when sufficiently tested, it provides one level of understanding of a given subject. In addition, it functions as a useful means of predicting new phenomena.

Relativity and Geometry

Modern scientific cosmology began in 1917 with a model of the physical universe derived by Einstein from his general theory of relativity. General relativity is a theory of gravitation that supersedes Newtonian physics.[8] Newton's formula for gravitation states that every body in the universe attracts other bodies with a force that is proportional to their masses, and varies inversely as the square of the distance between them.[9] Whereas Newton conceived gravity as a force of attraction between two bodies separated by empty space ("action at a distance"), general relativity is a field theory in which gravity is understood in terms of the geometry of space (or spacetime). Consequently, it dispenses with the idea of a *force* acting between bodies, focusing instead on the geometrical *structure* of the field surrounding them. In spite of conceptual differences, Newton's formula is now incorporated as a special case of the more general theory.

The philosophical basis of general relativity is the idea that the laws of nature must be the same for all observers, no matter where they are and how they are moving. This is the gist of what is known technically as the "principle of covariance":

> The principle asserts that the laws of nature must have expressions independent of the frame of reference in which they are represented—from any particular observer's view. This is equivalent to saying that the laws of nature are totally objective.[10]

Therefore, contrary to popular opinion about Einstein's theory of relativity, everything is *not* relative. Nature is viewed as being the same everywhere, though what we observe depends upon our particular frame of reference. Thus, the complex physical world of experience can be described by a few absolutely invariant laws. This captures the essence of genuine laws of nature, which (as we saw earlier) are characterized by their universality. In general relativity, for example, the law of gravitation is pictured as a curvature of space (spacetime) in the presence of matter. Planets circle the sun because the space surrounding it is curved, rather than being attracted by a force centered in the sun. But what does the "curvature of space" mean?

To begin with, there are different geometries available to cosmologists today. Three of them are particularly pertinent to relativistic cosmology, and can be distinguished from each other by their properties. For example, in Euclidean geometry only one line passing through a point outside a given line can be parallel to it, but Non-Euclidean geometry introduces two other possibilities. In one case, there is an infinite number of lines through a point that are all parallel to the given line; in the other case, there are no parallels at all. These three alternatives can be visualized in terms of two-dimensional surfaces. A flat plane extending infinitely in all directions represents Euclidean space; this kind of space is called *flat*. Newton took Euclidean geometry for granted in formulating his law of gravitation, since it was the only geometry known at that time. He assumed that Euclidean space was a passive container in which the interactions between material bodies took place. In Newton's theory, bodies were assumed to move uniformly in straight lines unless acted upon by external forces. These forces were needed to change the state of motion of a body (first and second laws of motion).

On the other hand, Non-Euclidean geometry with an infinite number of parallel lines through a point can be represented by a saddle-shaped surface; the space of this geometry is *open*. Finally, Non-Euclidean geometry with no parallels can be illustrated by the surface of a sphere; the space of this geometry is *closed*. All three geometries differ in other properties as well, such as the sum of the three angles of a triangle, the area of a circle, and so forth. The differences among them are completely general and can be extended to spaces of more than two dimensions, though they are impossible to visualize. Curvature is defined as an *intrinsic* property of a space and does not depend on our ability to imagine it in terms of higher-dimensional spaces. Which geometry best corresponds to the space of our universe is an empirical matter to be determined by measurements made entirely within it. The choice between alternative cosmological models is difficult, involving delicate observational techniques.

This is abstract mathematics so far, but it can be turned into physics by imagining the ideal geometrical lines as the paths taken by light rays.[11] The question then becomes a matter of which geometry the light rays obey as they travel through the universe. Is cosmic space flat, open, or closed? In an open or closed space, the paths of light rays are bent in accordance with the curvature of the surfaces referred to above. An answer to the question raised depends on how non-Euclidean geometry enters into general relativity. It involves the notion that space becomes warped in the presence of matter, making light rays (as well as other bodies) move in curved paths. The clue that led Einstein to this view is known as the "principle of equivalence." In one formulation, it states that the effects of gravity are equivalent to accelerated motion, thus allowing him to dispense with gravitational force as a fundamental concept in his theory.[12] It is only useful in certain frames of reference. All of this is summed up in *Einstein's equation*, which is the culmination of his efforts to develop a new theory of gravitation.

Einstein's Equation

Einstein's equation is among the most celebrated scientific equations because it connects geometry and physics in an elegant mathematical fashion. While space, time, and matter are experientially real, it suggests that they need not be fundamental entities in a unified theory of the universe. They are treated as interdependent aspects of a single comprehensive reality, whereas Newton conceived them as separate and independent of one another. Newton believed that God created material bodies and placed them in space, which he thought of as the divine sensorium.[13] Stars and planets resulted from the mutual attraction of these bodies. For Einstein, however, spacetime and matter are related modes of one physical system identified as the gravitational field. A recent book on this subject has the title *God's Equation*.[14] This may be going in the direction of hyperbole, but there is a point to be made here. Einstein was driven by a deep conviction of the harmony of the universe and confidence that this harmony could be expressed in conceptually simple laws. He spent ten years of arduous intellectual labor to arrive at the equation. His attitude in these years is reflected in a comment he once made that "God is subtle, but he is not malicious."[15] The great personal sacrifices he made aged him prematurely into the gray-haired and wrinkled wizard with whom we are familiar in later photographs. On several occasions, he referred to the inspiration that sustained him during these difficult years as "cosmic religious feeling." This seems to be a reference to cosmic consciousness, though it was heavily mathematicized by Einstein for scientific purposes. In his creative work, emphasis was placed on the cosmic aspect of harmony rather than on the immense variety of things that are encompassed by it. He once said, "I want to know God's thoughts . . . the rest are details."

Einstein often expressed his admiration for the rationalist philosopher Spinoza. But apart from some general observations about Spinoza's philosophy, he never embarked on a detailed exposition of it. His respect for Spinoza was so great that he considered such a course to be presumptuous. As he says:

> Many have attempted to present Spinoza's thoughts in modern language—a daring as well as irreverent enterprise which offers no guarantee against misinterpretation. Yet throughout Spinoza's writings one will find sharp and clear propositions which are masterpieces of concise formulation.[16]

What seems fairly certain is that Einstein saw in Spinoza a kindred spirit. He appreciated the philosopher's deep reverence for the universe and human life as a part of it. Spinoza was not particularly concerned with physics and didn't make any notable contributions to it. His primary interest was in developing a metaphysical system that would support his conception of a blessed life. He concluded that the highest form of thought is "to perceive things under a certain form of eternity."[17] This suggests a trace of cosmic consciousness, but Spinoza did not develop it any further. Curiously, he used the expression "the face of the whole universe" (*facies totius universi*) for the physical universe and identified it as a mediate infinite mode of God. His philosophy resonates with Einstein's own view of the world as summed up in the following passage:

> The individual feels the futility of human desires and aims and the sublimity and marvelous order which reveal themselves both in nature and in the world of thought. Individual existence impresses him as a sort of prison and he wants to experience the universe as a single significant whole.[18]

The impersonal conception of the universe that was characteristic of both Spinoza and Einstein, while not the whole of cosmic consciousness, is an important aspect of it. It provides a useful safeguard against the self-deceptions and dogmatic stances to which many well-meaning persons have fallen prey.

Einstein's equation is too complicated to be analyzed in depth here, but it can be schematized in the following way: Curvature of spacetime = 8π G x Matter. A statement attributed to the physicist John Wheeler captures the gist of this equation. He said that matter tells spacetime how to curve, and the curvature of spacetime tells matter how to move. The general equation is a symbolic expression in tensor form for ten separate field equations.[19] Tensors represent in concise mathematical notation the fundamental requirement of general relativity that the laws of nature must retain the same form under all possible transformations (principle of covariance). They can be expanded into an array of partial differential equations that describe the motion of bodies in a gravitational field.

The foremost feature of Einstein's equation is that the metric defines a four-dimensional spacetime field. In this case, the fourth dimension is not experienced time but a spatialized term that incorporates the measure of time. Spacetime as a whole, like a vast ocean, is one indivisible thing with motions occurring in it. These relative motions are responsible for the variations in our physical measurements. We experience space and time separately, but the combination of their measurements always yields the same invariant quantity. This suggests that they are different manifestations of a single continuum (spacetime). Although the metaphysical implications are far-reaching, we will not explore them at present. The structure of spacetime cannot be visualized but is nonetheless mathematically precise. No one knows for sure, moreover, what to make of spaces with more than three dimensions.[20] For practical purposes, it is sufficient to conceptualize spacetime in terms of geometry rather than as a substantive entity. Geometry describes the way light and matter move in a gravitational field and, in turn, matter determines the geometrical structure of the field. If this is kept in mind, we can avoid falling prey to logical conundrums like "What is outside space" and "What was before time?"[21]

When Einstein formulated his equation, he commented that the left side had been carved in marble, but the right side was made out of straw. The left side refers to the geometry of spacetime, which can be precisely defined, while the right side describes the general properties of matter and energy. General relativity tells us nothing about the nature of matter and energy in themselves. Much has been learned about this since Einstein's day; some of it will be considered when we discuss quantum mechanics. Einstein's equation, on the other hand, does tell us many important things about the physical universe. Gravity rules the universe at large, and this equation expresses the law of universal gravitation. It describes the forms of planetary orbits, the shape of galaxies, the curvature of light in gravitational fields, the slowing down of clocks by gravity, gravitational lensing effects, the collapse of stars into black holes, and gravitational waves in space. Above all, it traces the history of the universe from its origin in the big bang to its possible demise in the far distant future. One is tempted to say that it contains the entire physical world within its compact symbolism, but it takes prodigious mathematical powers to get all of this information out of it.

For all its successes, general relativity is basically a theory of gravitation, which is only one of the four fundamental forces of nature alongside electromagnetism and the strong and weak nuclear forces. Einstein was aware that his theory was incomplete, and driven by his central vision of cosmic harmony, he tried to extend it to include other forces in a unified field theory. Although this proved to be an insurmountable task for him, other approaches to unification are being made today along different lines. The most promising attempt so far is an insufficiently understood form of string theory known as "M-theory." Its mathematical subtleties, involving many hidden spatial dimensions, challenge the present capabilities of the human mind.[22]

Cosmological Models

Cosmological models are the core of scientific cosmology. An understanding of their nature and function is essential to a discussion of the role of relativity in cosmology. A cosmological model is a simplified theoretical representation of the universe at large.[23] Modern scientific models consist of a combination of general statements, geometrical assumptions, and mathematical equations characterizing a specific kind of universe. Prior to the advent of modern science, models of the universe were typically pictorial and did not include equations of the kind employed in physics today. This is still true in traditional cosmology, which is fundamentally qualitative in character. Some pictorial models have a cosmic significance far beyond the scope of conventional astronomy. In general, the universe should not be confused with a model of any kind, which is only a schematic outline possessing a built-in structure of its own. A given model is compared *in toto* with the available observations to determine how well it fits the observed universe. Thus, unlike creation myths, a cosmological model is subject to specific scientific tests. The fit is always partial and imperfect; this is not only the result of observational inaccuracies, but also because many aspects of the universe are inevitably left out of the model. There is consequently no such thing as a perfect model, complete in every detail.

Even if a final model were achieved, it would only be final for physics, since questions still remain about the origin and character of the physical laws on which it is based. Valid or not, a successful cosmological model tends to become identified as the real universe. In some cases, this has led to the model being incorporated into the worldview of an entire culture or historical period (compare the medieval geocentric cosmos, which held sway for over a thousand years). But as we saw in Chapter I, worldviews contain many nonscientific factors. Even though sometimes referred to as "cosmologies," the identification of worldviews with particular scientific models greatly impoverishes our understanding of the universe as a whole.

The *general statements* of modern scientific models include the accepted laws of physics (e.g., gravitation) and a few simplifying assumptions like the cosmological principle, which implies the homogeneity and isotropy of the universe. In the context of a cosmological model, the laws of physics become rules for defining the structure of the model rather than independent empirical statements. The justification for their choice lies in how well the model *as a whole* offers a coherent interpretation of the available observations. This can also be said of the simplifying assumptions that impose additional constraints on the model. Furthermore, the universe has spatial properties, so the model must include *geometrical statements* defining a specific kind of space. Until the twentieth century, Euclidean geometry was the only one taken seriously by cosmologists. Since the advent of the general theory of relativity, however, alternative geometries are now considered. At present, there is a choice of geometries available for the theoretical construction of cosmological models. In general relativity, geometry plays an essential role in the formulation of Einstein's equation; therefore, the geometrical aspect of contemporary models is inseparable from physics. *Mathematical equations* appear in them because the basic program of modern physics is concerned with the formal mathematical structure of nature.

Relativistic Cosmology

Specific solutions of Einstein's equation are difficult to find, even in this age of powerful computers, unless the distribution of matter is very simple. Therefore, the cosmological principle is employed as a simplifying assumption in relativistic models of the universe. Einstein's original model indicated that, in the special case of empty space, the curvature will be zero and the geometry Euclidean. But if there is a spherical mass present, like a star, the geometry in its vicinity will be Non-Euclidean and light rays will follow curved paths. Bodies that are not moving as fast as light may get caught up in the gravitational field and circle the star as planets. Relativistic cosmology, on the other hand, is not concerned with individual stars but with the universe at large. A simple way of constructing a cosmological model is to assume that matter is distributed uniformly throughout the universe like a rarefied gas; the density of this gas will then be the same everywhere. If this is assumed, Einstein's equation can be reduced to a geodesic equation that defines a particular cosmological model.

Early Relativistic Models

When Einstein formulated his first model in 1917, he believed that the universe was static, since astronomers had not yet discovered any evidence of its expansion. He may also have had philosophical reasons, derived from Spinoza, for rejecting a nonstatic world. To prevent a solution in which the whole universe collapses under the influence of gravity, he added an extra term to his equation that contained a constant (represented by the Greek letter lambda) now known as the *cosmological constant*. It was interpreted at that time as a repulsive force that counterbalanced gravity. When an expanding universe solution was found without lambda, its introduction proved to be unnecessary, and Einstein dropped it from his equation. Today, lambda has been revived with a new interpretation to account for recent evidence that the expansion is accelerating. If this is verified, it could indicate that space is a reservoir of enormous energies (now called "dark energy") that drive the expansion forward.[24] Einstein's universe was closed and finite, like a sphere, and nothing (not even light) could escape from it. In our soap bubble image, the entire universe can be visualized as embedded in the two-dimensional surface of the bubble. Although finite in volume, his universe was unbounded and light rays would travel in great circles, always returning to the place from which they had started.

In addition to the mistaken belief that the universe must be static, which led to the introduction of the cosmological constant into his equation, there is another consideration that Einstein found for the moment convincing. He believed at first that his equation implied that space could not exist without the presence of matter. This was a reaction against the Newtonian concepts of Absolute Space and Absolute Time, already repudiated in the special theory of relativity. Another solution of Einstein's equation, however, showed that under certain conditions space could exist and even possess a curvature without matter.[25] But at that time, Einstein was influenced by an idea he found in the writings of the Austrian philosopher Ernst Mach, who believed that the inertia of bodies was determined by the large-scale distribution of matter in the universe. This implies, for example, that the resistance we feel when pushing a heavy body is caused by its interaction with far-off galaxies. Therefore, the inertia of the body would be due to the retarding effect of the universe at large. Einstein dubbed this idea "Mach's Principle," and to the present day cosmologists disagree about whether, or to what extent, it should be incorporated as a special assumption in cosmological models.[26]

The situation was compounded by further developments in the theory. Shortly after Einstein's first model appeared, the Dutch astronomer Willem de Sitter introduced another that contained no matter at all. The most interesting feature of this model was its prediction that empty space is expanding with a velocity proportional to the distance between any two points within it. This resulted from the cosmological constant, which was interpreted as a repulsive force stretching space apart. In an empty universe, gravitation is absent, and there would be no attractive force to counteract cosmic repulsion. It was said that Einstein's universe had matter without motion, while de Sitter's universe had motion, but no matter. Nevertheless, they represent two complementary cosmological solutions of Einstein's equation.

Although de Sitter's universe was unrealistic because it was empty, it turned out that if it contained a few stars (or galaxies), they would be caught up in the general expansion of space, like corks floating down a river. Since their velocities of recession are proportional to the distances between them, they would satisfy Hubble's law. This law, however, had not yet been formulated. In effect, then, de Sitter's model predicted the cosmological red shifts of the galaxies that were, unknown to him, just being detected by American astronomers.[27] A further consequence of this model was that each star (or galaxy) had a horizon beyond which the rest of the universe was invisible. This is because the finite velocity of light places a limitation on how much of the universe can be observed at a given time. In the cosmic expansion, therefore, objects receding from one another faster than the speed of light would be invisible to each other forever.

All of this changed around 1920 when a Russian cosmologist, Alexander Friedmann, discovered a whole family of dynamic solutions to Einstein's equation. They included expanding, contracting, and oscillating models, with or without the cosmological constant. Of these, there are three important types, all with a zero cosmological constant; which one of them corresponds to the actual universe depends on the average density of the matter it contains. If the density is less than a certain critical value, the universe will be *open* and go on expanding forever. On the other hand, if it equals the critical value, the universe will be *flat*. In this case, the expansion gradually decreases as it approaches a limit asymptotically. The third possibility, where the density is greater than the critical value, yields a *closed* universe. Mathematically, such a universe could include more than a single cycle of expansion and contraction. These three cases are all determined by the *density parameter,* Omega (Ω), which is the ratio between the actual density and the critical density. The choice between models is an empirical matter to be determined by observation. At present, it seems that the universe will go on expanding forever, but this result may change with more accurate observations.[28]

In all the nonstatic models, after an initial phase of expansion the universe slows down; this is because gravity is acting against the force of expansion. Since the cosmological constant in these models is assumed to equal zero, gravity is the only force acting on the receding galaxies. We will see later that recent observations of supernovae in distant galaxies suggest that the cosmological constant is not zero. This could mean that the universe is actually accelerating into the future (vide Chapter V). An important feature of all three models is that there is at least one point (called a *singularity*) where the density becomes infinite and Einstein's equation breaks down. Not only does the equation fail to determine a unique model of the universe, but it also fails to give us any information concerning how the universe behaves in regions close to the singularity. As a consequence, this has led to the development of more complex cosmological models. In addition, there were new observations that had to be taken into account. General relativity, like previous scientific theories, must somehow be incorporated into a more complete theory. Yet its foundations are too substantial, and the knowledge of the universe it provides is too extensive, to be abandoned entirely.

Transition to the Standard Model

All of this theoretical work had been done before Hubble's observational discoveries established the scientific picture of an expanding universe of galaxies. Among the first to notice the connection between theory and observation was the English astronomer Sir Arthur Stanley Eddington, who publicized the idea of an expanding universe in a number of popular scientific books. Most of the early relativistic models involved a singularity at the beginning of the present expansion phase of the universe. The Belgian cosmologist Georges Lemaître gave the singularity a physical interpretation, calling it a "primeval atom." He supposed that this "atom" was unstable and dissolved into fragments as a result of radioactive decay. This gave rise to an expanding universe of galaxies similar to a display of fireworks. Eddington, on the other hand, found the idea of an abrupt beginning abhorrent and preferred a universe that had existed for an indefinite time as a static Einstein world before the expansion began. It then continues to expand until reaching the de Sitter state where repulsion dominates over gravity. Eddington thus united the worlds of Einstein and de Sitter into a single conception of cosmic history. He believed that the justification for this hybrid model lay in his discovery that the Einstein universe was unstable and could not remain forever in a static condition.

Around 1930, Einstein and de Sitter collaborated on a model of the expanding universe based on the idea of flat space. As we have seen, in this kind of space the universe continues expanding at a decreasing rate that comes to a stop at infinity. Although they took lambda equal to zero, they succeeded in preserving some of the features of Einstein's original static model. A discussion of the origin of the expansion, however, was pointedly avoided. This was justifiable at that time, since very little was known about the behavior of matter in the early universe. Even today, a flat universe remains the ideal toward which scientific cosmologists are striving. But the idea of a sudden, catastrophic origin of the universe could not be ignored for long. A succession of new discoveries was making it more and more likely that the universe really did have such a beginning.

In 1948, George Gamow introduced the idea of a violent explosion of hot condensed gases to explain the expansion of the universe. He based this idea on the discovery of nuclear fission, which had led to the building of the first atomic bomb. His picture of the early universe begins with a "primordial soup" of protons, neutrons, and electrons that he named *ylem*. There were also highly energetic photons making the universe so hot that the particles could not at first bind together into nuclei and atoms. The universe cooled as it expanded, and more complex structures were able to form.[29] Gamow's opponent, Fred Hoyle, called this theory the "Big Bang," and the name has continued to designate the more complex models that have succeeded it. The original version has been replaced by what is now called the "Standard Big Bang Model," which is the basis of contemporary cosmology. This model also has its shortcomings, and many attempts have been made to supersede it.

The major observational discovery fueling contemporary thinking about the Big Bang is the *cosmic background radiation*, discovered accidentally by Penzias and Wilson in 1965. Although Gamow had already predicted its existence, they were unaware that he had done so. It is composed of low frequency radio waves filling space uniformly in all directions. According to the Big

Bang model, this radiation was originally produced by the collisions of particles when the universe was much younger and hotter than it is now. At first, it could not escape because of these collisions. When the universe was about 300,000 years old, the collisions ended, allowing the radiation to travel freely thereafter. The cosmic background radiation now exists in the form of radio waves because of the expansion of the universe.

Another consideration brought into prominence by the Big Bang model is known as "Olbers' paradox." This problem was recognized in the seventeenth century by the German astronomer Johannes Kepler. He employed an early version of it in an argument against the idea of an infinite universe populated by an infinite number of stars; in this case, the universe would be ablaze with light both day and night. Why, then, does the sky appear to be dark at night? The paradox was reformulated by Olbers in 1823, and has since been known by his name. At the time, it was supposed that clouds of gas in interstellar space absorbed light from distant stars, which reduced the amount reaching us. But this will not solve the problem, because clouds that absorb light, if given enough time, would emit it again. After the discovery of the expanding universe, it was thought that the reddening of light from distant galaxies would be enough to account for the darkness of the night sky. The puzzle is now resolved in the context of the Big Bang model, for the discovery that the universe had a beginning means that it has a finite age. Light coming from very distant regions in space would not have had enough time to reach us yet. Hence the darkness of the night sky is the result of light traveling at finite speed in a universe that is not infinitely old.[30]

The Standard Big Bang Model

This model provides a picture of the history of the universe from about one millionth of a second after the start of the big bang down to the present time, ten to fifteen billion years later. Einstein's equation, supplemented by the results of contemporary particle physics, cannot take us back any further than this. There may even be a theoretical limit to how closely we could ever approach the original singularity predicted by general relativity. For, according to quantum mechanics, the smallest unit of time that can exist is the Planck time (10^{-43} sec); a smaller unit of time has no physical meaning. Nevertheless, within the given limits, we can obtain a general outline of the stages through which the universe has passed (Figure 3).

In the beginning, everything was so crowded together that nothing could be distinguished. At first, there was only the singularity, where the laws of physics as we know them break down. Then elementary particles of matter, antimatter, and light appeared, all mixed together in the "primordial soup." By one millionth of a second (10^{-6} sec), at the temperature of a thousand trillion degrees (10^{15} Kelvin), neutrons and protons began to form out of free quarks. After three minutes, the universe cooled enough (about one billion degrees Kelvin) for protons and neutrons to bind together into the nuclei of the lightest elements (hydrogen, helium, and lithium); this process is called *primordial* nucleosynthesis. About 300,000 years after the beginning of the universe, when the temperature had dropped to three thousand degrees Kelvin, almost all of the free electrons and nuclei became bound into atoms of hydrogen, helium, and lithium. As neutral atoms formed, photons of light broke loose from their interactions with unattached particles in a process called "decoupling," and the photons were now free to roam about in the universe. They are the source of the cosmic background radiation detected in 1965. Then gravity slowly began to draw matter together into stars and galaxies. In about one billion years, stars were starting to form, within which the heavier elements were eventually cooked; this process is known as *stellar* nucleosynthesis. The heavy elements, so crucial for the formation of planets and living organisms, were spread through space by supernova explosions.[31]

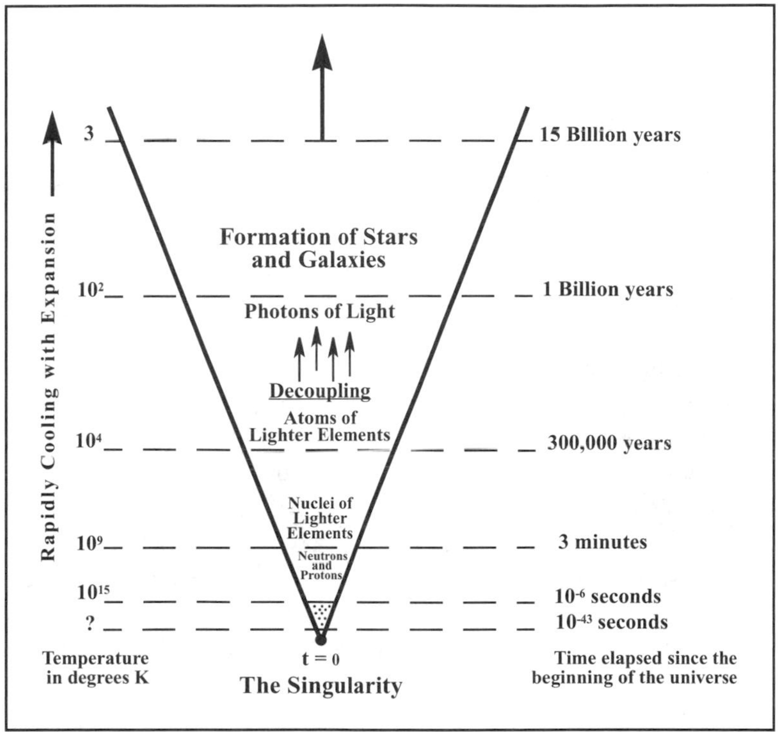

Figure 3. The Standard Big Bang Model

There are several misconceptions about this model that should be cleared up before we continue. One of them visualizes the big bang as an explosion that occurred somewhere in space at some time in the past. This is not so, because the big bang involves the entire universe, including space and time, which did not exist in their cosmic forms prior to it. We are in the midst of the big bang now, as evidenced by the cosmic background radiation uniformly surrounding us. Another erroneous idea is that the galaxies are flying away from one another like bullets through space. According to general relativity, however, the space between them is stretching and carrying them along with it.[32] In this theory, space has physical significance as a gravitational field, and hence contains energy.

The main supporting evidence for the Standard Model consists of (1) the cosmic background radiation, (2) the cosmological red shifts, and (3) the observed cosmic abundances of the light elements (which are accurately predicted by the model). The Standard Model is a great scientific achievement, but it hasn't really solved the problem of the origin of the universe. No one is certain about what, if anything, may have existed before the big bang, or whether such a question has any meaning. As we saw in our discussion of mythical cosmology, this may not be a purely physical question, because the origin of the universe could lie in a transition from the psychic to the physical state of being. Until recently, the general opinion among scientific cosmologists has been that the universe began at the singularity, and questions about what existed before the big bang were considered meaningless. Some theologians find this agreeable, because it is compatible with scriptural accounts of divine creation. The laws of physics may break down at the singularity, but this should be no obstacle to God. Surely, they believe, God could have created a singularity out of nothing and then started the universe off with a "bang." But why would God have chosen such an abrupt and violent beginning for the universe?

Physicists are suspicious of singularities and make every effort to eliminate them. We should not expect science to tell us very much about these peculiar mathematical entities, since they lie beyond the reach of the conventional laws of physics. But the singularity at the beginning of the universe cannot be dealt with as summarily as theologians would like us to think. The mind is hurled back upon itself as it confronts a dark impenetrable mystery looming before it. Later on, it will be seen that Sri Aurobindo calls this the "Inconscient," because consciousness is locked away deeply within it. It manifests physically as the inward pull of gravity toward destruction and self-annihilation. The Inconscient lies at the root of the entire universe and is forever closed to inspection by physical science. We will have more to say about this in Chapter VII on the evolving universe. A similar situation occurs inside black holes (stars that collapse to infinity), for there is a singularity at the core of each one of them. The singularity is still another version of the mythical boundary that separates the universe from its unmanifested source (see Chapter III). Lately, some scientific cosmologists have shifted toward sophisticated and far-reaching modifications of the Standard Model that may circumvent the problem of the singularity altogether. These will be reviewed in the next chapter. But first we survey a few earlier alternatives to the Standard Model.

The Oscillating Universe Model

One way of understanding what might have happened before the big bang is to assume an oscillating universe. This, as we saw earlier, is one of the Friedmann models derived from Einstein's equation. It bears some resemblance to the Hindu myth of cosmic cycles and suffers from the same ambiguity. Mathematically, the cycle of expansion and contraction, beginning and ending in singularities, can repeat itself forever. But if there were only one universe that is continually being regenerated from its own ashes, like the legendary Phoenix, there would be a problem with entropy. Richard Tolman demonstrated in 1934 that only a small number of cycles would have been possible up to now, because entropy increases from one cycle to the next and would eventually shut down the process.[33]

There are difficulties, however, in applying general relativity and thermodynamics to the extreme physical conditions that exist close to a singularity. So an oscillating universe may still be possible. Other suggestions have been made, such as counting each cycle as a new universe with different physical properties. The cycles could be separated by conditions of intense compression in which information about previous cycles is lost, or time could break down entirely so that talk about "previous" cycles would be meaningless. Hence the possibility of successive universes, in some sense, cannot be ruled out. Still, the existence of the singularity remains a great stumbling block, and we must go on to examine a different kind of model that rejects the big bang altogether.

The Steady State Model

From the time of Lemaître's introduction of the "primeval atom" hypothesis, many cosmologists have voiced objections to an abrupt beginning of the universe. In 1948, a trio of British scientists at Cambridge University, Thomas Gold, Hermann Bondi, and Fred Hoyle, introduced a new model based on the idea that the universe has always been the same with no beginning or ending in time.[34] They maintained that there was no unique creation event and that the universe always has the same appearance to all observers within it. The basis of the new model was an extension of the original cosmological principle (which states that on a large enough scale the universe is the same everywhere in space) to include time as well. Therefore, the universe is *always* the same with no overall change ever taking place. This constitutes a new principle, which is called the *perfect cosmological principle,* since it asserts the uniformity of the universe in time as well as in space. The idea is as old as the Presocratic philosopher Parmenides, and a version of it is even found in some Indian philosophies (e.g., Jainism). But in the present context, it must be shown to be compatible with the observed recession of the galaxies, which suggests that the universe is expanding.

In the Big Bang model, the universe gets less and less dense as the expansion proceeds. There is a "thinning out" process at work as the galaxies recede from one another; consequently, the universe becomes less dense as it gets older. This could not happen in the Steady State model, because it would be a large-scale change that is ruled out by the perfect cosmological principle. Therefore, it was proposed that as the universe expands and becomes less dense, more matter is being created to fill in the gaps; the average density would always remain constant. The process is called "continuous creation," which refers to the way that the universe is maintained in a steady state. It is asserted that matter is being created spontaneously out of nothing in the empty space left by the galaxies as they recede from one another. But this seems to violate the law of conservation of mass-energy. The originators of this model claimed that we do not know whether the conservation law applies exactly to the universe. They estimated that the rate of the creation of matter (in the form of hydrogen atoms) predicted by their model is well below the limits of our measuring instruments; thus, a violation of the conservation of mass-energy could not be detected. It is also maintained that the continuous creation of matter is no worse an idea than the abrupt creation of the universe implied in the Big Bang model.

A word of caution is required with regard to the term "creation." Scientific models never assert creation by God. All that is meant by creation is that the universe comes into existence in a way that does not violate the laws of physics. The Steady State model was suspect for a variety of reasons, but the final blow came with the discovery of the cosmic background radiation. There is no convincing explanation of this radiation in terms of the Steady State model, though it fits naturally into the conception of a primeval cosmic explosion. Since 1965, the Steady State model has been excluded from serious consideration by most cosmologists. Recently, however, it has drawn some interest in the context of Inflationary Universe models that imply the existence of multiple universes. We consider this kind of model in the next chapter.

V

THE BIG BANG AND BEYOND

In this chapter, we begin with a brief consideration of the foundations of quantum mechanics. It leads into a discussion of the most recent cosmological theories introduced to solve some of the puzzles associated with the Standard Model. We have seen that relativistic cosmology is derived from Einstein's equation, which is the core of the general theory of relativity. This equation is based on Einstein's deep intuition into the harmony of the universe and the unity of its laws. Einstein's equation sketches the large outlines of the physical universe, at least as far as gravitation is concerned. But *harmony* is only one aspect of the universe, the other being the *variety* of things filling it with overflowing abundance.[1] General relativity does not explain this variety, and physicists have had to turn elsewhere to account for it. Hence we must look at the other major theory that rules modern physics—quantum mechanics. Although Einstein was involved in the early development of the quantum theory, he later repudiated its foundations and spent the rest of his life trying to refute it.

The great scandal of modern physics is that these two theories, general relativity and quantum mechanics, seem to be logically incompatible. For general relativity is *deterministic*, being based on the principle that inflexible laws precisely determine every physical occurrence; everything that happens is assumed to be predictable on the basis of these laws. Quantum mechanics, on the other hand, is *indeterministic,* describing the world in terms of probabilities rather than certainties. This theory is concerned with the behavior of the elementary particles of matter and energy. Elementary particles can be studied in detail only where large amounts of energy are produced, such as in cosmic rays, the great particle accelerators that physicists have designed, and the very early universe close to the singularity. The uncertainty implied by quantum mechanics applies only to the atomic and subatomic worlds. But even though the behavior of individual particles is unpredictable, the statistical laws governing large assemblages of them lead to precise predictions when enough particles are involved. In spite of its strangeness, quantum mechanics has been widely confirmed experimentally. It provides the principles that account for the immense variety of the world, including atomic structure, chemical reactions, molecular bonding, and the initial formation of stars and galaxies—it may even be able to account for the origin of the universe. In addition, the theory is directly involved in modern technology, for it underlies most of the innovations in electronics, superconductivity, and lasers.

But what can quantum mechanics tell us about the universe at large, which is the concern of scientific cosmology? Its value for cosmology lies in the fact that as we get closer to the singularity at the origin, the universe gets smaller and matter breaks down into tiny particles. This is the region over which quantum mechanics holds sway, so the theory should tell us something about the conditions prevailing in the very early universe. For example, the later formation of galaxies cannot be explained unless we understand the behavior of matter close to the singularity that appears in all of the relativistic models. Physics as we know it breaks down at this point, because general relativity cannot account for the behavior of matter at the extreme temperatures and pressures existing in the early period. Something more is needed that general relativity cannot provide, since it does not deal with the microscopic world. This is the province of quantum mechanics, and we have to turn to it for knowledge about the very early universe. But, as already noted, this is an entirely different kind of theory than general relativity.

Although logically incompatible, both theories seem to work in complementary ways to account for the harmony and variety of the universe. General relativity is basically a field theory, and the outstanding property of fields is that they are continuous throughout space. All disturbances within them flow smoothly like waves from one location to another. In other words, there is no instantaneous action at a distance in the field. The picture of the world in quantum mechanics is quite different because nature is viewed as discrete at the microscopic level. Quantum mechanics makes use of fields, but they are associated with the particles that make up the atomic world. It seems that instantaneous action at a distance between particles might also be possible. At this level, the universe exhibits a predominantly granular structure. Large objects appear to be solid and impenetrable because we cannot perceive the inner structure of matter directly. The Planck length (10^{-33} cm) determines the graininess on the quantum level, since a smaller unit of length has no physical meaning. What this implies is that no measurable length can be infinitely divisible.

To sum up with an image, nature is like a sandy beach that appears to be a smooth white strip when viewed from a distance, but is seen to consist of innumerable tiny grains of sand when viewed at close range. Similarly, the universe is conceived as a continuous field from the standpoint of general relativity, while being granular in structure on the level of quantum mechanics. According to some physicists, the microstructure of spacetime itself may be a seething quantum foam out of which universes can arise spontaneously. Just as in the case of the sandy beach, however, it is the same universe that is being described from different points of view. This suggests that there is a deep principle of unity underlying the two theories. Consequently, the most promising way for physics to proceed is to combine them into a single comprehensive theory. A search is now underway for an ultimate theory that will unify the four fundamental forces and explain all the properties of elementary particles. But the mathematical construction of such a theory has proven to be extremely difficult.[2]

Present attempts to unify the two theories are highly speculative; they tend to be little more than ingenious computational exercises. None of them have been sufficiently tested, and some may even be untestable in principle. The human mind might not be able to accomplish unification through its own powers. Although it may possibly achieve an abstract formal unity, mind is basically an organ of analysis and division. It can never really unify the world, unless that unity already exists in nature. The mind combines a set of discrete symbols or numbers into a general formula that can be manipulated according to logical and mathematical rules capable of yielding predictions. There is no reason why scientists should stop doing this, since important discoveries about the physical world are possible through this approach. But the implication that they can arrive in this way at a final understanding of the universe is presumptuous. More to the point, unity is always an ideal worth pursuing, whether in science, religion, politics, or human relations.[3] Whatever the cosmological solution may be (if there is one), we first glance at the foundations of quantum mechanics. This theory underlies new developments in scientific cosmology aimed at eliminating the initial singularity altogether.

An Overview of Quantum Mechanics

Quantum mechanics is a mathematical theory that describes the phenomena of the microscopic world. It dispenses with the simple pictures of billiard balls and miniature solar systems that were once popular ways of visualizing the structure of the atom. The intricacy of the mathematics involved makes it difficult to discuss the theory in verbal terms, and this creates many paradoxes for the unwary. But the language of mathematics is perfectly adequate for a description of quantum systems, which lie below the level of everyday verbal discourse. We will only attempt to highlight a few salient features of the theory necessary for understanding its applications to cosmology. There are three basic ideas that characterize the quantum mechanical description of nature: the Copenhagen interpretation of the wave-particle duality, the Schrödinger equation and the wave function, and Heisenberg's uncertainty principle. A few words must be said about each of them.

The Copenhagen Interpretation

Physicists have been familiar with the wave-particle duality since the time of Newton and Christiaan Huygens, each postulating a different theory about the nature of light. Newton explained light in terms of material particles, which he called "corpuscles," and Huygens claimed that light consisted of waves in a continuous medium. Both pointed to experiments that seemed to support the views they held. The debate continued for some time, but by the end of the nineteenth century the wave theory enjoyed a brief period of triumph. Light was explained as waves traveling through a universal ether filling empty space. There still remained the difficulty of explaining the mechanical properties the ether must have in order to transmit light waves, though most physicists believed that the problem would eventually be solved. A serious blow to the wave theory came, however, with the appearance of Einstein's Special Theory of Relativity in 1905. This theory abolished the conception of a light-bearing ether, along with the concepts of absolute space and absolute time.

The debate revived when Einstein discovered that certain phenomena could only be explained in terms of particles of light (called "photons"). The situation was complicated further when it was found that matter possessed wave-like characteristics that were associated with elementary particles like electrons. Since then, physicists have had to live with the wave-particle duality as a fundamental feature of the physical world. For the basic constituents of matter and light have the characteristics of *both* particles and waves. Furthermore, the observation of a physical system on the quantum level seems to influence its behavior in this regard. In some experiments, for example, light behaves like a shower of particles, while in others it behaves like waves. But particles and waves have distinctive properties that cannot be reduced to a common principle. How can nature be explained in terms of two such contradictory ideas? Einstein summarized this dilemma in the following words:

> Is light a wave or a shower of photons? Is a beam of electrons a shower of elementary particles or a wave? These fundamental questions are forced upon physics by experiment. In seeking to answer them we have to abandon the description of atomic events as happenings in space and time, we have to retreat still further from the old mechanical view.[4]

This duality irked physicists until Niels Bohr and his colleagues developed what is now known as the "Copenhagen interpretation" of quantum mechanics. In this connection, Bohr developed the "principle of complementarity" as a means of understanding the wave-particle duality. He did not think that it was paradoxical at all, since the wave and particle aspects do not appear in the same experiment in a contradictory way. Rather, he saw them as complementary aspects of a single situation in which the one we are shown depends upon the nature of the experiment being performed. Thus, it would be meaningless to ask what a particle *really* is in itself. Bohr claimed that it is not the purpose of physics to answer questions about the nature of reality. The quantum world cannot be described independently of the mathematical formalisms constructed by physicists to make their observations intelligible. The state of a system at the quantum level is undefined before a measurement is made, and its physical properties depend on how the experiment has been carried out. Therefore, the quantum world is said to have no objective reality except when it is being observed and measured. According to the Copenhagen Interpretation, it is the *total situation* (including both the system observed and the measuring apparatus being used to observe it) that is relevant for physics.

The Schrödinger Equation and the Wave Function

If the Copenhagen interpretation is correct, there is no independent reality that can be discovered behind the observed universe. Hence the real world for physics is the one observed. This is a world of measured quantities susceptible to mathematical analysis. The mathematics allows physicists to predict the results of experiments; this is all that the Copenhagen interpretation requires. Their means for doing so is the *Schrödinger equation*, which is named after the Austrian physicist who first formulated it. This is the fundamental equation of quantum mechanics. Its solution is the wave function that describes the state of a quantum system.[5] The *wave function* contains all the information that relates to the system being examined. As its name implies, this function represents a wave, but it is not a real wave in the classical sense. Instead, it is a mathematical expression of the probabilities that certain states of a quantum system will actually occur; before their occurrence, they are merely "potentialities" without any definable properties. When a measurement is made, the wave function is said to collapse, and the potential thereby becomes an actual event in space and time. The background of potentialities, however, is not part of the world that we observe. Thus, the wave function is viewed by most physicists as only a way of making predictions about what will happen when certain conditions are specified. They do not consider it to be the description of a real world existing independent of observation. The trouble with this way of looking at things is that it confines the mind to its own constructions of experience, leaving the rest of reality unprobed. It may be sufficient for the purposes of physics, but could never really satisfy the soul.

If we look beyond physics, a philosophical question remains concerning the kind of reality that corresponds to the wave function. This is the most serious problem facing quantum mechanics. Werner Heisenberg, a major contributor to the theory, appealed to a world of *potentialities* containing all the possible states of a quantum system that can become actualized by observation.[6] But this world does not exist in space and time (or spacetime), which are the conditions for the existence of the physical universe. The wave function thus appears to imply a strange reality underlying the observable world. Many attempts have been made to interpret this function in terms of more fundamental ideas. They range from various kinds of "hidden variable" theories implying that the probabilities on the quantum level are results of our ignorance of the deeper aspects of the system being studied, to David Bohm's idea of an "implicate order" from which the observed world is ultimately derived. The implicate order defines a reality in which any element contains enfolded within itself the totality of the universe.[7] There is also a "many-worlds" interpretation asserting that every observation of a quantum system splits the universe into many parallel and disconnected worlds, each representing a result of the observation being made.

None of these attempts to account for the wave function have displaced the Copenhagen interpretation. They seem to be verbal pointers toward a reality existing that cannot be fully grasped in mental terms. Quantum mechanics has done more than any other scientific theory to undermine a purely materialistic version of the universe. Yet most physicists and philosophers who have tried to interpret it are still oriented toward some form of materialism, no matter how refined it might be. With the wave function, physics once more seems to have confronted a boundary between the observed universe and its unseen roots. As with the singularity in relativistic cosmology, we may have reached an invisible border between the physical and the psychic faces of the universe. The psychic face is manifested to us through the mediation of symbolic images. In the case of the wave function, the symbols are abstract mathematical ones representing the threshold that physics cannot cross. Heisenberg's world of potentialities could be a psychic realm whose characteristics are less confined than those of the physical universe. But, as we have already seen in our discussion of mythical cosmology, the symbols needed to gain a deeper insight into the psychic world are not those of mathematical physics.[8]

Heisenberg's Uncertainty Principle

Returning to the basic ideas of quantum mechanics, something must be said about Heisenberg's uncertainty principle, which has led to new insights into the origin of the universe. According to Richard Feynman, every statement in quantum mechanics is a restatement of the uncertainty principle. Just as general relativity is based on the principle of covariance, quantum mechanics is summed up by Heisenberg's principle. It is the result of a careful investigation into the limitations imposed on the measurement of a quantum system. The uncertainty principle states that we cannot know the precise values of certain pairs of observables (such as position and momentum, or time and energy) to a greater degree of accuracy than allowed by *Planck's constant* ($\hbar$); this is an extremely small quantity ($\hbar = 6.63 \times 10^{-34}$ joule-seconds) that sets the scale of all quantum mechanical effects. In mathematical terms, $\Delta x \cdot \Delta p \geq \hbar$, which states that the product of the uncertainties in position (Δx) and momentum (Δp) can never be smaller than the order of magnitude of Planck's constant.[9]

There is an intrinsic "fuzziness" of matter at the quantum level, which is a consequence of Heisenberg's principle. The exact position and momentum of an electron, for example, cannot both be known simultaneously. Surprisingly, the amount of fuzziness, or uncertainty, is precisely determined by Planck's constant. The uncertainty principle governs the whole make-up of the microscopic world of atoms and their constituent particles; the stability of atoms, and thus of the entire physical universe, depends upon it. This principle implies that we cannot localize an electron and at the same time determine its velocity with precision, since the fuzziness inherent in the electron prohibits it. Heisenberg's principle also applies to energy and time, for if a small quantity of energy exists during a brief interval of time the amounts of both together cannot be known with precision. We will see in the next section that this has an important cosmological application.

Many paradoxes are associated with the foundations of quantum mechanics, but their consideration is not germane to our present concerns. The relation of Heisenberg's principle to the universe merits comment. The uncertainty in our measurements of particles does not result from the limits of our measuring instruments, as is sometimes supposed; it is an intrinsic characteristic of the physical world. There seems to be a random element in nature that makes the fuzziness involved in our measurements more than merely a matter of human ignorance. Philosophically, some degree of randomness in the physical world could account for the immense variety of things appearing in it. A world that is too tightly structured would be restricted in the diversity of its contents. Physical randomness need not imply that the universe is the result of pure chance, since there may be a deeper reason for the exclusion of strict determination. All of these considerations apply to cosmology, where uncertainties in the microscopic world become important as we approach the singularity. Theoretically, this is the point from which the universe began, so the earliest stages can be treated in quantum mechanical terms. At the singularity, the concepts of space and time become blurred. Consequently, it is possible to replace the sharpness of a singularity by the fuzziness implied in quantum mechanics. Enormous complications are involved in this, and claims to understand the physical conditions near the singularity are dubious. But one physicist, Edward Tryon, made an interesting proposal along these lines in 1973.[10] His idea was later incorporated into the inflationary universe models that will be considered in section five of this chapter.

The Universe as a Quantum Vacuum Fluctuation

The Standard Big Bang Model, in which the universe begins at the singularity, seems to violate the conservation laws of physics because the law of the conservation of energy forbids creation out of nothing. This is an old idea, appearing in ancient Greek philosophy as the dictum that "nothing comes from nothing." Also, from the standpoint of physics, there is no obvious reason for the big bang to have occurred. But, according to Tryon, the universe did appear from nothing, and the law of the conservation of energy was not appreciably violated. This follows from quantum mechanics, which allows for "quantum vacuum fluctuations" in which particles apparently spring into being out of nothing and quickly disappear again. Energy conservation may be violated, but only for the brief lifetime of a particle permitted by Heisenberg's uncertainty principle. Moreover, in the equations of physics the gravitational binding energy of the universe is a negative quantity that exactly balances the total positive energy it contains. Therefore, the universe might have originated as a tiny fluctuation from zero total energy and, if Tryon is correct, this is just a chance happening.

The existence of quantum vacuum fluctuations is implied by Heisenberg's uncertainty principle when it is interpreted in terms of energy and time. This tells us that for very brief intervals of time the energy of space is indeterminate, preventing us from fixing a precise zero energy level for it. Consequently, in quantum mechanics one can only identify the lowest possible energy level of a system; this is called its *ground state*. In quantum systems, the ground state is never zero, so that it is possible for the energy of space to fluctuate. What this suggests is that even "empty space" has energy, which fluctuates like ripples on a lake: it is called the "quantum vacuum." This does not mean, however, that it is entirely without content. For the vacuum has some energy and should not be equated with total emptiness. Hence there is no such thing as a true vacuum (or "absolute nothingness"). In a way, the quantum vacuum can be compared to that of the classical ether, except that here the ether is not a material substance. But quantum mechanical nothingness is not absolute nothingness because it contains some energy.

According to Einstein's mass-energy equivalence relation (special theory of relativity), energy fluctuations in the quantum vacuum can be converted into material particles; they are called "virtual particles" due to their fleeting existence. The laws of physics do not place a limit on the size of vacuum fluctuations. It is possible that an energy fluctuation in a quantum vacuum could have given rise to the whole universe. In a certain sense, then, the universe may have appeared "out of nothing." This, of course, is not the same as the theological version of creation *ex nihilo,* where it is claimed that the universe was created out of absolute nothingness. The universe might simply be a fluctuation of the energy of some larger multidimensional space in which it is embedded.[11] But why should there be such a space in the first place, and why should it obey the laws of quantum mechanics? Is it to be taken as a brute fact, or would this also call for an explanation?

Another attempt to apply quantum mechanics to cosmology has been made by Stephen Hawking and his colleague James Hartle. In essence, they tried to find the wave function of the universe. The wave function describes the probability of particles behaving in certain ways and, with suitable alterations, this function may be assigned to a set of cosmological models. It could then indicate the probability for the occurrence of different kinds of universes. Hawking's analysis of the problem led to his "no boundary proposal" (1981), in which he suggested that the most probable universe had a *closed* spacetime with no boundaries or edges. Hence there would be no singularities and no moment of creation. One oddity of this proposal is that time has both real and "imaginary" components.[12] The so-called imaginary component, unlike real time, exists even before the big bang. All talk about the beginning and ending of the universe in time would become meaningless. The laws of physics would reign supreme, thus rendering the idea of a divine Creator superfluous for cosmology. Hawking offered this model only as a speculative hypothesis.

One advantage of the application of quantum mechanics to cosmology is that it could provide a scientific explanation for the origin of matter out of the quantum vacuum. The Standard Model simply assumes that the singularity existed at the beginning of things. On the other hand, physical laws may actually determine the initial conditions of the universe. It is hard to imagine something as large as the universe we inhabit originating in an infinitesimal point. But it could have begun small and later grew gigantic in size as the result of a rapid phase of expansion. Considerations like this have led to a new model based on the idea of inflation, which will be examined shortly. Before doing so, we describe a few other puzzles raised by the Standard Big Bang Model.

PUZZLES OF THE STANDARD BIG BANG MODEL

As pointed out earlier, the Standard Model is based on the assumption that the cosmological constant equals zero. This means that gravity is the only force operating in the universe at large, and it is slowing down the expansion. But recent observations indicate that gravity is opposed by another force. If the preliminary results are confirmed by further research, the Standard Model will be radically altered. Prior to this, cosmologists had already noticed other puzzles that led to significant modifications of the Standard Model. The most important of these are the "flatness problem," the "horizon problem," and the "smoothness problem." They are concerned with observations that place very strict conditions on the properties of the very early universe. The questions they raise involve what happened at the beginning that could account for the features of the universe that we now observe. These features must either be accepted as brute facts, or be somehow explained.

The *flatness problem* arises from the fact that the geometry of the observable universe is very nearly flat. If the actual density of the universe exactly equals the critical density ($\Omega = 1$), the geometry would be completely flat. The observations indicate a close balance between gravity and expansion, so the universe cannot be expanding too quickly or too slowly at the present time. An extremely slight difference (one part in billions), one way or the other, in the early expansion rate would have caused the universe to either collapse almost immediately or fly to pieces so rapidly that no stars or galaxies could have formed. Since the value of Ω could be any number at all, cosmologists find it surprising that it has the precise number that allows a universe like ours to exist. The situation may be further complicated if recent observations suggesting that the universe is accelerating are confirmed. In this case, the cosmological constant would have to be included in the value for Ω. An added factor in the puzzle is that our universe contains observers like ourselves, which means that its initial conditions had to allow enough time for humans to evolve into their present form. Considering the highly selective conditions necessary for this to happen, it is curious that we are here at all.

Another consideration is the *horizon problem.* It arises from the observation that the intensity of the cosmic background radiation is the same in all directions (isotropy), indicating that the universe is quite uniform. The puzzle is that unless the universe started off uniformly it would be difficult to explain why it looks so uniform now. For if it had begun with different regions expanding at different rates, it would not have been possible for these regions to have become homogenized. Large parts of the early universe would have been uncoordinated, since there could not have been enough time for causal influences to link them together. If they had not been in causal contact, however, it would be very difficult to explain the uniformity that we now observe. Even if they eventually did make causal contact, tremendous turbulence would have occurred, yielding temperatures preventing the formation of normal stars like the sun. This would make a low turbulence universe like ours very unlikely. Here again, cosmologists are surprised that the universe appears to be so uniform. In fact, if it were not, we very likely would never have existed.

The uniformity of the universe leads to a third puzzle, called the *smoothness problem,* because a perfectly uniform cosmos could not account for the birth of planets, stars, and galaxies. Thus, some minute and difficult to detect irregularities must have been present in the overall smoothness of the early universe. This has led many cosmologists to seek for some form of "dark matter" that could provide the gravitational pull needed to build the galaxies. But too much dark matter would cause the universe to collapse too soon in a violent implosion. In that case, a complex world including living observers like ourselves could not have developed.

New Concepts

We have now seen that the Standard Big Bang Model has a number of shortcomings. To account for these puzzles, adjustments to the Standard Model are necessary. These relate to conditions prevailing in the very early universe, where the known laws of physics are no longer reliable guides. There are other difficulties as well, many of them too technical to discuss here. A few, however, have led to the introduction of new concepts that take us beyond the Standard Model. The most important of these are fine-tuning, the anthropic principle, and multiple universes.[13]

Fine Tuning

Besides the aforementioned problems, cosmologists have wondered about the many apparently accidental "coincidences" among the various constants of nature. For example, the fundamental force strengths and particle masses observed seem to be precisely determined for the existence of a universe like ours. Slight deviations from the values of these constants would lead to a radically different kind of universe with extremely inhospitable conditions for life forms like our own. These apparent coincidences are sometimes referred to as examples of *fine tuning,* which implies that tiny changes in some of the basic features of the universe would make the existence of life in it impossible. Fine tuning, however, does not presuppose the existence of a cosmic "Fine Tuner," though it could be interpreted in this way if so desired. This might appeal to theologians looking for evidence of cosmic design, but most scientists would prefer to invoke either pure chance or the anthropic principle.

The Anthropic Principle

To begin with, "anthropic principle" is a misnomer since the term can be applied to any kind of sentient observer and has no special concern with man (*anthropos*). It is also misleading to call it a principle, if we mean by this an explanation of something, for in itself it does not explain anything. The anthropic principle simply asserts that the presence of life places limits on the universe, because we can only observe one that has properties allowing us to exist. Obviously, a universe without such properties would not contain observers like ourselves. Although stating an obvious truth, the anthropic principle has also been employed in explanations of fine tuning. It is a general way of thinking about the universe rather than an explanatory principle, and some cosmologists prefer to use the term "anthropic reasoning" to characterize this kind of thinking.

There are several versions of the principle that are called "strong" or "weak," but we can ignore the fine distinctions among them.[14] Misunderstandings here should be avoided. For example, the anthropic principle is not religious or teleological in intent, though widely construed in these ways; it says nothing about God or the role of purpose in the universe, yet it is compatible with them when additional conditions are imposed. Furthermore, it is not really anthropocentric, since it need not be restricted to human beings—any kind of observer would do. One interpretation implies that our existence *causes* the universe to possess life-permitting properties, but this is incorrect since the anthropic principle does not reverse the cause-effect relation. Its basic function is to call attention to a fact that might otherwise go unnoticed. Even though this principle is not in itself an explanation, it might become one when combined with other ideas. Most physicists are not fond of it, since they prefer to derive the properties of the universe from a fundamental theory rather than think solely in terms of what properties are favorable to life. So far, however, attempts to formulate a "theory of everything" have only resulted in untestable mathematical speculations.

Multiple Universes

We must now consider how the anthropic principle can be used to account for fine-tuning. Since the universe must possess some properties, one could claim that those it actually has are purely accidental; thus, no further explanation would be required. On the other hand, it is remarkable that the laws of physics allow a universe to exist with so much variety—one rich enough to enable intelligent life forms to appear in it. We can easily imagine universes that are so simple or short-lived that nothing very complex could develop in them. So it would seem that the immense variety allowed by our universe calls for some kind of explanation. The anthropic principle can play a role in this, though it is not sufficient by itself. It is employed in theological explanations appealing to God's purpose in creating a universe in which living creatures could exist, but this takes us beyond science. Another explanation is also possible, in which the anthropic principle plays a key role in conjunction with the assumption of multiple universes.

If there were a vast assemblage of universes, all differing in their properties, then observers would only exist in those rare examples that had life-permitting properties. This is similar to having a royal flush in poker: among all the hands that have ever been dealt, there have been some royal flushes, and if you are holding one in your hand right now, you know that at least one exists. The situation is similar with respect to the universe. If there are enough universes around, there may be a few that are life-permitting. Since we are able to observe our universe, we know that one actually exists (otherwise we would not be here to observe it). In this way, the assumption of multiple universes, supplemented by the anthropic principle, accounts for the existence of our observer-containing universe. But this argument only works if other universes actually exist; merely possible worlds, as supposed by Leibniz, will not do. In the perspective of multiple universes, anthropic reasoning can thus acquire genuine explanatory force, since it gives an account of why our fine-tuned universe happens to exist.

Let us explore the multiple universe scenario a bit farther, for it plays a role in a new cosmological model widely discussed today.[15] If multiple universes do exist, most would presumably be without life, because the appearance of life requires very precise fine-tuning. But the existence of a vast number of universes beyond possible observation is hard to accept unless they are included in an enormous Multiverse. The idea is not in itself unreasonable; we are already familiar with the classification of particular things (like trees) into general types. A variety of trees is certainly richer than only one tree. Our universe could well be a member of a class containing many universes. Speculations about a "plurality of worlds" are as old as ancient Greek philosophy, and the idea is also found in the mythical cosmologies of Hinduism and Buddhism. They may involve a succession of universes in time, universes existing simultaneously in space, or a combination of both. But the failure to provide a credible *mechanism* for producing multiple universes seriously hampered earlier speculations. Scientific defenders of multiple universes must provide a mechanism for producing them that is consistent with the known laws of physics. The most promising mechanism, as far as recent cosmology is concerned, is associated with the idea of an inflationary universe.

An imaginative attempt to do this can be found in Edgar Allan Poe's long cosmological essay, *Eureka,* in which he presents an elaborate account of multiple universes in terms of nineteenth century science.[16] At the beginning of a universe, Poe imagines God creating a "primordial particle" (singularity?), which then expands by "irradiation" spherically in all directions. As the expansion continues, gravity slowly takes over and matter condenses into stars and planets. He argues that our universe must be finite, for otherwise the sky would not be dark at night (Olbers' paradox). Since there are numerous universes, they must be so distant from one another that light from any one of them never reaches the others before they collapse. Furthermore, each of these isolated universes has its own God. The force of gravity eventually halts the expansion of a universe and contraction begins to set in. Matter will ultimately dissolve into the nothingness from which it came: "Let us endeavor to comprehend that the final globe of globes will instantaneously disappear, and that God will remain all in all."[17] God will then start another universe with "a new and perhaps totally different series of conditions."[18] Poe concludes:

> Guiding our imaginations by that omniprevalent law of laws, the law of periodicity, are we not, indeed, more than justified in entertaining a belief — let us say, rather, in indulging a hope — that the processes we have here ventured to contemplate will be renewed forever, and forever, and forever; a novel Universe swelling into existence, and then subsiding into nothingness, at every throb of the Heart Divine?[19]

This cosmic vision filled him with delight, and he declared that it was too beautiful not to be true.[20] Unfortunately, Poe lacked the scientific training necessary to sustain it, and his theological speculations were woefully inadequate. But he compensated for these shortcomings with a boundless cosmological enthusiasm. His book can still be warmly recommended to anyone with a serious interest in cosmology.

Inflationary Universe Models

Models of an inflationary universe were motivated by new theories in particle physics that are still incomplete. The idea of "inflation" appeals to scientific cosmologists because it explains many of the puzzles associated with the Standard Big Bang Model, such as the flatness, horizon, and smoothness problems. Inflationary theories assume that the early universe underwent a brief period of acceleration (about 10^{-34} sec) that increased its size exponentially (by a factor of 10^{60}). The energy for inflation is thought to come from scalar fields associated with the quantum vacuum.[21] These fields provide a mechanism that can generate rapid inflation. It is theorized that the universe began as a tiny quantum fluctuation that suddenly blew up to gigantic size, far exceeding that of the observable universe. A rapid inflationary period accounts nicely for the flatness and uniformity that we observe. In the case of *flatness,* the rapid expansion causes space to flatten out, just as the surface of a balloon becomes flatter as it is inflated. As for the *horizon problem,* inflation begins with a homogeneous region much smaller than in the Standard Model. It is then inflated to become large enough to include the observed universe.

The *smoothness problem* is also accounted for, because quantum fluctuations in the primordial soup would be enlarged to become seeds for the formation of galaxies. After the burst of inflation, the universe settled down to normal expansion as described by the Standard Model. In earlier versions, inflation was only concerned with our universe and was thought of as a modification of the Standard Model. Later versions, however, push beyond the big bang itself and supersede this model. They imply that there are many universes (of which ours is only one) existing in a vast Multiverse, or large assemblage of different domains. This Multiverse replaces what was previously called "the universe," since it contains everything that exists in the physical world.

One recent inflationary model is the eternally "self-reproducing universe" developed by Andrei Linde, a Russian cosmologist working at Stanford University. It is complicated in detail and remains controversial; only a general summary of its contents is attempted here.[22] Linde postulates a constantly inflating field that has always existed in what may be an infinite, multidimensional Superspace. Quantum fluctuations are continually occurring within it, as implied by Heisenberg's uncertainty principle. The total energy of this field is zero, because its negative gravitational energy cancels out the energy of the particles being created and annihilated by these fluctuations. It can thus continue to inflate endlessly with no loss of energy. Quantum fluctuations give rise to separate domains, or "bubbles," some of which inflate as a result of the intensity reached by the associated scalar fields.[23] These will eventually become large and independent worlds in their own right; hence they correspond to the different universes that make up the Multiverse. There are no limits to the number of such "bubble universes," and there can be an enormous variety of them because of the arbitrary values taken by the scalar fields. Linde called this process "chaotic inflation," since it exhibits a fractal pattern producing new bubbles *ad infinitum*.

Each bubble universe cools as it expands. At first, the various forces of nature are undifferentiated due to the high temperatures existing at its origin. As the bubble cools, however, the forces split apart in a process called "symmetry breaking," but the way this happens could differ from one universe to another. Symmetry breaking is likened to a phase transition, such as water freezing into ice, through which the perfectly homogeneous fluid differentiates into separate regions with distinct internal orientations. Under these conditions, particles would have different masses, depending on the intensity of the scalar fields associated with each universe. This would in turn have an effect on the force strengths in each universe, which are related to the properties of the particles it contains. All of these results are determined by the nature of the inflating field. The field is governed by the fundamental laws of physics (e.g., conservation laws), but each universe would have its own set of local laws. Bubble universes could differ in relative force strengths (e.g., gravity to electromagnetism), the mass-ratios of particles (e.g., proton to electron), expansion rates, degrees of turbulence, and so forth. Some of these universes would have life-permitting properties, and the anthropic principle reminds us that ours is one of them (and perhaps the only one). While physics gives us a picture of the formation of bubble universes, it has not yet provided an explanation for all of their properties. These may vary considerably from one bubble to another.

If this model is correct, inflation is not a part of the big bang model, but the big bang is itself derived from the inflationary model. The dominant image consists of expanding bubbles rather than violent explosions. Universes are bubbling up from some murky sea of inconscience underlying cosmic existence. This inconscience is the foundation of universes, though science cannot tell us what it is or why it is there. As was suggested in the previous chapter, the Inconscient lies deep within the psychic world beyond the reach of modern physics. A poem of Shelley's, in which he compares the formation of worlds to bubbles "sparkling, bursting, borne away" on an endlessly flowing river, expresses the gist of this view of multiple universes.[24] Some cosmologists have compared the Multiverse to the former Steady State model, because it is forever producing new worlds to replace others that have disappeared, thus maintaining the same overall pattern. But the difference is that we are now talking about a whole assemblage of universes rather than only one. The Multiverse combines harmony and variety on the largest imaginable scale, for an eternally inflating field gives rise to a multitude of universes in a lawful manner. Although much of this cosmic picture remains speculative, and may never be scientifically verified, it could be the next stage in a historical progression that began with Copernicus demonstrating that the earth was a planet circling the sun. Giordano Bruno followed him by including our sun among the stars, and Edwin Hubble later discovered that the Milky Way was a galaxy like other galaxies. Now the chaotic inflationary model suggests that our universe is but one among a large number of universes.

Responses to Fine Tuning

When confronted with the remarkably fine-tuned character of our universe, one can respond in several ways. There could be *multiple universes,* one of them being our own. Alternatively, if there is nothing beyond our universe, its properties may be either accidental or providential (created by God). A purely accidental universe is not very likely; we never believe this when there is a simple and direct way of explaining something. Compare, for example, the familiar situation in a movie where a poker player loses his money under suspicious circumstances. He doesn't assume that this is mere chance, but accuses the dealer of cheating—and may even shoot him. This is an unfortunate consequence. Given the circumstances, however, he is probably right in assuming that he has been cheated. In the case of the universe, we have *two* reasonable accounts available, one theological and the other scientific. The chances are that one of them could be right, yet it is also possible that both can be incorporated into a more comprehensive explanation. If so, at least some of the remaining mystery would be removed. Therefore, we proceed to examine this third possibility.

It was suggested above that the eternally inflating field is like an infinite sea with bubbles of foam appearing on its endlessly recurring waves. But one question remains: Why does the field exist in the first place? Science is mute about this, and theology is hard-pressed to explain it in terms of creationist ideas. One intriguing answer is suggested by the Hindu conception of creation as *līlā* (play, sport); this term is used to refer to the cosmic play or sport of God in the world. It expresses the divine delight of existence in an infinite variety of forms, which hardly suggests a restriction to only one universe.[25] In this context, the field serves as a support of the divine play.

Delight is the essence of creative activity. The inherent freedom of consciousness is veiled in an obscurity that the unaided mind cannot penetrate. A human work of art reveals potentialities that are incomplete until actualized through the creative work of the artist. The artist's freedom to create ensures that what is only a possibility can be actualized. Thus, we can know our latent powers in completed works of art. They are not known in detail beforehand, since to know them in advance would blunt the desire to discover something new. For an Infinite Artist, on the other hand, a single creative act would not suffice, because there are always other possibilities awaiting manifestation. We could say, then, that the Divine freely chooses to conceal itself in order to release delight in a variegated world. Without this self-imposed concealment, nothing about existence makes much sense. But it implies a last remaining veil between the universe and what still remains unmanifested. It also implies that *time* is necessary for the continued unfolding of hidden possibilities.

Creation of the universe as an expression of delight has been criticized on various grounds. Among the most serious objections is the charge that it seems to be incompatible with our notion of moral goodness. Critics maintain that an appeal to delight as the ultimate motive of existence trivializes our revulsion toward a universe as full of suffering as ours seems to be. This is a form of the traditional problem of evil that has always plagued theism. The question demands to know why there is so much suffering in a world created by an all-powerful and benevolent God. Numerous solutions have been proposed attempting to justify the divine purpose in allowing suffering to exist (theodicy), but they fail to completely convince. In the case of the *līlā,* however, the situation is mitigated by several other considerations. One is that there is no separation between the Divine and the universe as in conventional theism. The cosmos is viewed as a *divine manifestation* rather than a separate creation by God. Moreover, the soul itself is considered to be part of the Divine Being, so that God is not conceived as a judge presiding over fallible creatures different from himself. Finally, suffering is understood as a temporary distortion of the delight that is always present at the core of being.[26]

Admittedly, none of this entirely eliminates the nervous shock attending the experience of great personal tragedy, but no theodicy is capable of doing that. It is at least conceivable that the depth of suffering in this world is an unavoidable byproduct of the urge for an ultimate consummation of delight within it. Among the endless possibilities available to the Divine, one is to wrap itself in total darkness. But to remain in such a negative state is contrary to the divine nature. Like a starless night, it would be the prelude to a brighter dawn. Only time can reveal what this might be. The mind finds it exceedingly difficult to accept this, which largely accounts for the persistence of the problem of evil in human thought.

Theodicies are generalized intellectual solutions to a problem experienced on a deeply vital and emotional level, resisting any rationalization in mental terms. Consequently, theists are forced to fall back on an appeal to faith in the ultimate goodness and wisdom of God, despite all appearances to the contrary. Some people, on the other hand, find strength to endure relentless suffering in the belief that the laws of nature rule supreme. Others remain confused by an appalling mystery that they cannot fathom.

Still, the view of the universe as *līlā* is attractive on a number of counts. Although it favors delight as the primary impulse of creation, it does not exclude goodness altogether; great variety may itself be good in a larger sense than we ordinarily imagine. Greater goods always overrule lesser ones, and it seems impossible to satisfy all of them simultaneously. The Divine does not need to satisfy or conform to our limited standards of goodness; besides, if the universe is an evolving one, conflict and suffering need not be viewed as permanent parts of our destiny. A final judgment based upon what we may now believe would be premature, because it is possible that the world is in the process of changing into something better. Furthermore, a fully comprehensive perspective might convince us that we are never entirely abandoned by the Divine, no matter how dire the circumstances seem to be.[27]

A Runaway Universe?

Before leaving modern scientific cosmology, something more must be said about the recent discovery of the accelerating expansion of our universe. Up to now we have been dealing primarily with problems arising out of the postulated singularity at the origin of the universe. But the Standard Big Bang Model offers a variety of scenarios concerning the end of the universe as well. Here again, as in the case of cosmic beginnings, no firm answer is forthcoming. The three Friedmann models discussed in Chapter IV all differ from one another in this respect. In the case of the oscillating model, the universe expands to a maximum size and then contracts to a catastrophic end after a finite time has elapsed; everything within it would be completely annihilated. In the other two models, the universe goes on expanding to infinity, with stars and galaxies slowly dissolving into a uniform sea of heat energy. They differ only in that an open universe goes on expanding forever, while expansion in a flat universe slowly decreases as it approaches a limit. In all three models, the expansion slows down due to the retarding effect of gravity. Recently, however, the possibility that this is not so has become one of the most hotly debated topics in scientific cosmology.[28]

Two surveys made of supernovae in distant galaxies close to the edge of the observable universe provisionally show that the expansion is speeding up, rather than slowing down as predicted by the Friedmann models. As we saw earlier, a zero cosmological constant was assumed in the Standard Model. This left gravity as the sole force operating in the universe at large, acting to retard the expansion. If the expansion is accelerating, energy must be available to overcome the retarding effect of gravity. But where is the energy to propel the acceleration coming from? The suspicion is that it is related to the cosmological constant, which would represent the action of a new force (dark energy) in the universe.

Einstein introduced the cosmological constant (lambda) into his field equations in order to keep the universe static. The constant was interpreted as a repulsive force that exactly balances gravity to keep the universe from collapsing. He repudiated this once he saw that lambda was no longer necessary in the Friedmann models. It was later reinterpreted as the measure of the stored-up energy of space, but a positive cosmological constant would have an enormous value inconsistent with current observations. With the discovery of an accelerating expansion, a more reasonable value for the cosmological constant is possible. The constant is now thought to represent the energy content of space, making the universe accelerate ever more rapidly. If the present observations are being correctly interpreted, our universe faces a future in which all cosmic distances will grow at a rapidly increasing rate.

There is an interesting implication of this interpretation of lambda as dark energy. For, as we already know, energy has mass, and this could make up for the extremely low density of matter observed in the universe. Cosmologists have long been searching for the "missing mass" that would bring the total mass-density of the universe closer to the critical density; the density parameter (Ω) would then be nearer to one. Attempts to find enough missing matter have consistently failed, but it now appears that even without it, a positive cosmological constant would account for an Ω equal to one. In this case, Ω could be divided into two parts, one corresponding to the actual mass-density of matter and the other to the dark energy responsible for accelerating expansion.

The observations seem to indicate that the total Ω is close to one. This, incidentally, is the value predicted by the Inflationary Universe model. In the early stages of expansion, when the mass-density was very high, the energy density of space would have been very low (lambda close to zero). But, as the expansion continues, the mass-density decreases and the energy density of space increases to keep their sum equal to one. During a certain transitional period, both would become equal in value, and this is the period in which we now live. Eventually, however, the acceleration will rapidly drive the mass-density toward zero and dark energy will become the dominant force in the universe. No one knows what the universe would be like for people who might still exist at that time.

In one scenario, our galaxy would be left isolated in a space that was swept clear of most of the others. By that time, whatever influence distant matter exerts on the laws of physics might already have dissipated. If there is any truth to Mach's Principle, even inertia might gradually weaken. The universe would not look the same to observers who may still be living in our galaxy. It is premature to speculate about this on the basis of physics alone, since a great deal of scientific work must be done before the recent observations can be confirmed. But they suggest a future universe radically different from the one we now observe. A vast space beyond the Milky Way that is unpopulated with material bodies of any kind seems unlikely (compare the "Great Debate" among astronomers before Hubble). Yet there is no indication that ordinary physical matter would have much significance in the later stages of a runaway universe. Even our own galaxy would eventually dissolve in the general heat death of the stars it contains.

It may be that a new kind of universe made up of a more subtle physical matter, such as that mentioned at the end of Chapter II, will begin to take shape and replace matter as we now know it. If this were the case, our present universe of gross material substance would be in the process of being cast off like a broken shell. In other words, the World Egg spoken of in myth may be just starting to hatch. Physics cannot tell us anything about this, and speculations regarding it belong to mythical cosmology more than to modern science. Rather than trying to pursue the possible implications of the strange fate of the universe now being revealed by physics and astronomy, it will be more fruitful to inquire first into the remaining faces of the universe in the following chapters on traditional and evolutionary cosmology.

THE MAGICAL UNIVERSE

Regarding herself
In the dark mirror of space
She beholds the stars.

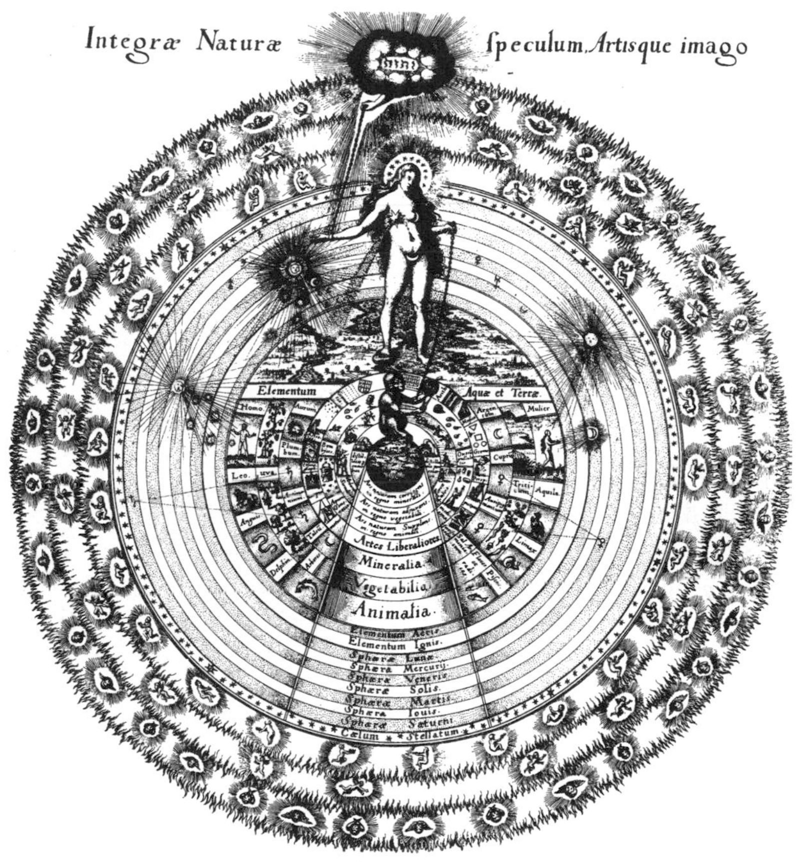

Plate VI. The Magical Universe

VI

TRADITIONAL COSMOLOGY

Modern science, when pressed far enough, is confronted by several impassable boundaries. Physics extends our knowledge up to these boundaries, but in doing so leaves us with an impoverished universe lacking a clear meaning or purpose. Although science today has rid itself of the absolute emptiness of Newtonian space, all that is offered as a substitute are impersonal fields of force and a vacuum filled with aimless energies. It spatializes time to the extent that its dynamic essence is all but lost, and a serious consideration of cosmic purpose is effectively abolished from scientific discourse. Life is reduced to a biological anomaly in a limitless expanse of space and time. The presence of fine-tuning does not account for the existence of life in a world that seems so hostile to it. Merely possessing life permitting properties doesn't guarantee that the universe will contain living beings. The actual appearance of life in it depends on many other factors: proximity to the right kind of star, the requisite chemical elements, appropriate climates, adequate warmth and moisture, and a host of other apparently coincidental conditions. Even so, we still might ask why life should exist in our universe at all.

Another face of the universe shows things in a different light. This is the magical face dealt with in traditional cosmology. In its cosmology, the universe is full of a life not restricted to biological organisms on the earth or other planets. It embraces many orders of living entities in the psychic world, including a "World Soul." The appearance of living organisms on earth is viewed as a special manifestation of a life-principle active everywhere in the universe. Traditional cosmology has a long history, antedating the rise of modern science by many centuries. It has been an integral part of many cultures, and has taken innumerable forms from sophisticated metaphysical theories to popular superstitions. Although theological prejudice and modern science have taken turns in driving it toward the fringes of conventional society, they have never succeeded in eradicating it entirely. Up to the seventeenth century, before its wholesale replacement by mechanistic modes of thought, traditional cosmology was valued as a viable form of knowledge.[1] Today, it still has much to offer a spiritually impoverished society like ours.

Macrocosm and Microcosm

Traditional cosmology views the universe as a manifestation of transcendent Being. If we use the term "science" broadly enough to include metaphysical knowledge (as is common among traditionalists), then traditional cosmology can be defined as "the science of the world inasmuch as this reflects its unique cause, Being."[2] It seeks beauty as well as knowledge, so art and imagination play important roles in it. The basic idea underlying the magical universe is the correspondence of the macrocosm and the microcosm, which we encountered, for instance, in the section on mythical cosmology. But in the present context, it is the defining doctrine of an entire cosmology, for it underlies the unique model of the universe in this tradition (designated here as the "Three Worlds" model). This kind of cosmology is concerned with clues that aid us in discovering the order and beauty of the cosmos. It presupposes the correspondence between the universe as a whole and one of its parts (preeminently man) as an epitome of it. The image is not taken as a mere "poetic fancy," nor can it be understood in terms of materialistic analogies based on supposed similarities between the human body and the physical world.[3] Although such reasoning has been employed to illustrate it in various ways, the point is that the universe is taken to be a living, intelligent being, whose nature is reflected in man. Elements of both the psychic and the physical faces are included in its compass. Not only are the universe and man mirrors of one another, but they are also mystically present within each other. They cannot be separated in reality, and whatever appears in one must somehow be represented in the other. Cosmic unity is thus established; the whole universe is ordered in terms of this correspondence.

The bond between man and the universe is explained in terms of a Universal Intellect (*Nous*), which holds them both in an indissoluble unity.[4] When man is taken as the microcosm, it suggests that he can gain cosmic knowledge and consequent power by employing his imagination in innovative ways. Such knowledge is based on the kinship between man and the universe. Even though all things mirror the world in their own ways, man is thought of as the most perfect exemplar of it. He can be regarded as the total image of the cosmos in all its aspects, ensuring access to the Universal Intellect as well. This offers the possibility for a systematic understanding of the universe and, even more, of mastering things through union with the Intellect. Experiencing such a unity would be another instance of cosmic consciousness, and in many traditional writings it is celebrated in comparable terms. A door was also opened for magic, astrology, alchemy, and other occult pursuits, which claimed to be based on similar principles. The vision embodied in this view of the universe is summed up in a short alchemical treatise known as the *Emerald Tablet* of Hermes:

> Tis true, without falsehood, and most real: that which is above [the macrocosm] is like that which is below [the microcosm], to perpetrate the miracles of One thing. And as all things have been derived from one, by the thought of one [Intellect], so all things are born from this thing [the One], by adoption.[5]

Related Doctrines

Traditional thought has taken different forms at various times and places, but they all possess certain common features. These features include a doctrine of emanation as opposed to creation *ex nihilo* and belief in the existence of a Universal Intellect containing the ideal forms of all things (Ideas or Archetypes). A conception of the hierarchical structure of the world with living beings existing on all levels (the "Great Chain of Being") is also an important part of this type of cosmology. The universe is geocentric in this tradition. In addition, it is divided into three interpenetrating worlds: the Intelligible, the Celestial, and the Elemental. Its operations are governed by an immanent World Soul. Traditional cosmology also places emphasis on the primacy of qualitative correspondences between different things, rather than the quantitative character of the universe favored by modern science. This issue rests on the distinction between the measurable properties of things, which are conditioned by external circumstances, and their essential qualities, derived from the Intellect. Finally, it appeals to intellectual intuition as the primary source of knowledge. This is based on the belief that the human mind participates in the ideal forms of the Universal Intellect, through which it can acquire direct knowledge of the nature of things.

Emanationism

Underlying the worldview of traditional cosmology is the idea that the universe is an emanation of a unitary divine principle. Although this idea has been blended with the revealed creationist doctrines of the major monotheistic religions, orthodox theologians have generally regarded it with suspicion. They have relegated it to the shadowy spheres of mysticism, pantheism, and the occult, which have always been at odds with orthodoxy. The traditional view is summed up in the *doctrine of emanation* as formulated by Plotinus. Emanation is a metaphor appearing in traditional cosmology as an alternative to the idea of creation *ex nihilo*. The doctrine asserts that all being streams forth necessarily (overflowing like water from an inexhaustible fountain) from a perfect and transcendent principle called "the One," on which everything else depends. Three metaphysical principles (*hypostases*) are postulated, the One, Intellect (*Nous*), and Soul in descending order, from which Nature and the universe are derived.

The One is the ultimate source of the other principles and is said to be beyond Being. Therefore it cannot be spoken of in the terminology of logical discourse. Theists sometimes refer to the One as God. This is not quite correct, however, since God is usually given the attributes of a personal being. In Plotinus's system, Intellect may be referred to as God. Even though derived from the One, it is the highest manifested principle. The process of emanation can be compared to light radiating from its source in the sun, but it is not to be understood in terms of mere physical causation. Beginning with Intellect, a lower principle follows from a higher one by means of contemplation (*theoria*), or self-reflection, which Plotinus conceived as a productive power. When objects are farther from the sun, the light is dimmer and, similarly, things possess less perfection when more distant from the One. Matter, which is identified with nonbeing, is at the opposite pole from the One. Soul is an intermediate principle existing between Intellect and Nature (a special adjunct of Soul). Since the universe contains matter, it is not identical with the Soul. Still, the latter is assumed to be present in some way throughout the entire manifestation.

The Great Chain of Being

Emanationism is the metaphysical source of the idea of the Great Chain of Being.[6] This is a popular metaphor for the traditional belief that all beings in the universe are arranged in an unbroken hierarchy. Every kind of creature occupies an allotted place in the hierarchy, being inferior to what is above it and superior to what is below. Consequently, everything that exists has a recognizable position in this order. The lower part of the chain is made up of stones, plants, and animals, and the upper part consists of God and the angelic orders. Both parts meet in man, the microcosm, who is the nexus between them. He is the crucial link in the chain, surpassing the lower levels by his intelligence and even superior to the angels in not being confined to the upper part of the chain. Whereas angels lack physical bodies and can operate on the lower levels only by influencing them, man can roam about freely in the world while participating in the upper levels through his intellect. As the microcosm, he includes within himself all the levels of the macrocosm. God and Prime Matter (the formless root of all material things) mark the two extremities of the chain.

Hosts of normally invisible beings are believed to exist on every level. They are known by a variety of names in different traditions and have given rise to an extensive mythology of gods, goddesses, angels, archangels, demons, elementals, and so forth. But despite the richness of the universe depicted in this image, hierarchical patterns suffer from several drawbacks. For one, they restrict the different orders of creatures to assigned categories, and hence stratify the various levels of being. There is little mobility between the levels, making the system essentially static. An additional shortcoming is that the linear mode of representation leaves the increasingly material levels of being dangling from God, who exists at the top of the hierarchy. Matter is clearly assigned an inferior status in the order of being. Consequently, there is a built-in bias against it that is revealed by a general disdain for earthly life.

The World Soul

Another doctrine essential for an understanding of traditional cosmology is that of the World Soul. Philosophically, it designates the immanent cause of order, life, and intelligence pervading the universe. Plato, in his dialogue the *Timaeus,* was the first to call it soul. He conceived the World Soul as a mediating principle between eternal being and temporal becoming, thinking of it as embodied in the circling movements of the stars and planets. All individual souls were believed to be derived from it. It became widely known in the Middle Ages by its Latin equivalent, *Anima Mundi.* Later, it was connected with the so-called "astral light," a subtle etheric substance that receives impressions of thought-forms and physical events. The World Soul is a feminine principle associated with Nature and nourishes the world with a vitalizing force. In her cosmic function, she governs the universe, maintaining the order of the celestial spheres and radiating planetary influences to the elemental world.

Hence, Soul ensures the interconnectedness of all things, uniting them in a network of sympathetic forces and correspondences.

Nature

The association of the World Soul with Nature is salutary. The word "nature" is derived from the Latin *natura,* which is a translation of the Greek *physis* (suggesting birth, growth, and procreation). Nature originally meant the power that brings forth and regulates the universe and all things within it. Hence it was often personified as the Great Mother, or the Goddess. The course of nature and its laws are manifestations of her force. She has many names and aspects, one of them being "Mother Nature," who is usually identified with the Earth. In her supreme cosmic aspect, she is the Mother of the Universe, though the full meaning of her relationship with God is not clear. It could be said that Nature without God cannot exist, and without Nature, God cannot manifest. This suggests that both are inseparable aspects of a single more comprehensive reality (see Chapter III). In traditional cosmology, however, Nature is usually conceived as a power subordinate to God and bound by his will.[7] Although traditional cultures have always viewed Nature as feminine, the modern scientific mentality has depersonalized her. Today, the word commonly refers to the part of the visible world that has not yet been interfered with by man. In spite of our changing conceptions of Nature, she remains what she has always been and offers much to those who are in harmony with her ways.[8]

PLATO'S *TIMAEUS*

One of the most important sources of traditional cosmology is Plato's great cosmological dialogue, the *Timaeus*.[9] What it pictures is not the magical cosmos of later Medieval and Renaissance thought, but it exerted a strong influence on the development of traditional views about the universe. It is embedded in a creation myth, apparently of Plato's own devising, which incorporates the essential principles of the Pythagorean mathematical philosophy pre-dating Plato. The exposition in the dialogue is presented by a Pythagorean astronomer named Timaeus, who invokes the gods before taking up what he considers to be a sacred subject. In the ensuing discourse, he describes the nature of the universe from its initial organization down to the creation of man, who is treated as the microcosm. Although this is not the first time that the idea of the microcosm appears in ancient Greek thought, Plato gives it a clearly defined place in his theory of the universe. The world is conceived as a living creature possessing reason and intelligence. Man and the universe are not identical in either structure or function, but there is a similarity between them underlying Plato's whole cosmological outlook.

Plato rejects earlier Greek speculations about the origin of the universe. He is not impressed by mythical images of biological reproduction or by philosophical theories that account for the generation of the world in terms of a evolution out of some pre-existent material stuff. Instead, a Divine Craftsman (Demiurge) is presented who designs a rational cosmos on the basis of a perfect world of immaterial Forms.[10] His function is similar to the creator god "born from the world egg" in mythical cosmology, and Plato may have been drawing from earlier traditions preserved in the Greek Mysteries.[11] The Forms are eternal and unchanging realities that are sharply distinguished from what is always in a state of flux. In an earlier dialogue, the *Republic,* Plato had compared the transitory visible world to a dark cave beyond which lay the bright world of Forms. The universe of the *Timaeus* is thought of as imperfect in relation to the Forms, but the goodness of the Demiurge ensures that it is the best possible copy of the perfect world. Immaterial Forms can be grasped only by rational thought, and in the later development of Platonism they were construed as eternal Ideas in the Divine Mind.

There is a clear contrast in the *Timaeus* between activity governed by intelligent purpose and the erratic movements of a material substratum. Pre-existing materials that were not created by the Demiurge represent blind necessity. He uses rational means to shape them into a cosmos of orderly motions governed by an indwelling World Soul. Throughout his work, the Demiurge is guided by aesthetic considerations concerning what objects would best reflect the perfection of the world of Forms. The body and the soul of the world are made by the Demiurge, who copies the all-inclusive Form of the ideal living creature. This Form is not in itself any specific kind of creature, but embraces the types of all living things.[12] In essence, the universe is patterned on the principles of life and intelligence, since this is deemed better than making it a dull, lifeless world. Plato through Timaeus cautions, however, that cosmology can only present a "likely story" of the process of world-creation.

The World Soul is constructed according to complex geometric and musical ratios that are meant to ensure its harmonious nature. Since it had to be capable of rational thought, the basic elements of logical discourse (sameness, difference, and existence) were blended in it to form its mind. For astronomical purposes, the principles of sameness and difference were shaped into intersecting circles that represent the two primary motions of the cosmos, because uniform circular motion was considered to be better than all other kinds of motion (Figure 4). The circle of the same became the celestial equator around whose axis the entire cosmos turns. Only the earth resisted this rotation, remaining stationary at the center of the world. On the other hand, the circle of the different represented the ecliptic, along which the sun, moon, and other planets move in the opposite direction. It was divided into seven smaller circles to account for their orbits. The two major circles intersect at an angle of 23.5 degrees, forming a *cosmic cross* that the sun passes over twice in its annual orbit—ascending above the celestial equator at the vernal equinox and descending below it at the autumnal equinox.[13]

Plato was also aware of the intricate patterns of the planetary orbits, such as direct and retrograde motions, but preferred to leave the details to astronomers. Elsewhere, he is reported to have

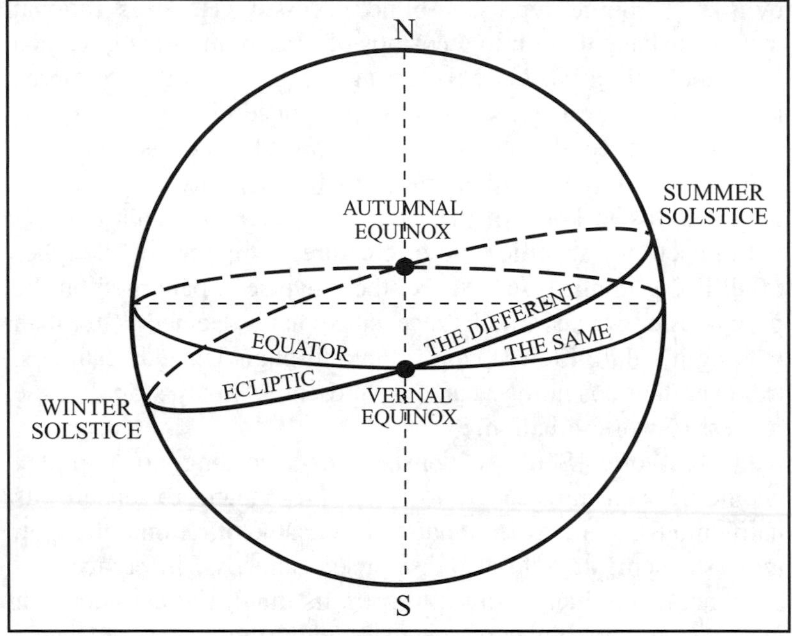

Figure 4. Plato's Circles

spoken of "saving the appearances," which meant that astronomers should try to account for the apparently irregular motions of the planets in terms of combinations of uniformly turning circles. Circular motion was considered to be the most rational and perfect (hence "divine") form of movement.

Because the sphere was deemed to be the most perfect and beautiful geometrical solid, the body of the world was given this shape and then joined to the World Soul. There was nothing material left outside the cosmos to threaten it, nor was anything else required for its sustenance. So there was no need for sense organs or means of taking in nourishment. In this way, it was unlike the body of any living creature within it. The cosmos was unique and self-sufficient, depending on nothing else to continue existing. Subsequently, the planets were set into appropriate circles to be the instruments of time. Their movements measured out and defined time, which is referred to as "the moving image of Eternity." Plato presumably meant by this that the everlasting circling of the cosmos was a fitting copy of the timeless eternity of the world of Forms. Time is not independent of the created world, since it comes into being only with the construction of the cosmos. But it brings into the world a measurable likeness of the order and constancy of the Forms. Timaeus sums up this part of his discourse by calling the universe "a shrine brought into being for the everlasting gods."[14]

The nature of the primitive chaos out of which a cosmos was formed is also addressed in the dialogue. Reasons are given for the choice of four elements (fire, air, water, and earth) to make up the world's body. Their volumes are arranged spherically in geometrical proportion, with fire on the outside and earth at the center. The universe is said to be held together in a unity bound by friendship (*philia*) of the elements:

> For these reasons and from such constituents, four in number, the body of the universe was brought into being, coming into concord by means of proportion, and from these it acquired Amity [*philia*], so that coming into unity with itself it became indissoluble by any other save him who bound it together.[15]

Since the universe is constructed geometrically, it presupposes the existence of space. Space (*chora*) is called the "receptacle of becoming" and is imagined as something vaguely material and ill-defined. The world needs the presence of a medium in which the elements can take shape. Plato compared this medium to a mirror in which the Forms are reflected. It is also the matrix of the universe, and is described metaphorically as the "nurse of becoming." This suggests that Plato thought of it as feminine. He presents space (mother) as a third principle, along with the visible cosmos (son) and its eternal prototype in the world of Forms (father). In this way, he employed the common mythological technique of representing cosmic principles in terms of family relationships.

Originally, the receptacle is agitated by restless vibrations occurring within it. Plato likens it to a plastic material lacking any structure of its own, which can be given any shape the Demiurge chooses to impose on it. The receptacle and its chaotic contents are imagined as existing prior to the formation of an ordered cosmos. It is shaking all over, like "a winnowing basket," causing a separation of dense and heavy things from those that are rare and light. Primary bodies are given the form of the regular geometrical solids, bringing order and structure into the confusion of the original chaos. Their surfaces are constructed by the Demiurge out of special triangles that form a kind of mathematical atomism. Fire is composed of tiny tetrahedrons, air of octahedrons, water of icosahedrons, and earth of cubes. The dodecahedron, composed of twelve regular pentagons, is reserved as a representation of "the whole heaven," presumably because it most closely approximates the sphere enclosing the entire universe. Rational order is thus established among the primary constituents of the material world. Transformations of matter are accounted for by interchanges of the elementary triangles that compose the faces of the composite solids.[16]

Four classes of living creatures are created in a hierarchical order that is correlated with the four elements, beginning with the gods (fire) and descending through birds (air), animals (earth), and fish (water). The rational soul of man is created by the Demiurge out of the same essence as the World Soul, but the creation of his irrational parts is left to the lesser gods. Each human soul is assigned to a star, to which it can return after death. Souls not yet morally perfected must be reborn on earth in different bodies through a cyclic process of transmigration that continues until they reach perfection. To accomplish this, the mind must become attuned to the orderly revolutions of the cosmos. A systematic study of these revolutions is the means of bringing about harmony between man (the microcosm), whose mind is deranged by the pangs of birth, and the macrocosm. The dialogue ends with Timaeus observing that:

> Here at last let us say that our discourse concerning the universe has come to its end. For having received in full its complement of living creatures, mortal and immortal, this world has thus become a visible living creature embracing all that are visible and an image of the intelligible, *a perceptible god,* supreme in greatness and

> excellence, in beauty and perfection, this Heaven single in its kind and one [italics added].[17]

Plato imagined this picture of a rationally ordered universe to support his ethical view that a moral life governed by reason was the best one for human beings. It influenced succeeding cosmologies in different ways. Greek astronomers from Eudoxus to Ptolemy focused on the geometrical circles and devised increasingly complex mathematical models of the planetary motions. Their work culminated in Ptolemy's intricate theory of epicycles, eccentrics, and equants, which dominated astronomy for over a thousand years up to the time of Copernicus. In another direction, Plato's philosophical successor, Aristotle, turned the purely geometrical circles of the *Timaeus* into solid material spheres rotating around a central earth. His geocentric world system became the prevailing physical model of the universe in medieval European cosmology, and also left a deep impression on Islamic culture.

Christian theologians saw the myth of the Demiurge as a philosophical parallel to the creation story in the Book of Genesis. Neoplatonic philosophers, beginning with Plotinus, included the Platonic Forms in an elaborate system of hypostases emanating from the One. But most of these thinkers were more interested in attaining mystical union with the One than in studying the universe. The cosmological picture of the *Timaeus* was eventually incorporated into an astral religion that came to dominate the thought of the later Hellenistic world. It was brought to a focus in Egypt, where it became associated with traditional beliefs surrounding the worship of Thoth, the god of learning and magic. The Greeks identified him with their god Hermes, so the cosmology that developed in this tradition is called Hermetic. Although continuing throughout the Middle Ages as an esoteric alternative to orthodox theology, it surfaced briefly in the Renaissance as the foundation of belief in a magical universe. Historians refer to it as the "Hermetic Tradition," or Hermeticism.

THE HERMETIC TRADITION

In this section we concentrate on the Hermetic Tradition as an influential version of traditional cosmology. This tradition derives from the *Corpus Hermeticum,* a group of writings associated with Hermes Trismegistus ("Thrice Greatest"), who was a legendary figure linked with the Egyptian god Thoth. These books were written in Greek and are now thought to have appeared in Egypt around the second century C.E., but they may have roots in remote antiquity.[18] For the Alexandrian Hermeticists, Trismegistus was a semi-divine figure who functioned as the mediator between gods and men. The original texts were mystical and cosmological in character, and were soon associated with other writings on alchemy, astrology, number mysticism, and geomancy. Later they were widely influential in the Renaissance, after Marsilio Ficino translated them into Latin, because early Christian writers had placed Hermes in the same period as Moses. As will be seen, they embody a distinctive picture of the universe that for a short time rivaled the mechanistic predilections of early modern scientists. The Hermetic Tradition, mixed with some Kabbalistic ideas, offered an alternative approach to the universe that played a significant role in the early stages of the Scientific Revolution (1500-1700 C.E.). Yet the worldview it expresses is very different from that of scientific cosmology as understood today. Because of its distinctive cosmological orientation, this tradition was associated with all three monotheistic religions, regardless of their specific dogmas. It helped to mitigate the sharp differentiation between God and the universe that was presupposed in these religions.

The more philosophical Hermetic texts, with their lofty mystical aspirations, are usually distinguished from the occult works that are also parts of the Hermetica. There is, however, a broad unity between them. Magical practices, for example, took place within a cosmological framework that is found in both types of literature. The relationship between the macrocosm and the microcosm, already employed by Plato in the *Timaeus,* became a central idea in this body of literature. Human nature mirrored cosmic existence, uniting within itself the three worlds of traditional cosmology. Inner experience was considered to be a direct route to cosmic understanding. The human intellect, which participates in the Universal Intellect, connected man with the macrocosm: through the proper use of his intellect, man could know and become all that he wills. This idea took root in the Renaissance and became an important source of inspiration for artists, magicians, and philosophers. It held an irresistible attraction for those who believed in the creative power of the imagination. As noted by Frances Yates, the Hermetic Tradition had a strong influence on Giordano Bruno, whose thought was permeated with Hermetic ideas. Bruno regarded the Hermetica as the basis of an Egyptian religion antedating Christianity. He also believed that it could be made the foundation of a general reform of religion in his time. This would have been seen by the Inquisitors at his trial as a much more serious offense than his espousal of Copernican ideas, for his thought was permeated by Hermetic ideas.[19]

A unique form of the Hermetic Tradition is known as Rosicrucianism. The term "Rosicrucian" surfaced mysteriously in the early seventeenth century, the period when modern mechanistic science was beginning to replace the waning magical tradition. At that time, a few anonymous manifestoes appeared announcing the existence of a secret order of adepts, who declared that their mission was to bring about a general reformation of the world based on Hermetic principles. In a Rosicrucian manifesto of 1614, for example, it is proclaimed that "finally man might thereby understand his own nobleness and worth, and *why he is called Microcosmus,* and how far his knowledge extendeth into Nature [italics added]."[20] Aside from this, no one can be sure about anything connected with the existence of a "Brotherhood of the Rosy Cross." Yates suggests that in the seventeenth century the term "Rosicrucian" signified a certain way of thinking that was shared by many people during this critical era when the foundations of European society were rapidly changing.[21] There was widespread pessimism about the new mechanistic trends in scientific thought and the ability of the Roman Catholic Church, which was riddled with doctrinal disputes, to stabilize European society. Some people hoped that a return to older Hermetic modes of thought could bring about a utopian solution of the world's problems.

Rosicrucianism survives today in the doctrines and rituals of a number of esoteric societies. They usually make wildly extravagant claims about being the only true Rosicrucians, with connections going back to ancient mystical schools. None of this can be verified, and these societies are mere anomalies in the context of modern society. There is a note of spirit-matter dualism in it, which is inconsistent with the Neoplatonic doctrine of the One. Still, the persistence of Rosicrucianism is noteworthy, despite being associated with such vague ideas (or perhaps *because* of them). Its survival may be partly due to the appealing image of the Rose-Cross. One version depicts a wooden cross with a red rose affixed to its center, which suggests the divine soul flowering on the cross of matter. This is an incomplete rendition of the soul's development, however, since a red rose signifies the moral purification of human passions without implying further evolution of the soul toward perfection. We have already noted in the cosmological symbolism of the cross a suggestion of the descent of higher spiritual powers into the material world.[22]

A Pictorial Representation

All the principles of traditional cosmology come to a focus in the picture of a magical universe. Nevertheless, we should be clear about how the term "magic" is to be understood in this context. There are two meanings of the word that must be carefully distinguished. One of them is *natural magic,* which is based upon knowledge of the essential qualities of things. These qualities are construed to be emanations from the Divine Intellect; the universe, as a visible reflection of the Intellect, provides signs enabling its hidden structure to be discerned. Since the form of an object is taken to be a sign of its essential power, this theory is known as the *doctrine of signatures*. The intent of the magician (or *magus*) is to discover these signs in the universe and bring about useful effects through his acquired knowledge. From this point of view, the aim of magic is not very different from the practice of modern science, except that the worldviews and methods of inquiry employed are so dissimilar. Our interest is in the kind of universe implied by natural magic. Another kind of magic is *ceremonial;* its goal is the summoning of angels or demons to do one's bidding. Although an offshoot of the conception of a magical universe, it has no cosmological significance and is generally frowned upon as an egregious aberration within the total cosmic picture.

Attempts to visualize the magical universe are very diverse. The example to be discussed here is culled from a large collection that can be found in seventeenth century esoteric books. It originally appeared in a compendious work by the English physician Robert Fludd.[23] He was a defender of Rosicrucianism, though there is no conclusive evidence that he ever succeeded in contacting any member of this elusive Order. His books are filled with magnificent illustrations of the magical universe, one of which we examine in detail (Plate VI). The cosmological model it represents is strikingly different from those found in modern scientific cosmology. Examples of the latter, as we have seen, relate exclusively to the physical world. They depend heavily on the use of mathematical equations expressing the quantitative features of the universe considered to be important by modern physicists. Models in traditional cosmology, on the other hand, point to psychic worlds whose imagery is reflected in nature. They are full of pictorial symbols rather than mathematical equations and convey a distinctive feeling about the universe that is inseparable from their subject matter. Cosmological pictures included in Fludd's works are beautiful examples of the high quality of the engraver's art found throughout the extensive literature on traditional cosmology. The one chosen here to illustrate the essential cosmic principles in this tradition is titled

"The Mirror of the Whole of Nature and the Image of Art." It is one of the most comprehensive pictorial representations of the magical cosmos.[24]

When we look at this picture, the figure of the nude goddess stands out among its other features. Who is she, and what does she represent? The iconography is traceable back to earlier Hermetic depictions of Isis, the Egyptian Mother Goddess. She represents Nature, or the World Soul, who sees herself reflected in the universe (the "Mirror of Nature"). One foot is placed on land and the other in the sea, while her head resides in the world of stars. Milk flowing from her right breast indicates her status as a cosmic representative of the Great Mother. Her right arm is chained to the cloud-hidden Deity, identified by the Tetragrammaton, showing that her true being lies there. It may correspond to the highest world, Atzilut, in the Kabbalistic scheme of four worlds. In her left hand she holds another chain, reminiscent of the Great Chain of Being, which links her to a man-ape who is measuring the world with dividers. He is the "Image of Art" (or applied magic), the imitator or "ape" of Nature exemplifying the human mind striving to master the world by dividing it into parts and measuring it.[25] Man owes his being to Nature, but doesn't really understand her. A statue of Isis in the ancient Egyptian city of Saïs had an inscription carved on its base: "I am everything that was, that is, that shall be. . . . Nor has any mortal ever been able to discover what lies under my veil."[26] And so she remains to the present day.

The man-ape is sitting on the earth, his cosmic home. His head touches a circle enclosing others that allude to the arts and sciences through which he attempts to improve his life on earth. Below the sphere of the moon, the four elements are indicated along with other symbols. Fire and air have their own circles, but water and earth are depicted as a realistic landscape. Some of the inner circles show representative specimens of the mineral, vegetable, and animal kingdoms. The sublunary region includes everything found in the *Elemental World*. Above it are the spheres of the sun, moon, planets, and fixed stars. They represent the middle division of the cosmos, the *Celestial World,* which contains the invisible astral light. It is pictured by the starry spheres because the astral light is believed to affect the lower world through emanations from the stars and planets. Three zones of spiritual fire, with various angelic figures representing the divine Ideas, exist beyond the stars; this is the *Intelligible World* of the Universal Intellect operating on the cosmos through its spiritual powers. These worlds correspond to the three lower worlds of the Kabbalah. The planetary forces acting on the sublunary region are shown by dotted lines, with the man at the left facing the sun and the woman on the right facing the moon.[27] There are many other details contained in this extraordinary picture, but they are unrelated to our present concerns. We proceed instead to a discussion of the cosmological model embodied in it.

The Three Worlds Model

The magical universe is divided into different regions represented by the "Three Worlds" model. These regions include major levels of the psychic world that are superimposed on a picture of the physical universe as then understood. They can be visualized as concentric spheres with the earth located at their center (Figure 5). Although a geocentric picture, it is not identical with the well-known Ptolemaic astronomical model. The latter is primarily a mathematical description of the planetary orbits as observed from the earth, though Ptolemy also imagined a system of solid shells surrounding each planet. His model was a scientific elaboration of the cosmological theories of earlier Greek philosophers, who had abandoned the ancient conception of a universe consisting of horizontal layers of earth, atmosphere, and sky. On the other hand, the whole cosmos of traditional cosmology includes, but is not exhausted by, its physical contents. In this model, the universe is treated as a totality whose various parts interact with one another as in a living organism.

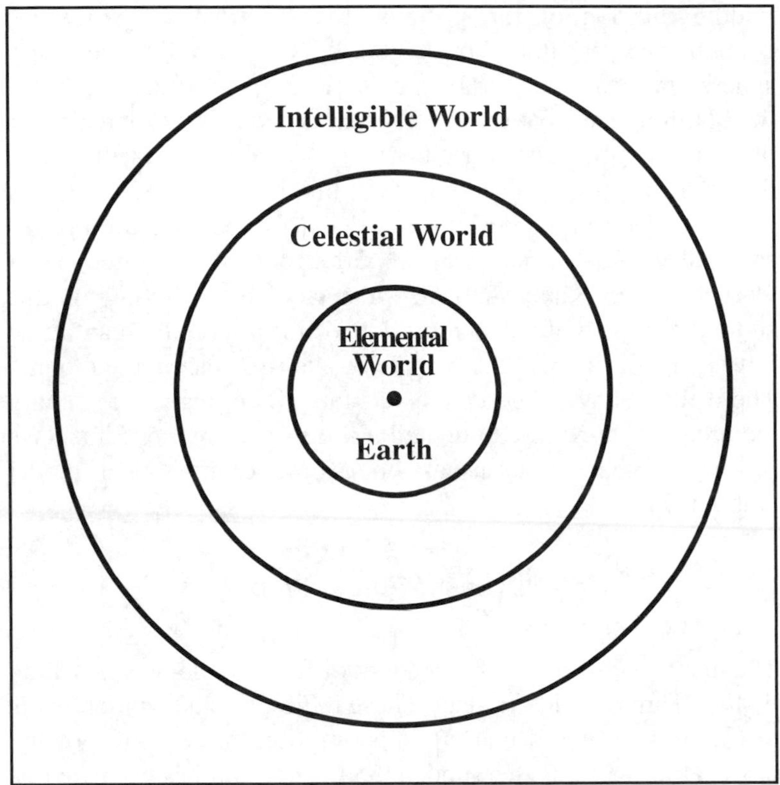

Figure 5. The Three Worlds

On a physical level, the three worlds model appears to be the antithesis of the modern scientific picture of the universe, which arose after Copernicus placed the sun at the center of the world. But the contradiction holds only if we take these views literally rather than symbolically. Copernicus's heliocentric system is not factually true either, because the sun is not really at the center of the universe. The geocentric model corresponds much better to our immediate sensory experience than the more abstract heliocentric system. We still refer to the sun rising and setting daily, and moving annually through the zodiac, rather than to the motions of the earth. This is the way it actually appears to move from an earthly standpoint. The geocentric picture puts the earth in the middle of the universe, the place from which we observe our cosmic surroundings. In this sense, we are at the microcosmic center of the macrocosm. An attempt to imagine the world from the perspective of an observer on the sun requires a feat of abstraction that few people can manage, even when raised in a scientific culture. For most of our daily activities it is not necessary to do so. It can even contribute to a habit of believing things blindly on the basis of authority instead of trusting one's own senses.

A Copernican point of view is necessary to learn modern astronomy, but otherwise it is a matter of selecting the appropriate frame of reference for the task at hand. Therefore, there is some freedom of choice available in describing what we observe. Even the Copernican model is not sufficient, since modern scientific cosmology employs the center of our Galaxy (or the local cluster of galaxies) as a reference frame. No cosmological model is applicable to every situation, since the universe can be described in terms of different spatial and temporal coordinates according to the purpose being served. Progress in scientific cosmology consists in achieving greater range and generality rather than approximating toward some final truth. This is because we exist *within* the universe, and there are no absolute reference points outside it. We are like clever fish trying to describe the limitless ocean that contains them.

The three worlds model can also be approached from a spiritual viewpoint. In this model, the order of the spheres reflects the Neoplatonic levels of emanation, where each sphere proceeds from a higher one containing it. By inwardly reversing the order of emanation, the soul can return to the source from whence it came.[28] This is represented spatially in the three worlds model as the ascent of the soul through the starry heavens to the higher realms above. The planetary spheres symbolize the stages of the mystic's inner journey toward reunion with the One. In addition, the outermost celestial sphere containing the whole universe, whose revolutions are the primary measure of time in this model, represents the boundary between time and eternity. When the soul crosses this boundary, it leaves behind its temporal abode in this world and merges with timeless being. The three worlds model thus offers a visual expression of man's spiritual destiny as conceived in traditional cosmology.[29]

Even the heliocentric system has symbolic significance, since the traditional symbol of the Intellect is the sun. This was known long before Copernicus presented an astronomical model that brought it down to a mundane plane. Judging from certain statements Copernicus made in *On the Revolutions of the Heavenly Spheres* (1543), he was himself influenced by the magical view of the universe. Similarly, the kind of mystical Copernicanism that attracted Kepler, and to a much larger extent Giordano Bruno, was deeply indebted to it. The Copernican system, however, was later used to discredit the three worlds model, along with the spiritual meaning that was attached to it. In the end, a worldview resulted that reduced man to a mere speck in an infinite and featureless space, where his existence was nothing more than an accident without meaning or purpose.[30] What was forgotten altogether is that the universe can be viewed as the content of consciousness and that the soul, which experiences existence from a deeper standpoint, is the spiritual center of things. This is reflected in the three worlds model, where man is placed in the middle of a cosmos that revolves around him.

The heliocentric system can be interpreted as a symbolic representation of the Universal Intellect, in which the physical world is peripheral to that of the spirit. It complements the geocentric view, since man is believed to be able to participate in the Intellect and contemplate the universe from a higher standpoint. Even the denial that there is a unique center of the universe, incorporated into science as the cosmological principle, can be traced back to a Hermetic statement that God (and, by extension, the universe) is "a sphere of which the center is everywhere, and the circumference nowhere."[31] For without a circumference, a unique center cannot be defined. In sum, even though every scientific model of the universe is incomplete, some of them can be given a significant spiritual interpretation.

On a more commonplace level, if the three worlds model is understood as a symbolic structure, there is no basis for a conflict between it and modern scientific cosmology. The geocentric and heliocentric models, for example, are alternative ways of describing our relations with the rest of the universe; as noted above, they are useful for different purposes. They are mutually supportive ways of gaining a fuller understanding of the world and our place in it. One may be earth-centered, another sun-centered, and so forth, but no model is adequate for all purposes. Taken together, they open our eyes to a much wider and richer universe. Nonetheless, the traditional view has certain limitations. As in the case of mythical cosmology, it does not offer an acceptable account of the existence of the physical world. Matter is identified as the negation of being and deemed to be completely passive. In the metaphor of emanation, it is equated with darkness (nonbeing), which is the absence of light (being). Although the One unites all forms of being, its relation to nonbeing is left ambiguous. In addition, the structure of the universe is determined by the Great Chain of Being that, despite a few hints to the contrary, excludes evolution.[32] Before treating evolutionary cosmology, we pause to examine a distinctive kind of traditional cosmology developed in ancient China.

CHINA: AN AESTHETIC COSMOLOGY

An unusual form of traditional cosmology appeared in China at an early period.[33] The philosophical principles of this cosmology can be found in classics like the *I Ching* (Book of Changes) and the *Tao Te Ching* (Book of the Way and its Virtue). Its experiential content is best expressed in the marvelous landscape paintings of the Sung Dynasty (960-1279 C.E.). This was an *aesthetic* cosmology, because it sought to discover something essential about the universe through *feeling* rather than scientific inquiry. The ancient Chinese also developed scientific models of the universe. Unlike their European counterparts, who were still under the influence of Greek cosmology, Chinese cosmologists avoided circles and spheres. They did not think of the stars and planets as being attached to concentric crystalline spheres, as did medieval cosmologists influenced by Aristotle. One important Chinese model pictured the celestial bodies floating about in an infinite expanse of space. Furthermore, they were inclined to observe the sky carefully for signs of change. Their view differed in this respect from that of Europe, where the heavens were believed to be absolutely unchanging; therefore, they did not ignore or misinterpret the signs. In China, the prevalence of change was considered a general characteristic of the entire universe.[34]

In addition to change, which accounted for the variety and multiplicity of nature, the universe was thought of as an organic whole with Heaven above, Earth below, and man as an intermediate being having the characteristics of both within himself. He was thus a microcosm of the grand totality. Perceptions of continual flux and cosmic harmony were basic in the Chinese worldview. Since the powers of Heaven were rain and sun, and those of Earth were associated with the fertility of the soil, it followed that Heaven and Earth interacted to produce living creatures. Mutual interaction was believed to account for all beneficial changes, including those that took place within the human sphere. The goal of life was to establish harmony between the individual, society, and nature. Two opposing principles were thought to be acting in the process of change, one called *yin* and the other *yang*. *Yin* was a receptive power identified as dark, cold, and feminine (Earth), and *yang* a dynamic force associated with light, warmth, and masculinity (Heaven). Harmony lay in the interplay of these principles. When *yin* yields to forceful *yang*, it absorbs and overcomes *yang*. A new situation is produced thereby, just as when rain and sunlight from heaven fall on the fertile earth to foster the growth of crops.

Change was thus conceived in terms of *yin* and *yang;* it was symbolized by simple geometric devices that grew into a complex system of signs in the *I Ching*.[35] *Yang* was represented by a solid line — and *yin* by a broken one – –. They were combined into groups of three to form eight trigrams associated with various images drawn from nature and family relationships. Each trigram was given a name that corresponded to some aspect of the world, such as

and so forth. When one trigram is placed above another, it becomes a hexagram. In this way, the eight trigrams become a total of sixty-four hexagrams. Their meaning was interpreted in a cryptic fashion, which led to the widespread use of the *I Ching* for divination purposes. The hexagrams represent a large number of situations that can arise in the ongoing process of change. For a given situation, a hexagram can be constructed and its interpretation looked up in the *I Ching*. The relevant hexagram is determined at random by the fall of yarrow sticks or the throwing of coins.

Although the pattern embodied in the hexagrams can be either auspicious or foreboding, no hexagram justifies a clearly positive or negative response to the questions asked. Most of the readings suggest caution before proceeding, and the responsibility for deciding what to do rests solely with the person consulting the book. The primary role of change is emphasized throughout, and the right decision depends upon how well the questioner is able to establish an inner resonance with the developing situation. A statement like the following is typical of advice given in the *I Ching:*

> Thus the superior man stands firm
> And does not change his direction.[36]

A popular diagram that represents the trigrams grouped around the symbol of the "Great Ultimate" (*T'ai Chi*) summarizes the whole conception. This symbol depicts the interaction between *yin* and *yang* in the process of change (Plate VII). *Yang* is represented by the white area inside the circle and *yin* by

Plate VII. The Great Ultimate

the dark area. Significantly, there is a small portion of *yin* in the *yang* area, and vice versa. Between the two areas there is a curved line, presumably indicating that a sharp division does not exist between them.

This view of change was developed further by a group of "Naturalists," who introduced the theory of five elements.[37] These elements, or "agencies of change," provided a more detailed explanation of natural phenomena. They were symbolically identified with wood, fire, metal, water, and earth. Their combinations were correlated with the cyclic passage of the seasons. Underlying this conception was the idea that hidden powers were responsible for the various transformations occurring in nature. The five elements were ultimately related to the universal principles of *yin* and *yang*. These, in turn, accounted for the genesis of the universe through a fundamental tension between opposing forces. The problem of how *yin* and *yang* themselves originated was more difficult. Chinese cosmologists did not have a profound creation myth that could throw much light on the problem. Still, some philosophers were not satisfied with the cosmic dualism implied by the twin forces of *yin* and *yang*. They fell back on the conception of one ultimate reality that became differentiated into *yin* and *yang*. This reality was called *Tao,* or the "Way" of Nature.

The characteristic Chinese attitude toward the universe is expressed in the *Tao Te Ching,* the great classic of Taoism ascribed to the ancient sage Lao Tzu. Although the pervasiveness of change is recognized in it, emphasis is placed on the unity and perfection of nature. To follow *Tao,* man must free himself from all aggressive tendencies and artificial social constraints. But even though *Tao* is usually translated as "Way," this translation can be misleading. Certainly, there is a characteristic way that nature behaves, and this is inseparable from nature itself. Yet, at the same time, *Tao* is the original source from which nature is derived. It is not a personal deity, nor is it "supernatural" in the sense of being above or beyond nature. As the ultimate reality underlying the universe, it is said to be indescribable. The *Tao Te Ching* states that:

> The Tao that can be told is not the eternal Tao.
> The name that can be named is not the eternal name.[38]

Tao is thus the indefinable principle that unifies the universe as an organic whole. It underlies the continuity of change, and all transformations in nature depend on it.

Although *Tao* is indefinable, the *Tao Te Ching* offers a number of similes that can help us relate to it. As the essence of nature, it can be regarded as feminine—"the mother of ten thousand things."[39] At the same time, it is identified with emptiness in relation to substantial things, being compared to the space within an empty bowl. It is yielding like water, simple like an uncarved block of wood, and lowly like a valley:

The valley spirit never dies;
It is the woman, primal mother.
Her gateway is the root of heaven and earth.[40]

Tao underlies the cyclic process of change reflected in the annual seasonal round, which always returns to its source:

Returning is the motion of the Tao.
Yielding is the way of the Tao.[41]

While *Tao* never asserts itself, nothing in nature happens without it. Its characteristic activity is called "inaction" (*wu-wei*), for there is no unnatural striving in Tao to become what it is not. Hence it is the principle of harmonious living toward which human beings should aspire. It is the inner "Spirit of Nature," and wise men will choose to live united with it. The whole conception is summed up in the following passage:

The great Tao flows everywhere, both to the left and to the right.
The ten thousand things depend upon it; it holds nothing back.
It fulfills its purpose silently and makes no claim.

It nourishes the ten thousand things,
And yet is not their lord.
It has no aim; it is very small.

The ten thousand things return to it,
Yet it is not their lord.
It is very great.

It does not show greatness,
And is therefore truly great.[42]

Obviously, this type of cosmology has implications going well beyond mere curiosity about how the universe works. Nevertheless, the later development of Taoism became involved with occult sciences like magic, alchemy, and geomancy. Unlike similar activities in Europe, however, the Taoists were primarily concerned with the pursuit of longevity. Consequently, Taoism, like Hermeticism, gave rise to two forms of literature, one relating to philosophical principles and the other to magical practices. The latter are concerned with manipulating the vital force (*ch'i*) believed to be stored in the body. The so-called "hard sciences," such as astronomy and mechanics, were also important in ancient China, but they served social and political purposes that were foreign to the Taoist world view. In pure Taoism, emphasis was placed on aesthetic experience of the unity and wholeness of the cosmos; consequently, it was felt that unity is better expressed by art than by scientific knowledge. Landscape paintings replace scientific models in this tradition, since the object is to cultivate a certain feeling about the universe rather than to explain it.

Chinese cosmology thus became associated with the practice of landscape painting, which reached its peak during the Sung Dynasty. This genre is unique in the art of China, and perhaps in world art as well. Landscape painting is described as *shan-shuei* ("mountain/water"), both usually entering into the pictures. Man and his works are also present, but they play a subordinate role to nature. The landscape artist found his inspiration in contemplating things around him. He saw the various aspects and moods of nature as clues to the essence of *Tao*. A painting of this type was considered to be the most effective way of expressing unity with *Tao;* through this he could enjoy harmony with the cosmos. The painter's object was to portray the reality of *Tao* in a schematic picture, which functioned as a microcosm reflecting the monumental character of the macrocosm. These paintings were meant to capture the spirit of nature rather than the substantiality of material things. Sung painters wished to identify with *Tao,* and their works testify to the depth of the cosmic consciousness that they were able to attain. They were not interested in depicting the surfaces of nature, but aimed instead at being absorbed into it. This attitude is illustrated in the story of a Taoist painter who was preparing to paint a landscape. After contemplating the scene for several years, it took him only a few minutes to actually paint the picture. When he had finished, it is said that he entered into his own painting and never returned, suggesting that the painting had become the abode of the artist's spirit.[43]

An outstanding example of this art is *A Solitary Temple Amid Clearing Peaks* (Plate VIII), which is usually attributed to the Northern Sung master Li Cheng (fl. 940-67 C.E.). The painting depicts clearing skies after a late autumn shower. A temple stands on a hill in the center of the picture, its position indicating that it represents the spiritual union of Heaven and Earth being sought by the pilgrims below. In the background are two towering mountain peaks rising above the secluded valley, which is filled with mist suggesting the mysterious presence of Tao. Trees with only a few remaining leaves are reminders of approaching winter. Several waterfalls replenish the waters of the stream below, just as *Tao* is the inexhaustible source of all movement and change in nature. Tiny figures of peasants and courtiers are seen dining and relaxing in the cool evening under the shadow of the mountains. At the lower left, travelers are moving steadily toward the inn that receives visitors to the temple and promises food and shelter for the night. The whole scene evokes a sense of deep contentment in the harmonious blending of man and nature. Clearly, the spiritual quality of a painting like this captures the inner unity of the universe in a way that expresses an entire worldview. Chinese scientific cosmology failed to keep pace with that of Europe, but it offers a great deal in the aesthetic cosmology so beautifully expressed in landscape paintings like this.

Plate VIII. A Solitary Temple Amid Clearing Peaks

THE EVOLVING FACE

Rising and falling
Like a wave spreading outward
In circles of light.

Plate IX. Sri Aurobindo

VII
EVOLUTIONARY COSMOLOGY

The concept of evolution entered modern cosmology by way of biology rather than physics and astronomy. While it was not a new idea by any means, its influence on modern thought was enhanced by the success of the Darwinian theory of evolution through natural selection. Darwin's theory is limited to the biological development of life on earth and is not a wide-ranging cosmological model. Yet it brought to the forefront the idea that the universe, unlike the fixed typal structure of traditional cosmology, is a dynamically changing entity capable of producing novel forms. Darwinian ideas became associated historically with a broadly materialistic worldview that had already taken hold through the work of the English philosopher Herbert Spencer. They were further reinforced by Victorian beliefs in unlimited progress and the improvement of the human lot through science and technology. Darwin himself was ambivalent about Spencer's philosophy, but accepted the basic picture of scientific materialism without going very deeply into its philosophical foundations.[1] The modern development of these ideas is known as *Darwinism,* which forms the core of evolutionary biology. Today this field is the focus of heated controversy. We look now at the leading tenets of Darwinism before examining the cosmological implications of evolution.

EVOLUTIONARY BIOLOGY

Evolutionary biology is now viewed as a historical science differing in methodology from exact sciences like physics and chemistry. The task of science is generally regarded as a search for laws of nature that can become the basis for making predictions. Evolutionary biology, though, only offers retrospective explanations in place of predictions. Because of the lack of sufficient data, it can sometimes offer nothing at all.

Instead of establishing universal laws by experiments, historical narratives are invented and then compared with the existing evidence. Explanatory concepts are emphasized—such as natural selection, competition, and adaptation—which cannot be reduced to the laws and theories of the physical sciences. There is an inescapable element of contingency in biology, and its concept of natural selection has not offered a complete account of evolution. Strict Darwinists are prone to sweep aside such contingencies as nonessential elements in the evolutionary record.

Biologists who recognize the immense complexity of life have developed a view of evolution known as "contingent history." They are impressed, for example, by the variety of bizarre creatures discovered in the Burgess Shale in Canada, many of which are totally unknown today.[2] These early oceanic creatures existed at the beginning of the Cambrian period, about 550 million years ago. At that time, in an explosion of creativity lasting no more than ten million years, nature produced an astonishing array of multicellular organisms that became the ancestors of virtually all creatures now existing on earth. Many of these organisms were unlike any known today. Only a few kinds still survive, but there is no obvious reason why they lasted while the vast majority disappeared forever. Had conditions been only slightly different, the present life forms on earth might never have developed. Biological evolution is consequently a contingent affair, with the conditions prevailing at any given time having a major influence later on. The path taken is unpredictable because each development is subject to the uncertainties of changing conditions. No particular outcome is inevitable; all one can do in looking back is to construct various historical scenarios that may have led to the actual phenomena.

Population Thinking

Evolutionary biology faces the overwhelming diversity of life on earth, and attempts to find some principle of order within it. Prior to Darwin, the prevailing idea of order was that of the Great Chain of Being as it was understood in traditional cosmology.

This view is called *essentialism,* which stresses the existence of a limited number of unchangeable types exemplified by individual things. General types were believed to form fixed natural classes, or species, whose individual members all possessed the same essence. Variations among individuals within each class were considered nonessential and purely accidental; thus they could not be an effective means for the evolution of new species.

Darwinism counters this typal view of the world with what is called "population thinking." Groups of living organisms are considered as populations consisting of innumerable, uniquely different individuals. Furthermore, the groupings represent statistical averages rather than eternal essences. Emphasis is placed on the variability of individuals in a given species. Whereas essentialists see the type as the fundamental principle and variation as secondary in importance, population thinkers view the type as a mere abstraction and individuals as the only realities. This is a biological version of the philosophical theory of *nominalism.*[3] Population thinking underlies Darwin's discovery of natural selection. The success of the latter as an organizing principle in biology has led Darwinists to believe that the deeper issue of universals versus particulars has finally been resolved. This is questionable, because scientific methodology neither proves nor disproves a philosophical theory. For the latter may include principles that are not presently accessible to empirical modes of investigation. Moreover, whatever evolutionary mechanism is at work may still require the descent of a higher typal principle that can establish itself in nature when the appropriate material basis has been developed. Only then could something really new enter into the physical universe.

Natural Selection

The central problem for Darwin was to account for the appearance of new species of living organisms, now interpreted as populations rather than fixed types. Assuming that new species develop over time, and that all life is linked through common ancestry, he wanted to explain how the process worked. Darwin proposed natural selection as the governing principle of evolutionary change. Just how evolution actually occurs is not clear; it could be only through natural selection or by other means as well. Darwinists are convinced that natural selection is the primary factor at work. Suppose we have an abundant population of living things, with a wide range of variation among individuals. This vast multitude of living organisms represents a random element in nature that cannot be predicted in advance; it is simply accepted as the starting point of the process. Overpopulation is followed by competition for the available means of livelihood, which results in the elimination of those individuals that fail to adapt to the existing environmental conditions. Over long periods of time, it is assumed that this process leads to the appearance of new life forms through the accumulation of advantageous traits.

The gist of this idea is that the elimination of organisms unable to compete for the available resources follows naturally from the original abundance of living creatures. Evolution is thus given a direction; even though the original overpopulation is a random factor, the elimination of those individuals that fail to adapt follows necessarily from the ensuing struggle for existence. Natural selection thus includes elements of both chance and necessity, thereby avoiding the age-old philosophical controversy over which one rules the world. Evolutionary change is the result of both, with randomness preceding necessity in time. Variation is not predetermined, and even the kind of selection involved can change from one generation to the next as environmental circumstances vary. But even though natural selection is a useful hypothesis for explaining adaptive change, it is not a physical force like the ones described by the laws of physics; its significance lies in the elimination of individuals who are unable to adapt to the existing conditions.

Besides placing emphasis on the idea that species undergo change through time, Darwin also pictured evolution as a growing tree. The image suggests that all species of living things on earth are descended from a single root. Darwin's tree pictures evolution with a common trunk from which branches diverge in different directions, each in turn sprouting numerous twigs.[4] This view contrasts with the traditional image of the Great Chain of Being, where living organisms are arranged in a hierarchical order from higher levels to lower ones in the scale of being. Early evolutionists like Lamarck thought that lower species reached toward the next higher level in a constant striving that drove evolution upward. But according to Darwinists, each species has a unique history influenced by many contingent factors that determine whether or not it will survive. Thus, no species can be placed "higher" or "lower" in the scale of nature; each simply adapts to changes in the environment. The issue is far from being closed, for many people still consider evolution to imply progress toward a higher goal. We will pursue this question further in the next section.

Another issue facing Darwinism concerns whether evolution is a gradual process without breaks in continuity, or one that proceeds in short discontinuous leaps. Darwin envisioned evolution as a progression of tiny changes slowly leading to the appearance of new species over immense periods of time. The concept of Darwinian gradualism, though, has been challenged by some biologists. In an attempt to account for peculiarities in the fossil record that seem to contradict gradualism, Stephen Jay Gould and Niles Eldredge proposed a new model of evolutionary change called "punctuated equilibrium." Rather than the gradual change that Darwin imagined, they suggested that species remain stable over long periods of time, but their stability may be "punctuated" by short periods of rapid change, implying discontinuities or "jumps" in the evolutionary sequence. Darwinists disagree on how much emphasis should be placed on this, a few seeing it as a revolutionary new concept and others maintaining that it is easily assimilated into mainstream gradualism. Punctuated equilibrium offers an interesting variant of Darwinism, but remains tied to belief in natural selection as the only acceptable explanation of evolution.

Natural selection fails to give any hint about the origin of life. It presupposes that there already is an abundance of organisms available for the process of elimination to begin its work. This leaves open the question of where life came from in the first place. If we go back far enough in time, it is assumed that there were chemical elements on earth capable of combining into complex organic molecules. Nevertheless, biology cannot explain how these molecules turned into something that is alive.[5] Ever since 1953, when Miller and Urey succeeded in artificially producing amino acids (the building blocks of proteins), laboratory experiments have produced many of the chemical components of living tissue. But these have never been successfully assembled into a living molecule. The constant failure to create life chemically in the laboratory, or to find it happening spontaneously in nature, has led to a search for other approaches to the problem. Some scientists have suggested that it came to earth from somewhere else in the universe; this, however, simply pushes the question back to another time and place.[6] The enigma is deepened if one asks whether something as fundamental as life could ever be explained satisfactorily in terms of chemical reactions alone. Yet Darwinists steadfastly refuse to look beyond matter for an original principle of life. This is a circumstance that itself calls for explanation.

A Materialistic Worldview

Although evolutionary biology seems to be inextricably linked to Darwinism, it is important to distinguish between Darwinism as a science and Darwinism as a worldview. In its fullest sense, evolution is not merely a scientific theory but a whole philosophy. Natural selection is concerned with some facts about natural history but is not a fully articulated philosophy of evolution. From its inception, it was part of a materialistic worldview thought to be implied by science. A worldview, however, involves a complete cosmological perspective that cannot be deduced from science alone.[7] Unfortunately, Darwinists generally ignore this distinction in the heat of public controversy, giving the impression that their materialistic view is derived from science. To some extent, this is the result of the nineteenth century intellectual milieu in which Darwinism arose. At that time, most people believed that the world had been divinely created. They accepted the claims of theologians that God had imposed laws to ensure the perfect adaptation of all living organisms to one another and to their environment. Scientific materialists, of course, objected to this belief.

With the rise of Darwinism, the perennial "warfare of science with theology" became intensified.[8] Its most controversial aspect became the materialist's denial of teleology or purpose in nature. Evolutionary thinkers before Darwin still accepted some version of the Great Chain of Being, viewing evolution as a purposeful march toward greater perfection. This process is known as *orthogenesis,* or goal-directed evolution; it implies that there are progressive evolutionary trends independent of natural selection or other external factors.

Teleological discussions, however, can easily become confused because of an ambiguity in the meaning of the word "purpose." Broadly speaking, there are two ways of understanding the idea of a cosmic purpose. One way sees the universe in terms of the action of a Divine Designer, whereas the other refers to an internal goal-directed process that may or may not be the result of external design. Whichever the case, the latter kind of teleology (but not the former) is incompatible with mechanism, which denies the idea of purpose altogether.[9] The issue becomes further complicated by a disagreement over the amount of spontaneity allowed in a teleological process.

Many Darwinists reject orthogenesis because they interpret teleology as progress toward a *predetermined* goal. This is called "finalism," but teleology need not be finalistic. It is true that both mechanism and finalism are deterministic theories, in so far as they leave no scope for spontaneity or indetermination, but an internal teleological force in the universe need not mean that everything is already determined by a goal. It may simply be an appeal to a principle of order that supersedes the hegemony of a blindly operating mechanism. In short, the Darwinist interpretation of orthogenesis seems to conflate different ways of understanding causation. Avidly opposed to natural theology, which saw evidence of design in the orderly patterns of nature, Darwinists consistently avoid the introduction of teleological views into biology. This extends to cosmology as well, because their worldview has little use for a purposive universe. Buoyed by the successes of natural selection in biology, they claim that science does not substantiate the existence of cosmic purpose in any sense. But purpose has already been eliminated by definition in their materialistic worldview, and worldviews are more resistant to change than scientific theories.

Belief in teleology has been a part of cosmology ever since the ancient Greeks. Aristotle, for example, made final causes the basis of his understanding of the structure of the universe, and Plato assumed that a Divine Craftsman shaped the cosmos. Their thinking dominated explanations in natural philosophy and theology during the Middle Ages. Although Descartes later abolished teleological explanations from his mechanical physics, they continued to play a role in cosmology. At the end of the eighteenth century, Immanuel Kant returned to such principles in his *Critique of Judgment,* after an unsuccessful attempt to account for biological phenomena strictly in terms of Newtonian ideas. Darwin swept aside all such considerations, but the concept of natural selection is only part of the total picture. As the historian John C. Greene has pointed out, the all-embracing philosophical synthesis achieved by Herbert Spencer had a large influence on the early development of Darwinism.[10]

Spencer's worldview was materialistic and saw evolution as a necessary consequence of the laws of matter and motion. His famous (or infamous) definition of evolution as "an integration of matter and concomitant dissipation of motion; during which the matter passes from an indefinite, incoherent homogeneity to a definite, coherent heterogeneity" set the philosophical tone for Darwinian thought.[11] But Spencer was not a biologist, and evolution interested him mainly as a universal principle of explanation. Everything, from the formation of a primordial nebula to the appearance of man, was considered to be the result of transition from a relatively simple state of undifferentiated matter to more and more complex and differentiated forms. He wavered on the possibility of an ultimate goal for evolution, yet his conception of the universe was fundamentally mechanistic. His views were purely speculative and had little influence on biology as a science. Nevertheless, they infused Darwinism with a materialistic mindset that survives to the present day. A forthright interpretation of this kind by T. H. Huxley (Darwin's "bulldog") gave a strong impetus to evolutionary biology. One recent version, championed by Richard Dawkins among others, further reduces evolution to a genetic determinism in which survival and reproduction are favored at the expense of everything else.

To sum up, the ideas proposed by Darwin, bolstered by the materialistic philosophy of Spencer, stood in sharp conflict with the tenets of natural theology. The controversy continues unabated in today's opposition between scientific creationists and evolutionists. Neither side seems to appreciate the deeper philosophical issues involved. One is reminded of Plato's reference to "a Battle of the Gods and Giants" in his dialogue, *The Sophist*.[12] He identified the "gods" with the idealists of his day and the "giants" with the materialists, and suggested that the battle was an interminable one. It is still going on among us, though in different terms. Plato, unlike many debaters today, believed that the issue could be resolved in a reasonable manner. What is at stake is a difference of worldviews—and more than two are available. Conflicts between them are too subtle to be settled by simply advocating or rejecting scientific theories. Attempts to derive a worldview from biology alone, whether of the Darwinian sort or that of so-called "creation science," are seriously misguided. For the evaluation of worldviews is not a strictly scientific affair, nor is it only a matter of appealing to the infallibility of religious scripture. Judgments of this sort require a more flexible approach based on the careful comparison of different ways of understanding the universe. An issue of this magnitude cannot be settled legalistically in courts of law. Such recourse is little more than a battle of wills rather than an appeal to clear thinking.

PHILOSOPHIES OF EVOLUTION

After Darwin, many efforts were made to place evolution in a larger context than that of natural selection with its Spencerian overtones. This led to the revival of *evolutionary cosmology,* which is an attempt to account for the universe as a whole in terms of the idea of evolution. "Evolution" means an unrolling or unfolding in an orderly process of development through successive stages to a more integrated whole. As used in science, it connotes little more than a mechanical change from simple to complex forms. But the term also describes developmental theories of life and consciousness, suggesting an inner potential moving toward some further result or goal. Consequently, it already carries a teleological sense that makes its application to the process of natural selection questionable. There is an ambiguity in the meaning of evolution that contributes to widespread misunderstanding of its import. Besides a purely Darwinian picture of complex speciation rising out of primordial slime, it can also suggest the cumulative descent of divinity in a succession of advancing organic forms. We will address this in greater detail later in this chapter.

Philosophically, evolution implies an energetic universe developing in time. Many cosmologies could account for this, but the scientific situation is more restricted. Biologists are primarily interested in the mechanisms responsible for the appearance of new species of living things on earth. Darwin's idea of natural selection is one kind of mechanism, but it is far from a cosmological theory. Whether or not its limited successes in biology justify the application of a non-teleological philosophy to the entire universe depends upon how committed we are to a materialistic worldview.

Darwinists find materialism a useful hypothesis for pursuing biological research. They are fascinated by the endless proliferation of life-forms that Nature seems to produce so indiscriminately. Darwin himself became lyrical over a "tangled bank" in the woods:

> It is interesting to contemplate a tangled bank, clothed with many plants of many kinds, with birds singing on the bushes, with various insects flitting about, and with worms crawling through the damp earth, and to reflect that these elaborately constructed forms, so different from each other, and dependent upon each other in so complex a manner, have all been produced by laws acting around us.[13]

In a materialistic worldview, "Nature" is merely a metaphor for the natural world around us. But it can also be viewed as an aspect of the Great Mother, who looms so large in mythical cosmology. In the guise of Mother Nature, she is charged specifically with the evolution of life on earth. Her manner, however, has been tentative and experimental; she evidently enjoys the play of possibilities in the proliferation of life, while caring little about the macabre consequences of the struggle for existence. The meandering ways of Nature lead into many blind alleys, which are eliminated when they can no longer adapt successfully. One would not expect to discover unambiguous evidence of an evolutionary purpose by paying exclusive attention to her whimsical play with the transformations of species.

A deeper search is necessary if we wish to find a teleological factor at work in evolution. To begin with, the scope of evolution must be broadened to include more than a biological interest in the mutability of species. Matter, Life, and Mind are the general categories of philosophical discourse about evolution. They designate the basic principles being employed in the philosophies of evolution we are about to examine. Although some philosophers maintain that they are mere abstractions from experience, this ignores their role as effective powers acting in the world. As Sri Aurobindo points out in an early essay, "Not Matter alone, but Life and Mind working upon Matter help to determine evolution."[14] He continues:

> Thus the whole view of Evolution begins to change. Instead of a mechanical, gradual, rigid evolution out of indeterminate Matter by Nature-Force we move towards the perception of a conscious, supple, flexible, intensely surprising and constantly dramatic evolution by a superconscient Knowledge which reveals things in Matter, Life and Mind out of the unfathomable Inconscient from which they rise.[15]

Any one of these categories can be taken as a fundamental principle in the development of evolutionary cosmology. Darwinists prefer to assume that living things evolved out of primordial Matter, but some philosophers seek to avoid the materialistic implications of Darwinism by finding cosmic roles for Life and Mind in the universe.

Speculative cosmological theories about an evolving universe can be divided into two classes. One class consists of materialistic theories that exemplify a mechanistic account of natural processes. They include Spencer's evolutionary ideas as well as others, like those professed by the German biologist Ernst Haeckel, who published an immensely popular book, *Die Welträtsel* (The Riddle of the Universe), in 1899.[16] The other class is made up of various types of nonmechanistic theories that attempt to account for evolution in less materialistic terms. After reviewing several of these theories, we will consider Sri Aurobindo's markedly different view of evolution. Nonmechanistic philosophies of evolution were developed by Henri Bergson, Samuel Alexander, and Pierre Teilhard de Chardin in the first half of the twentieth century. All three accept evolution as a fact, but differ in regard to its interpretation. They represent a new and more comprehensive form of cosmology based on the idea of evolution rather than the laws of physics. Although each enjoyed a brief period of popularity, none gained widespread philosophical approval. In passing, note that a comprehensive evolutionary cosmology allows the laws of physics to change with time, since they would then be subordinate to the principle of evolution. These laws may be viewed as conditions required for maximum variety and complexity to evolve in the universe.[17]

Creative Evolution

The French philosopher Bergson offered a theory of *creative evolution* based on the idea of a cosmic life force, or vital impulse (*élan vital*), which is driving the universe forward in an ever-growing complexity of forms.[18] It reveals itself dynamically in living things, spurring the evolution of instinct and intelligence in them. Contrary to Darwinism, he sees evolution as a creative process continually producing new forms in a spontaneous and unpredictable way. Life improvises as it goes, its action being comparable to a rocket bursting into numerous sparks whose spent cinders fall back as dead matter. In this way, matter is a product of the life force, counteracting its upward thrust with a downward inertial tendency. For Bergson, the universe is a continuous, nonrepetitive movement of life without any static background or ultimate purpose. Life is identified with pure duration and can only be known through intuitive feeling. Intuition is opposed to intellect, which cuts reality into pieces and is unable to grasp the world as a continuous whole. Only intuition, a kind of intellectual sympathy, can enter into the inexpressible heart of things and identify with the pure flow of duration.

Bergson rejects teleology as well as mechanism, because he interprets the former in a finalistic sense: the end *determines* the direction of evolution. Since both teleology and mechanism are deterministic for him, determination by the future (finalism) is just as restrictive as determination by the past (mechanism). If mechanism and teleology are both deterministic, then no scope would remain for freedom and novelty in the world. Bergson dismisses them both in favor of his idea of *creative* evolution. In his view, evolution is a continuous march toward novel creations which are not determined by either the past or the future. But, again, finalism is only one way of interpreting teleology. An end or purpose need not be something imposed on the universe from outside. Even an internal purpose does not imply absolute necessity; on the contrary, it can suggest that some orderly non-mechanical process of development is at work in the world. Change without any ordering principle is nothing more than an indiscriminate display of energy that leads nowhere. Thus, Bergson's attempt to introduce pure freedom and spontaneity into the evolutionary process fails to offer a reasonable alternative to Darwinian mechanistic ideas. But his theory stresses that evolution is a cumulative process inherent in time itself. He sees reality as the steady advance of the *élan vital* involving perpetual novelty rather than mechanical repetition. While his universe lacks a universal purpose to guide it, ample room remains for the attainment of lesser goals in Life's blind, unquenchable thirst for fulfillment.

Emergent Evolutionism

Another attempt to develop a nonmechanistic theory of evolution was the *emergent evolutionism* of the English philosopher Samuel Alexander. He presented his ideas in a massive book entitled *Space, Time and Deity.*[19] Alexander called the ultimate reality "Space-Time," arguing that space and time are interdependent and cannot exist as separate entities. This original cosmic stuff is prior to matter, being identified with pure motion. Matter is composed of motions made up of the point-instants of Space-Time. Matter, Life, and Mind are universal qualities that emerge successively from Space-Time, influenced by a creative urge (*Nisus*) that carries the universe upward through various emergent levels. Evolution is expected to continue beyond Mind to a higher level called "Deity." This is a relative term, however, since it always refers to the next level that is still to emerge. Just what quality Deity will possess is unpredictable before it appears. Each emergent quality in evolution is the result of the complexities attained at the previous level, but cannot be reduced to it. There is therefore a discontinuity among the levels that renders new qualities genuinely novel; this is the meaning of "emergent evolution," which stands in sharp contrast to Darwinian mechanism.

Emergence of a new quality in the universe is not the direct outcome of preceding conditions but an entirely unanticipated event that seems to render evolution inexplicable. For Alexander, the process is said to begin with Space-Time, the basic stuff of reality, though devoid of life and consciousness. How then shall we understand the emergence of higher principles like Life and Mind from it? Alexander's conception of *Nisus* as an evolutionary urge inherent in Space-Time is also suspect. Their relationship is not clear, since an insentient reality like Space-Time could not have creative urges. Alexander thus does not account for the mysterious *Nisus* that is supposedly responsible for evolution. The failure to offer an explanation for the discontinuous jumps between successive levels seems to admit an irrational element into his philosophy of evolution. Nevertheless, he raised an important issue with the conception of an evolutionary progression that does not end with the emergence of Mind in the universe.

Evolutionary Theism

Our last example of a nonmechanistic theory is the type of *evolutionary theism* found in the writings of Teilhard de Chardin.[20] He was not a professional philosopher like Bergson and Alexander, but a paleontologist and Catholic priest. This dual vocation led him to a lifelong endeavor to reconcile the claims of biology and Christianity in an all-embracing evolutionary synthesis. He accepted evolution as a fundamental fact, while differing from Darwinism by claiming that everything in the universe has dual aspects, the inner psychic and the external material. Accordingly, there is an evolution of consciousness going on simultaneously with physical evolution. The entire universe, from elementary particles to man, is governed by a "law of complexification" that carries it in the direction of greater complexity and increasing consciousness.

Like Bergson, he saw a special nonmechanical agency at work in evolution, which he called "radial energy." It is an internal psychic force that intensifies with the development of more complex forms. Radial energy causes things to become more integrated, both "within" and "without," being responsible for the major transitions from matter to life and mind. When a physical system becomes more highly organized, its psychic interior will be more fully developed. Man is the most recent form to appear in the evolutionary progression of nature. His capacity for self-conscious thought and the formation of cultures has added a new layer to the earth's ambience—the "noosphere," or layer of reflective thought. The noosphere is a unique environment that sets man apart from other creatures, characterizing the "phenomenon of man." Through the noosphere, all human societies are projected to unite in a single world culture.

Teilhard believed that evolution converges toward a point called "Omega" where it reaches its final goal. The "Omega Point" is a mystical concept, but it is not wholly unworldly, since the physical and the psychic aspects of the universe are inseparable. Omega is the focal point of their convergence, corresponding to God in so far as it determines the direction of cosmic evolution. The process is orthogenetic, though not in a finalistic sense, because Teilhard makes some allowance for chance events. The culmination will be reached when all individuals unite in a single community through love. He invests his vision with religious significance by identifying it as the "Divine Milieu," during which the spirit of the "Cosmic Christ" becomes fully manifested in the universe. In this way, he hoped to unite his personal religious convictions with science.

Teilhard's interpretation of evolution—a view he hoped to ground in science—fails to connect with mainstream scientific practice, which knows nothing of a psychic interior of physical matter. Ideas like "radial energy" and the "Omega Point" seem to be more fiction than science. They may have been intended to support his belief that the scientific view of evolution was not in conflict with Catholic theology. On the religious side, however, there was some uneasiness about Teilhard's emphasis upon God as the end (Omega) of cosmic history rather than its initiator (Alpha). His ideas also conflicted with theological dogmas regarding the fall of man and original sin. As a consequence, they were not widely accepted in orthodox Catholic circles. Teilhard's vision of an evolving universe remains purely speculative without having much support from either science or theology. But his optimistic faith in the future progress of humanity is praiseworthy and still has many avid adherents.

The work of Jean Gebser, particularly in *The Ever-Present Origin*, goes even farther than Teilhard in stressing the emergence of a new type of consciousness on earth.[21] According to Gebser, humanity advances culturally through successive stages, or "mutations," toward an arational and aperspectival integral consciousness. This is not conceived as a linear progression in which later stages replace earlier ones. Instead, the successive stages are cumulative, representing comprehensive integrations of all that preceded them. The various mutations through which humanity passes are regarded as partial manifestations of a single "ever-present origin."

Gebser was concerned with a detailed examination of the different structures of consciousness rather than with cosmology *per se*. He supported his thesis by a wealth of etymological, literary, and artistic evidence. Although his book displays remarkable originality and penetrative insight, it is only tangential to our present concern with cosmology. To recapitulate: the heart of cosmology is a distinctive mode of awareness identified by Sri Aurobindo as cosmic consciousness, which permeates all four faces of the universe.

SRI AUROBINDO

The evolutionary cosmologies just considered are the speculative philosophical theories of individual thinkers who stretched their mental powers as far as they could. We now examine a different kind of evolutionary vision derived from spiritual resources ordinarily unavailable to philosophers. It originates with Sri Aurobindo, whose multifaceted genius makes it impossible to classify him in conventional scholarly terms. He was not a philosopher, yet in *The Life Divine* he wrote an elaborate philosophical treatise on evolution. Not a scientist, his approach to the yogic life was nonetheless scientific in spirit. He was, though, a poet of extraordinary ability who wrote a magnificent epic poem, *Savitri,* which we present in the next chapter. Cosmology was a fraction of his enormous output, but it provides a broad context for understanding his treatment of evolutionary transformation.

Sri Aurobindo saw evolution as a spiritual process having as its goal the transformation of our present existence into a divine life. In his view, earth is a unique scene for the emergence of divinity from its encasement in matter.[22] It is important to emphasize at the outset that this was not the result of mere speculation. It was rather the outcome of a lifetime devoted to an intensive investigation of the nature of consciousness. Although his vision of an evolving universe holds its own as a purely philosophical theory, to reduce him to a philosopher would miss Sri Aurobindo's status as a great seer and fully accomplished yogi. His spiritual collaborator and compeer, the Mother, was instrumental in giving a practical focus to his vision. Following an earlier meeting in Pondicherry, she joined him there permanently in 1920. Subsequently, she organized the Sri Aurobindo Ashram to accommodate a growing number of aspirants from all over the world. Her collected works are a spiritual treasury and present pragmatic insights into the practice of transformative yoga.[23]

Sri Aurobindo was born in India in 1872, but was sent to England as a child to be educated in English schools. He studied classical literature at Cambridge University, winning prizes in poetry and passing examinations with high honors. While in England, he familiarized himself with the cultural achievements of Western civilization. After leaving Cambridge, he returned to

India and began a serious study of Indian culture. From the moment of his arrival there, a deep peace descended upon him; a great love for India blossomed. Later, Sri Aurobindo became a leader in the nationalist movement for independence from British rule.[24] He took up yoga as a means of gaining inner strength for his political work. Under the direction of a teacher named Lele, he quickly realized Nirvana, the experience of the Silent Brahman of Vedanta. This established him in a transcendent consciousness that never left him thereafter. But it was only a beginning, leading ultimately to the working out of a new yoga of human and world transformation.

During a year of imprisonment by the British for his revolutionary activities, he had a powerful realization of the Cosmic Divine. This convinced him that the achievement of Indian independence was only part of a larger work to be done. Released from prison, he eventually settled in the French colony of Pondicherry on the Bay of Bengal, where he remained for the rest of his life. In Pondicherry, he originated the unique form of yoga that led him to an understanding of spiritual evolution and the writing of his major works.[25]

In 1914, Sri Aurobindo began a monthly journal, *Arya,* in which the substance of his later books first appeared. Some of this work was concerned with the civilization of ancient India. In *Foundations of Indian Culture,* he reviewed the whole range of traditional Indian religion, art, literature, and politics from a spiritual point of view. Besides this, he wrote a brilliant exposition of the *Bhagavad Gītā* (*Essays on the Gita*), as well as translations and commentaries on several Upanishads. He made a careful study of the *Ṛg Veda,* the fountainhead of Indian culture, translating many of its hymns into English and offering an illuminative interpretation of their mystical content.[26] In addition, he achieved a masterful integration of the traditional yogic disciplines of India in *The Synthesis of Yoga.* Yoga was for him the practical basis for integrating spirit and matter on earth, rather than only a means for liberating the soul. Other books, such as *The Human Cycle* and *The Ideal of Human Unity,* were devoted to an examination of the development of human society and its progress toward world unity. In *The Future Poetry,* he considered the role of poetry as an effective instrument for the evolution of the soul. Noteworthy among his shorter works are *The Mother,* describing the four powers and personalities of the Divine Mother, and *The Supramental Manifestation upon Earth* (published in America as *The Mind of Light*), a series of articles exploring the possibility of a perfected humanity evolving prior to the manifestation of a supramental being.

The two books that best express his comprehensive approach to the universe are *The Life Divine* and his epic poem *Savitri*. In *The Life Divine,* he presents a synthesis of the philosophical systems of East and West based upon the idea of spiritual evolution. This he founded on an inspired vision of the divine nature of existence. The culmination of his enormous literary output was *Savitri,* which infused a sustained intensity and profound spirituality into the traditional form of the epic. The poem runs into nearly 24,000 lines of blank verse. After 1926, Sri Aurobindo gave increasing attention to its composition, revising it over and over whenever possible to match his deepening realizations. He also answered innumerable letters daily, for hours at a stretch, regarding all aspects of spiritual life. Our concern in this chapter is with the vision of evolution that he developed in *The Life Divine*.

THE LIFE DIVINE

Sri Aurobindo's magnum opus, *The Life Divine,* is an involved and complex work with a clear methodology. He presents a series of topics in the context of a developing argument, examines several viewpoints relating to each topic, and always concludes with his own position. Since he summarizes each perspective fairly and convincingly, we must distinguish his view from the others. A favorite ploy of philosophers for solving difficult problems is to offer a solution that logically eliminates possible alternatives. But rather than cut the Gordian Knot in this way, Sri

Aurobindo carefully unravels its various strands. He then integrates the partial truths they represent into a more comprehensive synthesis. His purpose was not to add one more theory to those already available but to deepen our understanding of the destiny of the soul (psychic being) and explain how we can continue to evolve. A final statement of his thought comes in the last six chapters, after a long winding development like the course of evolution he describes. In these chapters, Sri Aurobindo emphasizes that a divine life is a life lived in and for the Divine and that spiritual evolution must take place in this world.

The first chapter of *The Life Divine* sounds the keynote for everything that follows. It merits our careful attention because the general principles introduced are developed more fully later in the book. Chapter I, "The Human Aspiration," begins with a reference to the age-old longing of the human spirit for a more perfect life on earth:

> The earliest preoccupation of man in his awakened thoughts and, as it seems, his inevitable and ultimate preoccupation,—for it survives the longest periods of scepticism and returns after every banishment,—is also the highest which his thought can envisage. It manifests itself in the divination of Godhead, the impulse towards perfection, the search after pure Truth and unmixed Bliss, the sense of a secret immortality.[27]

Sri Aurobindo points out that, even though these ideals seem to contradict our normal experience, they can be realized by an evolutionary manifestation of Spirit in Matter. Nature's method is to seek harmony among opposing forces: the greater the apparent discords, the more they act as a spur toward more subtle and powerful harmonies. But if evolution is the means for achieving this, there must be something deeper that lies behind it:

> We speak of the evolution of Life in Matter, the evolution of Mind in Matter; but evolution is a word which merely states the phenomenon without explaining it. For there seems to be no reason why Life should evolve out of material elements or Mind out of living form, unless we accept the Vedantic solution that Life is already involved in Matter and Mind in Life because in essence Matter is a form of veiled Life, Life a form of veiled

> Consciousness. And then there seems to be little objection to a farther step in the series and the admission that mental consciousness may itself be only a form and a veil of higher states which are beyond Mind.[28]

The reference to higher states beyond Mind is significant, since evolution proceeds in this direction. The text continues: "For if evolution is the progressive manifestation by Nature of that which slept or worked in her, involved, it is also the overt realisation of that which she secretly is."[29] To seek the greater manifestation of divinity in this world is what Sri Aurobindo considers to be our highest and most legitimate end. Since "the secret will of the Great Mother" will not allow us as a race to reject the evolutionary struggle, it is better to accept our destiny in the clear light of reason than to be driven by blind instinct. The chapter ends with a reference to a supramental status of being, which is identified as the goal toward which we should aspire:

> For it is likely that such is the next higher state of consciousness of which Mind is only a form and veil, and through the splendours of that light may lie the path of our progressive self-enlargement into whatever highest state is humanity's ultimate resting-place.[30]

The rest of *The Life Divine* works out the details of this vision. Our focus is on three topics comprising the essential features of Sri Aurobindo's vision of evolution. They are creation and evolution, the principles of being, and spiritual evolution.

Creation and Evolution

Sri Aurobindo arrived at the metaphysical principles necessary for understanding evolution by a yoga that took him deep within the so-called "unconscious" of the psychologists, which he found to be actually full of consciousness. His yogic experiences revealed the complex structure of our inner being and reaffirmed the Vedantic conception of the Self recorded in the Upanishads.[31] The ancient seers had extended subjective knowledge of the Self to include the universe in accordance with their intuition of the correspondence between the macrocosm and the microcosm.[32] As we saw in Chapters II and III, this intuition was the original source of creation myths that trace the beginning of the world back to an unmanifested darkness veiling the divine source of things:

Darkness = Unmanifested Reality
Light = Manifested Universe

In Genesis, for example, God said: "Let there be light," but he remained hidden in the darkness above. Similarly, the Stanzas of Dzyan refer to the unmanifested status of absolute Being as the "Night of the Universe." Both of these myths imply an intangible boundary separating the darkness from the light. In reality, there is no darkness above, just as there is no darkness for the sun, which is shining even when hidden from us. This suggests that consciousness always exists everywhere, though we may not be aware of it, because in myth light represents consciousness and darkness unconsciousness.[33] Sri Aurobindo turns the relationship between light and darkness around by putting the light (identified with Consciousness) above the darkness representing Matter:

Light = Consciousness
Darkness = Matter

He also discovered (or had revealed to him) something else about this spiritual light that seems never to have been noticed before. In his view, *light is pressing down into the world in response to an aspiration from the darkness below.* The fullness of Spirit manifests gradually in an evolutionary advance with many turnings, but moves forward and upward beyond the previously attained stages.

Evolution is better represented by a spiral rather than the straightforward linear progression that is generally supposed. For there are exploratory byways that diverge from the main course, and also many returns to take up what was left behind by the upsurge of a new leap forward. Anything ready to be assimilated at a given stage will be lifted up to a higher level. In this kind of evolution, a descent of Spirit into its apparent opposite (Matter) leaves nothing completely untransformed. A gradual unfoldment is necessary, since an immediate descent of the infinite light would shatter the material foundation in which it is to be manifested.[34] With the advent of life, evolution became a ruthless and bloody affair so violent that the mind recoils from it in horror. The Victorian poet Tennyson expressed it as "Nature, red in tooth and claw."[35] He tried to reconcile this grim view of nature with faith in a loving Creator, but failed to penetrate into the deeper roots of the mystery:

> What hope of answer, or redress?
> Behind the veil, behind the veil.[36]

We are faced with a grisly spectacle of the immense struggle and untold suffering that life has undergone in the long course of its evolution on earth. In Sri Aurobindo's view, creation is the free play of divine delight and needs no justification for its action. Still, if evolution is the unfoldment of a Divine Reality, it should not be an arbitrary movement without a goal. Mind and life are limited principles, and neither of them could be the final goal of spiritual evolution. No mental attempt to justify suffering can remove all of the problems it raises, but mind is not the ultimate arbiter of truth in these matters. Only the power of Divine Knowledge, conscious of the total truth, could remove the last vestiges of mystery underlying the world-process.

Nevertheless, we may ask how evolution is related to creation. Sri Aurobindo suggests that "a Consciousness-Force, everywhere inherent in Existence, acting even when concealed, is the creator of the worlds, the occult secret of Nature."[37] Evolution must then be part of a continuous act of creation that is producing higher forms of being. Creation and evolution, far from being antagonistic, are really complementary means for fulfilling the divine purpose. Contrary to the views of contemporary "creationists" and "evolutionists," they are not wholly different processes. Evolution continues the act of creation, for Spirit first becomes absorbed in an abysmal inconscience and then re-emerges to discover itself in sequential fashion. All the powers of the Divine are manifested in this way. Evolution follows from the involution of higher principles into matter, instead of being the blind natural process presupposed by Darwin. The movement is not arbitrary or haphazard, since it develops in an orderly manner by reversing the path of involution. Instead of being restricted to a momentary act at the beginning of the world, creation is a continuous process of divine manifestation in which we are all taking part. Sri Aurobindo sums up the whole conception:

> The manifestation of the Being in our universe takes the shape of an involution which is the starting-point of an evolution,— Matter the nethermost stage, Spirit the summit
> . . . . In the descent into the material plane of which our natural life is a product, the lapse culminates in a total Inconscience out of which an involved Being and Consciousness have to emerge by a gradual evolution.[38]

The manifestation of Spirit is being brought to a focus on earth, which is viewed as a microcosm where the evolutionary impulse is now pressing forward. But to understand this process more fully, the essential principles operating in it must be clearly identified. For this purpose, Being can be imagined as a great sphere containing them.

The Principles of Being

According to Sri Aurobindo, Being is divisible into two hemispheres, the upper hemisphere representing Spirit and the lower, Matter (Figure 6). The terms "Spirit" and "Matter" are employed as general categories to designate the major divisions of Being; they are further differentiated into a number of distinct principles. The hemispheres are separated by a "Golden Lid."[39] The implied spherical image is an analogue of the linear Chain of Being found in traditional cosmology, without the suggestion implicit in the latter that the material world is an inferior form of existence. In Sri Aurobindo's view, even Matter is implicitly divine, being an aspect of Spirit. The Golden Lid consists of spiritual light, which is massed at the interface between the two hemispheres and effectively covers what exists above it. Consequently, there is an intensely bright boundary between the manifested universe and the transcendent realms that have yet to become organized in matter. As evolution ascends from below, the Golden Lid will gradually open to a downward flow of light into the darkness, eventually uniting the two hemispheres in a luminous sea of Consciousness. In our present condition, we cannot penetrate beyond the Lid into the upper regions without losing contact with the lower hemisphere, but evolution is bringing the light down into the material darkness in the course of time.

There is a graded series of principles, four transcendent above the Golden Lid and three cosmic levels below it. The transcendent principles are Existence, Consciousness-Force, Bliss (or Delight), and Supermind. They are essentially one infinite and eternal Consciousness, though distinguishable in the successive stages of involution. Each appears in turn, while the others are concealed behind it. *Existence* is the principle that begins the series of transformations. As Absolute Being with unlimited possibilities of existing, it is comparable to Brahman in Vedantic thought.

Consciouness-Force emerges next as the creative energy (*Śakti*) that brings forth the universe and carries evolution onward through time. This energy functions as the Divine Mother bearing and nurturing all beings. Sri Aurobindo calls the concentrated force by which Consciousness acts upon itself to create the universe *tapas* ("heat"). This corresponds exactly to the cosmic origin depicted by the big bang model, whether it is interpreted as a point-singularity or a compact nugget of vibrating energy as in string theory.

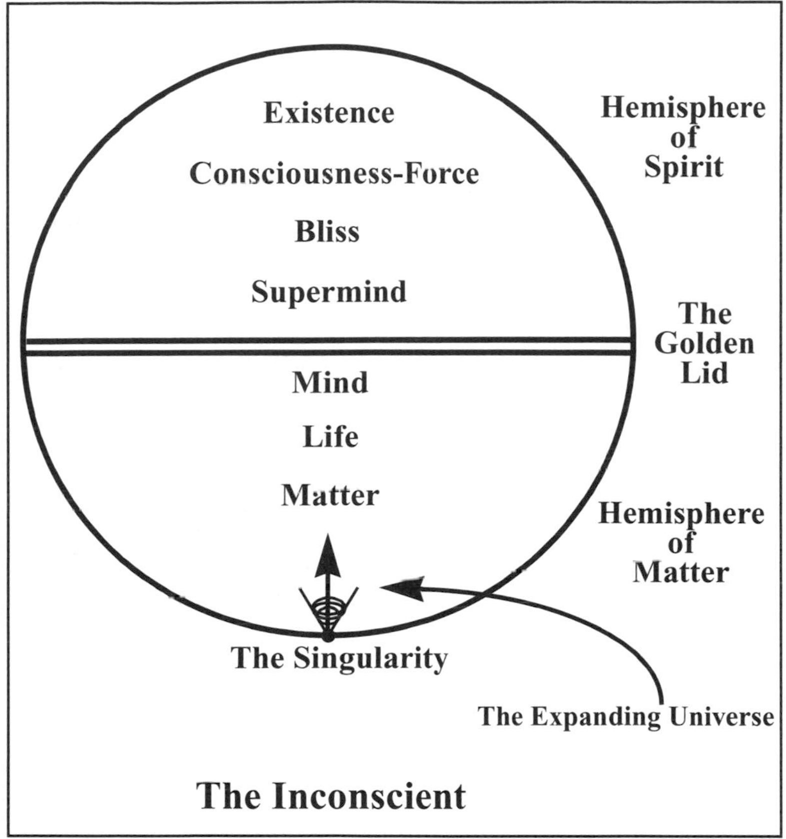

Figure 6. The Principles of Being

Delight is the third transcendent principle, sustaining the divine play of self-manifestation in a vast multitude of worlds. In our universe, the divine Līlā has taken an evolutionary path to cosmic fulfillment. Ordinarily, this principle is identified as the bliss that a liberated soul experiences when released from bondage to the world. Thus, the question why the universe was brought forth in the first place is left unresolved. Sri Aurobindo sees the answer to this question in the context of divine delight manifesting creatively in the world.

The last principle in the upper hemisphere, *Supermind,* is the key to Sri Aurobindo's understanding of the universe. He gave a great deal of attention to it, because its unique status as the link between the upper and lower hemispheres had not been fully recognized before.[40] Supermind is the principal source of selection and organization in the cosmos. For example, the exquisite harmony and variety of the physical universe, from the majestic whirl of the galaxies to the minutest details of subatomic structure, are founded on its action. Without it there could not be an ordered world anywhere.

Sri Aurobindo distinguishes three poises of the Supermind. They are aspects of one transcendent Consciousness that are necessary to facilitate its deployment in space and time. There is a *comprehending consciousness* holding all things together in their potentialities, an *apprehending consciousness* by which consciousness contemplates itself from multiple centers without losing its awareness of their unity, and a *projecting consciousness* through which it becomes involved in each of them to experience the universe from a variety of different standpoints. Realization of their ultimate unity would be the fulfillment, as well as the foundation, of the cosmic process. In essence, the delight of divine play would be the object of it all. Significantly, he likens this to what takes place imaginatively in a poet's mind. The latter contains various mental images of things, sees their mutual relations with one another, and identifies with them in order to create a unified poem.

Supermind presides over the course of evolution and also represents an important stage in its consummation. It supports the appearance of multiplicity in the universe, while holding things together in an interlocking unity. Sri Aurobindo refers to Supermind as the supreme "Truth-Consciousness," or "Real-Idea," because it comprises both Divine Knowledge and Divine Will. This should not be confused with the Intellect, or Universal Mind, which was discussed previously. Intellect belongs to the level of the divisive and constructive Mind, and lies in the region below the Golden Lid. The delegated light of Supermind poised in concentration at the Golden Lid is called Overmind. From there it turned away from its divine source, plunging in a series of descending levels into deepening darkness and ignorance.[41]

The three cosmic levels of Mind, Life, and Matter exist below the Golden Lid. They belong to the lower hemisphere, where Mind and Life have already entered into the evolution of material forms. These levels are related to the higher spiritual principles, since Matter is the inverse of Existence, Life of Conscious-Force, and Mind of Supermind. Mind and Life exist on their own levels prior to becoming organized in physical matter. Although these levels are not in themselves evolutionary, they play an important role in evolution because powers derived from them enter into matter at critical junctures of the process.[42] At the opposite pole from the Divine is the Inconscient, which lies far below even Matter. It represents the total oblivion, or trance, into which Consciousness sinks prior to creation. The Inconscient (as its name implies) conceals Consciousness, just as life lies hidden in the seed of a flower; all that exists on the higher levels is latent within it. As suggested in Chapter IV, it appears in the equations of physics as the notorious singularity where the laws of physics break down.

When matter first springs into manifestation in the "big bang," it is already imbued with a dumb, obscure impulse to evolve; though not overtly conscious, its activity is described as somnambulistic. Far from being a barren wasteland without redemptive value, as maintained in some traditions, it is viewed here as a rich soil prepared for the release of hidden potencies in response to the nurturing influences from above. This, incidentally, reveals the inner relation between the physical world and the Divine. As we saw earlier, neither mythical cosmology nor the traditional view gives a satisfactory account of the existence of matter in a world issuing from a higher spiritual principle. Scientific cosmology, on the other hand, accepts matter as real but cannot derive the psychic cosmos from it. In Sri Aurobindo's vision, matter is a form of Spirit that plays a necessary role in the complete manifestation of the Divine.

SPIRITUAL EVOLUTION

All of these principles are implicated in the evolution of Spirit on earth. To quote from Sri Aurobindo's description of the process of involution and evolution:

> The Divine descends from pure existence through the play of Consciousness-Force and Bliss and the creative medium of Supermind into cosmic being; we ascend from Matter through a developing life, soul and mind and the illuminating medium of Supermind towards the divine being. The knot of the two, the higher and the lower hemisphere, is where mind and Supermind meet with a veil between them. The rending of the veil is the condition of the divine life in humanity; for by that rending, by the illumining descent of the higher into the nature of the lower being and the forceful ascent of the lower being into the nature of the higher, mind can recover its divine light in the all-comprehending Supermind, the soul realise its divine self in the all-possessing all-blissful Ananda, life repossess its divine power in the play of omnipotent Conscious-Force and Matter open to its divine liberty as a form of the divine Existence.[43]

The levels above matter are typal (not evolutionary) and each possesses powers characteristic of its own nature. As the evolutionary ascent proceeds, something from the next higher level descends into the evolving being and raises it to a new status. The process is not a mechanical one, since aspiration to evolve must also be present. This presupposes that the potential for the higher is already involved at the lower level. Life descended into fertile matter and living organisms were brought forth on earth. Later, mind descended into a few advanced organisms to engender mental beings (of whom man is now the leading representative). In *The Supramental Manifestation upon Earth,* Sri Aurobindo speaks of a "Mind of Light" that is in the process of being manifested. It is a special action of Supermind, accessing truth-consciousness but expressing this only in mental terms.

The outcome of this phase of evolution would be a perfected form of humanity intermediate between man as he now is and a fully supramental being. For all of its promise, the Mind of Light is only a precursor of the supreme creative and ordering Intelligence behind the cosmos. Evolution has resulted in the appearance of complex forms, from plants and animals to human beings, and is projected to extend beyond man to Superman. It proceeds from above, though initiated by an aspiration from below; thus it would be fruitless to look for biological mechanisms that could account for this development. Sri Aurobindo is therefore not really concerned with the biological transformations of species, but anticipates the descent of greater powers of Spirit yet to manifest in the universe.[44]

Man is viewed as a transitional form, half-animal and half-divine, on the way to a supramental or gnostic being. The key to his evolution is the soul, or psychic being, for the conventional word "soul" is too ambiguous to convey the precise meaning intended. The psychic being is the true center of a person's existence. Everything we experience is mirrored in it. Unlike the aggressive ego, it is not involved in the ordinary mix of our contacts with the world. While not overtly active, it becomes influential when clearly recognized. Its essence is divine love, which can swallow up the whole world in its vast scope. For, according to Sri Aurobindo, the world is the Divine in the act of progressive Self-manifestation. Soul is the indispensable means for this, because it is a form of the Divine enjoying its own unfolding splendor.

The psychic being is the true Immortal residing in the secret recesses of the heart. Once it has been identified, our awareness begins to widen, eventually embracing the entire universe. It is the divine seed in Nature, born into the world to evolve through many lives into a fully manifested divinity on earth.[45] The vast scale of spiritual evolution implies repeated rebirths, but the psychic being is much more than a person's temporary personality. In itself *it does not go anywhere,* though putting forward a succession of different personalities by which it evolves. Like a seed, it grows upward by assimilating the experiences of past lives. While we give something of ourselves to it, the soul will eventually evolve beyond our human mode of existence. As evolution continues, it will outgrow the psycho-physical vehicles through which it now functions, acquiring a more supple material envelope wholly transparent to the spirit within. There are also reaches of consciousness above it that can descend like sunlight when we are prepared to receive them. Moreover, the growth experienced as the soul evolves can spark the inner potential of others as well, since everyone is linked together in an all-embracing unity.

Soul is hidden within us (though we do not "contain" it), but when its influence is felt in our lives an aspiration is awakened to evolve further. It is drawn toward the world, where it appears again and again in different guises, moved by a secret will to manifest the Divine in resistant and seemingly unconscious matter. Divine delight has infused itself into matter as the soul, which is meant to evolve *in the world* rather than leave it untransformed.[46] The convoluted march toward transcendence is propelled by cosmic love, the sustaining power of our efforts. This is the soul's love of the universe in which the Divine is manifesting more and more of itself.[47] The link between them is love, because the soul's love of the Divine in its multitudinous manifestation is identical with the Divine's delight in its own cosmic form.

Love resolves the mystery of our existence in an outwardly impersonal world, where life sometimes seems doomed to endless frustration and despair. It carries us beyond all mental doubts and reservations about who we really are and why we are here. No earthly power or nervous recoil can impede its course forever. Delight in manifestation is the ultimate *raison d'être* for the existence of universes, but it is expressed in this one as a cosmic play of self-concealment and rediscovery. As for the future, we will have to wait and see what takes place, for there are many obstacles still to be worked out, individually and collectively. Whatever our destiny may be, Sri Aurobindo reaffirms his vision of spiritual evolution in the concluding paragraph of *The Life Divine:*

> If there is an evolution in material Nature and if it is an evolution of being with consciousness and life as its two key-terms and powers, this fullness of being, fullness of consciousness, fullness of life must be the goal of development towards which we are tending and which will manifest at an early or later stage of our destiny. The Self, the Spirit, the Reality that is disclosing itself out of the first inconscience of life and matter, would evolve its complete truth of being and consciousness in that life and matter. It would return to itself,—or, if its end as an individual is to return into its Absolute, it could make that return also,—not through a frustration of life but through a spiritual completeness of itself in life. Our evolution in the Ignorance with its chequered joy and pain of self-discovery and world-discovery, its half-fulfilments, its constant finding and missing, is only our first state. It must lead inevitably towards an evolution in the Knowledge, a self-finding and self-unfolding of the Spirit, a self-revelation of the Divinity in things in that true power of itself in Nature which is to us still a Supernature.[48]

At this point, we pass beyond cosmology as presently understood and simply note that evolution can happen only in a universe possessing properties that permit it—which is another way of stating the anthropic principle. It implies that the laws of physics are precisely those necessary at the current stage of cosmic development. This could mean either that the universe was deliberately designed to allow evolution to occur, or that the singular properties of our universe provided the opportunity for an influx of Spirit into Matter. As we saw earlier, this is not an issue that can be finally decided by the mind.

CONCLUSION

Prismatic colors
Bearing in the shifting light
Tidings from the sun.

Plate X. The Mother

VIII

COSMIC POETRY

INTRODUCTION

It seems appropriate to conclude our study of cosmology with a consideration of cosmic poetry. Many of the universal themes associated with the four faces of the universe cry out for poetic expression, since the universe can only be grasped in its full significance as a grand poem disclosing our place and destiny within it. Poetry is a power of consciousness that, if we open ourselves to it, can uplift and even transform the mind. The traditional source of inspiration for poetry is a form of the Divine Mother known by various names in ancient cultures. In Vedic India, she was called Vāc, the goddess of Speech. She is the bearer of the Mantra, the inspired Word, which is the fountainhead of all great poetry. The Greeks, who did not have a separate category for cosmic poetry, recognized one of the Divine Mother's emanations as Urania, the Muse of astronomy. They linked her with the goddess of love and beauty, *Aphrodite Urania,* the Celestial Aphrodite. She signified the calm beauty of the starry sky to Greek poets and philosophers alike.

Although most poems are not intentionally cosmological, they still rest upon assumptions about the universe of which the poet may be only vaguely aware. There is usually some relationship between a poem and the world upon which it is commenting. Even when it does not involve the idea of a complete cosmos, the existence of something is presupposed from which elements of order can be extracted. For poetry is not just a spontaneous emotional outburst, but a way of giving coherence to what our feelings tell us about the world. It is an ordered vision that reveals the possibilities inherent in nature. A well-conceived poem aids in the discovery of the enduring aspects of things that feeling is able to reveal. At its best, it can show that the universe not only includes us among its contents but is also responsive to our highest ideals and aspirations.

The contrast between a deliberately organized cosmological poem and one less structured can be illustrated by the difference between Dante's *Divine Comedy* and T.S. Eliot's *The Waste Land.* In the *Divine Comedy,* Dante presents a finite, tightly ordered cosmos that includes a clearly defined goal. He knows what his world has to offer and can show how to achieve fulfillment in it. Every stage along the way toward spiritual perfection is correlated with a specific level of the universe. In addition, the whole journey is sustained by the power of Divine Grace. A poem like *The Waste Land,* on the other hand, reflects an indefinite world without coherence or purpose; all Eliot can do is present disconnected fragments of a life. Readers have to make sense out of it for themselves, if this is indeed possible in such a world. We are left seeking for meaning in a universe that is indifferent to whether or not any reason can be found for existing in it.

The cosmology of a poem may be mythical, scientific, traditional, or evolutionary. Each type of cosmology will influence the way that we respond to the poem as a whole. Philosophical worldviews may have an imaginative aspect, but the role of imagination is central in cosmic poetry. Although these poems may not always reflect contemporary cosmological knowledge, they can be judged by their success in awakening appropriate feelings about the universe. There are many kinds of poetry that are capable of expressing such feelings, but the form we will be concerned with is epic poetry. The large scope of an epic renders it uniquely capable of doing justice to the grand theme of the universe and our place in it. Memorable cosmic poetry of this kind is a rare occurrence, however, because it requires the conjunction of a number of uncommon qualities in a single poet. These include, besides consummate poetic gifts, an imagination large enough to encompass the entire universe, extensive learning, and a rich store of life experiences upon which to draw. An epic poet must also be able to visualize human destiny in a cosmic setting. Above all, a great heart is needed to beat out the vast rhythms of the universe. It is no wonder that only a few individuals have ever possessed all of these qualities.

Another reason that cosmic poetry on an epic scale is so rare is the difficulty involved in sustaining the reader's attention when the universe itself is the major theme. Poems of this sort tend to become purely didactic. The more interesting ones are those that relate the universe to serious human concerns. They usually identify a specific problem of life and draw upon a vision of the whole universe for its solution. For this purpose, any one of the four types of cosmology can be utilized to resolve the issue posed by the poem. In this way, readers are able to comprehend why the problem arose and how it can be solved. Finally, a great cosmological poem reconciles knowledge and feeling in a unified vision that relates man intimately to the universe in which he lives.

Readers will have personal favorites in this regard, but the four cosmic poems considered here have been chosen because each represents a type of cosmology that has been examined previously in this book. Except for the *Bhagavad Gītā,* they are all epic poems written by identifiable poets. Even the Gita is part of one of the great epics of India, the *Mahābhārata*. The Gita is also the only religious scripture among the four, being widely recognized as a sacred text of Hinduism. The *Mahābhārata* is ascribed to the compiler Vyasa, a name associated with a large body of Hindu literature, but he cannot be positively identified as a historical figure. In discussing these poems, the following classification will be employed:

1. Mythical Cosmology: *The Bhagavad Gītā*
2. Scientific Cosmology: *De Rerum Natura* (Lucretius)
3. Traditional Cosmology: *The Divine Comedy* (Dante)
4. Evolutionary Cosmology: *Savitri* (Sri Aurobindo)

All four poems celebrate the harmony and variety of the universe. They convey a sense of cosmic consciousness, though it is felt from different levels of experience. Correlating the poems with the various types of cosmology may not be exact in every detail, but each one relies heavily on a given cosmological perspective.

THE BHAGAVAD GĪTĀ

The *Bhagavad Gītā,* or "Song of the Divine," is a universal spiritual classic that transcends religious and cultural boundaries. Despite its Hindu context, burdened by centuries of sectarian disputes, it speaks directly to the human heart everywhere. It has been translated into English on numerous occasions, each translation giving a slightly different nuance to the text. Many commentaries have been written on it, only a few of which are really helpful for understanding its spiritual message. Three outstanding commentaries are available in English: (1) Sri Aurobindo, *Essays on the Gita,*[1] (2) Sri Krishna Prem, *The Yoga of the Bhagavat Gita,*[2] and (3) Sri Jnaneshvar, *Jnaneshvari.*[3] Each interprets the Gita from a point of view based on deep inner experience. In the following exposition, we prefer Sri Aurobindo's approach, because it captures the originality of the Gita better than the others. We should not forget that, besides its value as a religious scripture, the Gita is a cosmic poem of immense power and beauty. Read as an illustration of cosmic poetry, it provides us with a complete worldview.[4]

The problem of life with which the Gita deals occurs at the very outset of the work. It is the result of circumstances leading up to a fierce civil war fought at some time in India's legendary past. Arjuna, the most skilled warrior on the side of the forces destined for victory, is the representative man of his world. He is a great hero to whom the people look for leadership in the coming battle. His brother, the rightful king, wished to regain the throne out of which he had been cheated, and Arjuna supported his claim. Their ultimate goal was to establish a universal rule of peace and justice in India. The usurpers who opposed them were heroic according to the standards of the time, but their honor was stained by hypocrisy and self-aggrandizement. Before the battle began, Arjuna had his chariot driven out between the armies so that he could view the enemy forces. As he surveys them, he recognizes many relatives and former teachers arrayed against him. Realizing the horrific social and moral consequences of war, he loses his taste for battle and refuses to go on, declaring "I will not fight."

> Having thus spoken on the battlefield, Arjuna sank down on the seat of the chariot, casting down the divine bow and the inexhaustible quiver (given to him by the gods for that tremendous hour), his spirit overwhelmed with sorrow.[5]

This dilemma concerning what should be done when we are called upon to act in a less than perfect world is the central problem of the Gita.

Arjuna's charioteer has other ideas, for he is Krishna—an incarnation (*avatāra*) of the Supreme Person (Puruṣottama) or Godhead. In reality, he is a transcendent Being active in the world while remaining detached and immovable in the midst of action. The whole universe is a manifestation of this Being, and an Avatar is his special embodiment on earth at a critical moment in its history. According to Sri Aurobindo, the inner purpose of a descent like this is to reveal a previously undeveloped power in the world. The Avatar accepts the limitations of human birth and shares the difficulties and struggles it entails. He inspires and supports man's efforts to establish a higher life on earth. In the present crisis, the Supreme Person has become Arjuna's charioteer in order to awaken a larger, more universal consciousness in mankind. Greed and hostility toward an enemy, being rooted in aggressive egoism, usually motivate wars. The consciousness represented by Krishna, however, knows the Godhead within itself and all other beings, even enemies. This consciousness is the real basis of social stability, as well as the key to spiritual liberation. Its appearance on earth requires a divine descent, since it could not come to light through the ordinary course of human events. When it manifests, forces resistant to a decisive change in the world rise up against it. Thus, life's immediate challenges must be faced courageously, and the way to do this is the burden of Krishna's teaching in the Gita.

Krishna has chosen to reveal the deepest truth about reality to Arjuna, who is a high-minded and disciplined person responsive to the inner guidance of the Divine. He explains that the universe consists of conflicting forces of Light (the Daivic) and Darkness (the Asuric), which are represented on earth by the warring factions facing each other. There are two natures, one lower and the other higher, both being manifestations of the Godhead but acting differently in the world. The lower nature consists of the material principles of body, life, mind, and ego, which are only instruments of the Divine Will. In contrast, the higher or divine Nature is the power by which this Will works in the world. It is the Divine Mother of some traditions, but in the Gita she is treated as an aspect of the Supreme Person:

> Know this to be the womb of all beings. I am the birth of the whole world and so too its dissolution.
>
> There is nothing else supreme beyond Me, O Dhananjaya. On Me all that is here is strung like pearls upon a thread.[6]

Individual souls are eternal portions of the Godhead and should not be confused with the principles of the lower nature. They are manifestations of the Supreme Person in the cosmic arena. As Krishna declares, "It is an eternal portion of Me that becomes the Jiva [Soul] in the world of living creatures and cultivates the subjective powers of Prakriti [Nature], mind and the five senses."[7]

The war in which Arjuna finds himself takes place in this cosmic setting. Krishna wants him to lead the forces of Light against those of Darkness, who would crush all progress toward a higher consciousness that threatens their domination of the world. Arjuna is offered the chance to participate in this conflict by fighting in the vanguard of the forces of Light. But he must do so without the egoism entrenched in the lower nature, which is the barrier that stands in the way of establishing a new consciousness on earth. The choice is his, and he has Krishna as his charioteer waiting to carry him to victory. Nevertheless, even this inspired teaching fails to shake Arjuna out of his lethargy. An Avatar not only teaches a doctrine but may also reveal it through his own transfigured body. The scope of the higher consciousness preparing to come forth must be seen with the spiritual eye and not merely explained in words. Arjuna is vouchsafed a climactic vision of the World-Spirit, the universal form of the Godhead.[8] In this vision, the cosmic background of life on earth is depicted vividly so that Arjuna will participate with full comprehension in the task he is called upon to perform. He must grow into the knowledge of divinity by recognizing the Godhead in the immensity of the universe as well as within himself and others.

The Vision of the World-Spirit is a powerful experience of cosmic consciousness conveyed in the symbolic terms of Hindu mythical cosmology. Arjuna sees the entire universe, with a multitude of beings inhabiting the various cosmic levels, all unified in the luminous body of the Godhead "as if a thousand suns had risen at once in heaven."[9] This all-encompassing vision, presented with unsurpassed poetic power, overwhelms the imagination without sacrificing clarity and precision of form. At first, the aspect of terror and destruction is given full sway, and a voice declares:

> I am the Time-Spirit, destroyer of the world, arisen huge-statured for the destruction of the nations.[10]

Eventually the sense of a larger harmony and purpose prevails, and all the apparent discords are resolved. The whole scene displays the inexhaustible variety of the universe being held together in the unity of the Godhead.

Arjuna is told by Krishna that "By Me and none other already even are they slain, do thou become the occasion only."[11] Thus, if he chooses to fight he will not be the slayer but only the instrument for clearing away the obstructions to a new mode of life in the world. Elsewhere in the Gita, the methods for establishing the higher consciousness firmly within an individual are outlined and its major attributes described. Arjuna is situated in the midst of the action and his voluntary cooperation is being sought. Krishna's ringing call to the embattled soul in man sums up the message of the Gita: "thou who hast come to this transient and unhappy world, love and turn to Me."[12] In the end, Arjuna consents to enter the fray against the hostile forces that would stifle the further advance of humanity. United with the Supreme

Person, who has become his charioteer, all that is meant to be done will be accomplished. This resolves the issue with which the Gita began.

De Rerum Natura

It is difficult to find a great cosmic poem about scientific cosmology. Poems of this kind are usually concerned with the universe itself rather than man and his problems, except in so far as he is a representative part of the material world. Nothing related to this type of cosmology can surpass *De Rerum Natura* ("On the Nature of Things") by the Roman poet Lucretius. Written in the first century B.C.E., it presents a general picture of the universe similar to that found in modern science. This poem is based upon the image of an infinite universe of atoms flying about in limitless empty space and randomly combining into innumerable worlds. The universe is governed by inexorable law—even the gods, whose existence Lucretius does not deny, are nothing more than combinations of atoms existing in the eternally peaceful regions between the worlds.[13] In his view, the gods are as indifferent about the destiny of human beings as they are about the nature of things. We, on the other hand, must know the nature of the universe in order to achieve happiness, brief though it may be. We might desire to prolong our lives indefinitely, but all of us are doomed to die; thus the central problem that life poses for Lucretius is the fear of death. This fear is compounded by our religious superstitions concerning hell and divine judgment after death. After a long passage decrying the fear of death in a universe where life is only a passing phenomenon, he states:

> Men feel plainly enough within their minds, a heavy burden, whose weight depresses them. If only they perceived with equal clearness the causes of this depression, the origin of this lump of evil within their breasts, they would not lead such a life as we now see all too commonly—no one knowing what he really wants and everyone for ever trying to get away from where he is, as though mere locomotion could throw off the load.[14]

Lucretius quickly points out that the solution to the problem lies in understanding the nature of the universe in which we live:

> In so doing the individual is really running away from himself. Since he remains reluctantly wedded to the self whom he cannot of course escape, he grows to hate him, because he is a sick man ignorant of the cause of his malady. If he did but see this, he would cast other thoughts aside *and devote himself first to studying the nature of the universe.* It is not the fortune of an hour that is in question, but of all time—the lot in store for mortals throughout the eternity that awaits them after death [italics added].[15]

But what kind of universe does the poem reveal? Lucretius proposes to explain the ultimate nature of reality, which he says is composed of material atoms:

> I will set out to discourse to you on the ultimate realities of heaven and the gods. I will reveal those *atoms* from which nature creates all things and increases and feeds them and into which, when they perish, nature again resolves them.[16]

The universe consists of an infinite number of atoms and an infinite void of space that contains them. Everything can be explained by the combination of atoms interacting through mechanical sequences of cause and effect.[17] Even if the gods exist, they do not interfere with the working of nature and it is childish to fear them. There is no divine will or design governing the movements of the atoms; world-systems are continually forming and dissipating everywhere in space by chance collisions.

We happen to exist in one of these systems enclosed by "the flaming ramparts of the world." All appear and disappear with time but the atoms themselves are everlasting. Atoms did not come into being, nor will they ever pass away, since the great principle that governs the universe ensures that nothing can arise from absolute nothingness or be completely annihilated. As for *creation:*

> *Nothing can ever be created by divine power out of nothing.* The reason why all mortals are so gripped by fear is that they see all sorts of things happening on the earth and in the sky with no

> discernible cause, and these they attribute to the will of a god. Accordingly, when we have seen that nothing can be created out of nothing, we shall then have a clearer picture of the path ahead, the problem of how things are created and occasioned without the aid of the gods.[18]

The second part of this all-embracing principle concerns the nature of *destruction*:

> *Nature resolves everything into its component atoms and never reduces anything to nothing*. If anything were perishable in all its parts, anything might perish all of a sudden and vanish from sight. There would be no need of any force to separate its parts and loosen their links. In actual fact, since everything is composed of indestructible seeds, nature obviously does not allow anything to perish till it has encountered a force that shatters it with a blow or creeps into chinks and unknits it.[19]

This completes Lucretius' statement of the fundamental conservation principle, which, *mutatis mutandis,* still underlies much of modern scientific cosmology.

His vision of an impersonal Nature blindly creating and destroying worlds that are made out of everlasting atoms is presented with admirable poetic skill. The philosophy behind the poem did not originate with Lucretius himself, but is drawn from the writings of the Greek philosopher Epicurus (c. 300 B.C.E.), who built upon the theories of earlier Greek atomists.[20] His primary interest, however, was in the ethical implications of their ideas. He believed that a life reduced to a few simple pleasures that did not disturb one's peace of mind was the most one could hope for. Our souls are themselves composed of atoms of a finer type than those that make up our bodies. Death is the end of personal life, for it consists in the scattering of soul-atoms into space after the destruction of the body. Since death means the total extinction of an individual person, there is no basis for the fear of divine judgment afterwards.

Understanding that the universe is only composed of atoms moving about aimlessly in infinite space eliminates the fear of death (though not its *finality*) for Lucretius, thus solving the problem with which the poem is concerned. The impersonal principles of the universe convince him that it is futile to lament about our pending doom. Although it cannot be avoided, death has lost its sting because it is the dissolution of personality into insentient atoms. This bleak picture of human destiny is based upon an imaginative vision of Nature in which everything from the birth of a flower to the decay of a world is governed by mechanical process. Impressed by the inexhaustible power of Nature, Lucretius tried to show the impotence of man and the gods. For him, the achievement of inner peace is possible only by embracing this sobering view of universal and everlasting Nature. As he says:

> This dread and darkness of the mind cannot be dispelled by the sunbeams, the shining shafts of day, but only by an understanding of the outward form and inner workings of nature.[21]

THE DIVINE COMEDY

The Divine Comedy is not specifically about the magical universe, but it employs several of its leading themes. These include a geocentric cosmos, a moralized version of the three worlds with Hell located inside the earth, and an emphasis on the power of the divine feminine. In accordance with Christian tradition, the universe has been swept clear of gods but abounds with angels who perform various functions within it. Dante based his vision on the traditional theme of a journey through the cosmos as an allegory of the soul's spiritual ascent to God. The poem was ostensibly a portrayal of the worldview of medieval Catholicism but strayed from the outlook of the Church in a number of ways. Since Dante was a poet possessing extraordinary gifts, his imagination could not be constrained within the bounds of theological orthodoxy. At the beginning of the poem, his problem is a deepening sense of despair over the corruption and brutality existing at all levels of the social order. He is seen wandering in a dark wood from which he tries to flee by climbing a nearby hill. But he is driven back by three symbolic beasts, a leopard (lust), a lion (violence), and a she-wolf (treachery), each representing one of the defects of human nature. As Dante is about to lose all hope, the spirit of the ancient Roman poet Virgil, whom he revered, appears and offers to be his guide:

> Therefore, I think and judge it best for you to follow me, and I shall guide you, taking you from this place through an eternal place, where you shall hear the howls of desperation and see the ancient spirits in their pain, as each of them laments his second death; and you shall see those souls who are content within the fire, for they hope to reach—whenever that may be—the blessed people.[22]

We soon discover that Virgil is an instrument of Divine Grace, which is acting on Dante's behalf, for Grace is the saving power in the cosmos of the poem. It flows from the Virgin Mary, who is identified as the Queen of Heaven, the Mother of God, and the dispenser of mercy to suffering mankind. Divine Grace is open to all, but it can only operate effectively in those persons who are disposed to receive it. Presumably Dante is one of them. For his benefit, Grace functions through a succession of intermediaries ranging from Lucia (light) and Beatrice (love), who was Dante's youthful beloved, to Virgil (rationality). They intervene at this critical juncture in Dante's life to guide him through the various levels of the universe up to God. The symbolic meaning of each cosmic level is described along the way showing him how we are related to the cosmos. Only thus will he be able to arrive at a complete resolution of the psychological problem introduced in the opening Canto. Knowledge of man's true place in the universe is indispensable for the removal of our blindness concerning God's purpose in creating the world.

The universe of the poem is divided into three main regions corresponding to Hell, Purgatory, and Paradise (Figure 7). In accordance with medieval cosmological tradition, the earth is a sphere placed at the center of the cosmos, and the geography of the poem is based on what was then known about the surface of the earth. Europe, Asia, and Africa, the three great land masses of the Northern Hemisphere, were represented schematically by the so-called "T-O maps" of the time. These maps divided the known world into three parts, with Asia at the top, Europe to the lower left, and Africa to the lower right. The continents were enclosed within a circle and surrounded by the Ocean Sea. Jerusalem, as the most important city in the Christian world, was placed at their geographic center. The largely unexplored Southern Hemisphere was considered to be mostly water. But, in Dante's cosmos, there is an island in its midst on which the Mountain of Purgatory stands. It is located at the antipodes to Jerusalem. This mountain rises through the four elements of the terrestrial region to the sphere of the moon. Above it are the celestial spheres, ranged in order up to the sphere of the fixed stars. Beyond lie the *Primum Mobile*, which moves the other spheres, enclosing them all in a finite cosmos, and the *Empyrean* or eternal abode of Light surrounding God.

Hell is placed inside the earth, depicted as a conical cavity with narrow ledges leading down to the nadir of the cosmos where Satan (Dis) is embedded in a frozen lake. His impotent figure is incarcerated at the point farthest removed from the dwelling-place of God in the Empyrean. There are unregenerate spirits on every ledge, and Dante learns much about the frailties of the human condition by seeing and conversing with them. At first, he feels only pity for their sufferings. Later, however, as he descends deeper into the nether regions below, he is appalled by the depths of cruelty and treachery into which these spirits have sunk. They are responsible for crimes that violate every shred of human decency, and he realizes that they are in Hell because of their own misdirected wills. It is their adamant refusal to open their hearts to the power of Divine Grace that keeps them there. When he reaches the bottom of the pit, he is stunned into silence by the monstrous form of Dis. Contrary to popular depictions of Hell as a flaming inferno, Dante's Hell is frozen to symbolize the utter coldness of a heart without love. To his horror, he discovers

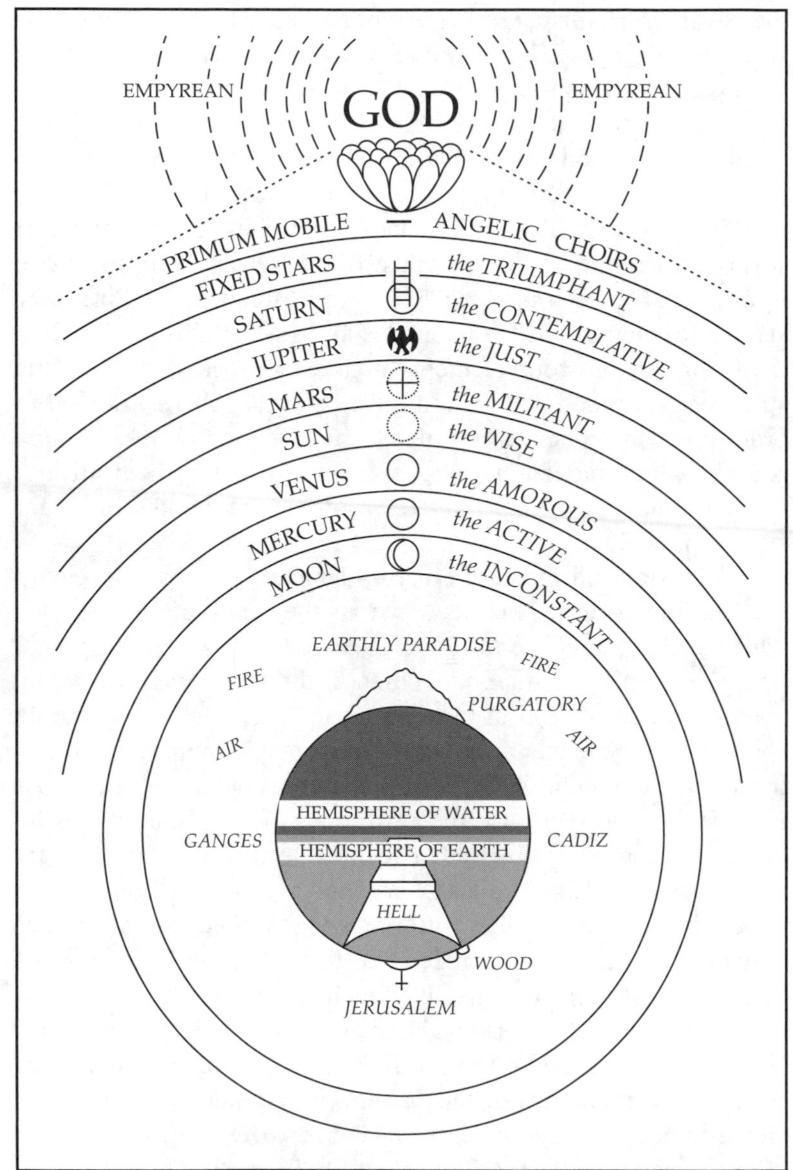

Figure 7. Dante's Cosmos

that this embodiment of depravity must be traversed in order to regain the relative safety of the earth's surface. Clinging to Virgil, he is carried down the hairy body of Dis through the world's center of gravity and then up to the open air above:

> My guide and I came on that hidden road to make our way back into the bright world; and with no care for any rest, we climbed—he first, I following—until I saw, through a round opening, some of those things of beauty Heaven bears. It was from there that we emerged, to see—once more—the stars.[23]

Upon exiting Hell, Dante finds himself on an island in the sea at the other side of the earth, where the Mountain of Purgatory is located. The top of this mountain lies just below the sphere of the Moon and is occupied by the Earthly Paradise. There is an atmosphere of hope on this island that raises his spirits after the long journey in darkness:

> To course across more kindly waters now my talent's little vessel lifts her sails, leaving behind herself a sea so cruel; and what I sing will be that second kingdom, in which the human soul is cleansed of sin, becoming worthy of ascent to Heaven.[24]

Dante climbs the terraces that spiral up the mountainside, learning from the souls he meets what each terrace signifies. The souls in Purgatory represent persons who tried to lead exemplary moral lives but were hindered from doing so by various obstacles. They are there because it is the place where, as Dante says, "the human soul is cleansed of sin." When its purgation is finished, a soul simply rises and passes on to Paradise, for there is nothing more to hinder it from doing so. After reaching the top of the mountain, Virgil, the Pagan Poet, can go no further. He relinquishes Dante to Beatrice whose love will draw him up through the celestial spheres into the Empyrean. After drinking from the reviving waters of the river Eunoe, he is ready to ascend into the heavens:

> From that most holy wave I now returned to Beatrice; remade, as new trees are renewed when they bring forth new boughs, I was pure and prepared to climb unto the stars.[25]

As they move through the heavens, Beatrice explains the significance of the angelic apparitions that are encountered along the way.[26] Blessed souls reside in the Empyrean near God, but Dante sees their reflections in the appropriate celestial spheres. Even in Heaven there is a hierarchy of souls ranked according to their spiritual merits. Nevertheless, each soul is content with its station, for all are one in the bosom of God. When Dante reaches the Empyrean, he is at first blinded by the Light but gradually discerns a great White Rose symbolizing Divine Love. The Virgin Mary, surrounded by the souls of the blessed, is seated there in the Divine Light.[27] Beatrice is replaced by St. Bernard of Clairvaux, the great medieval mystic and devotee of Mary, who now appears at Dante's side. In a magnificent prayer, he implores Mary to grant Dante the mystical vision of God.

> Lady, you are so high, you can so intercede, that he who would have grace but does not seek your aid, may long to fly but has no wings. Your loving-kindness does not only answer the one who asks, but it is often ready to answer freely long before the asking. In you compassion is, in you is pity, in you is generosity, in you is every goodness found in any creature.[28]

In response to Bernard's prayer, Dante is granted the coveted "Beatific Vision" that was fervently sought by Christian mystics as the culmination of their spiritual exercises; with it comes the peace that passeth all understanding.

The *Divine Comedy* closes with Dante's hesitant attempt to describe this Vision. He tells us that his gaze was fixed upon the "Eternal Light," in which the whole universe was "ingathered and bound by love into one single volume" and the disharmonies among things vanished. Three circles of different colors appeared that were interrelated within the Light. In the second circle, he saw a faint image of the Archetypal Man, in whom humanity and God are united in perfect harmony. As he pondered this vision, he suddenly lost all sense of separateness. Then words failed him, his desire and will being moved like a uniformly revolving wheel by "the Love that moves the sun and the other stars."[29] The power of Divine Grace emanating from the Virgin Mary has brought

Dante to the pinnacle of bliss, and he now understands the purpose of life in the universe. In this allegory of the soul projected onto the vast canvas of the cosmos, we are shown the spiritual Light that is reflected in human beings. Henceforth, Dante can live contentedly in a state of grace that will protect him from further psychological distress. Since his predicament at the beginning of the poem is the same as that of every sensitive person, the allegory can apply to anyone who is ready to undertake the mystical journey.

SAVITRI

Once again we return to Sri Aurobindo, who in addition to his other attainments was an accomplished poet with a sizable collection of poetry to his credit. It includes exquisite short poems, lyrical drama, narrative and epic poetry—almost all written in English. He employed various verse patterns, experimented with quantitative meter, and made a careful study of poetic form. Further, he attempted an epic in Homeric hexameters, *Ilion,* but left it unfinished with almost nine of twelve books completed. Sri Aurobindo also spent roughly three decades working on his masterpiece, *Savitri: A Legend and a Symbol,* an epic poem in twelve books totaling nearly 24,000 lines of blank verse (roughly twice the length of Milton's *Paradise Lost*).[30] *Savitri* is based on a legendary story, found in the *Mahābhārata,* about an Indian princess whose great devotion won back the life of her deceased husband, Satyavan, from the God of Death. She was connected with the Sun-Goddess (also named Savitri) who had granted the boon of a daughter to her childless father, King Aswapathy, in response to his religious austerities. After Savitri married, her life with her husband was happy but filled with a foreboding of his death, which occurred a year later. When Yama, the Lord of Death, came to claim the soul of her husband, her courage and devotion compelled him to release it. Sri Aurobindo saw in this legend a symbol of divine involvement in the process of world evolution.[31]

There are critical moments in evolution when the oceanic abyss of the Inconscient threatens to rise up and engulf the evolving soul. Only a direct intervention from above can defeat the oppressive forces at work in the deep.[32] These forces are symbolized in Sri Aurobindo's epic by the menacing figure of Death. In *Savitri,* the problem of life is of far greater scope than was entertained in the poems we have already discussed. The urgency of the situation is indicated in the opening Cantos, where Savitri is shown meditating in the forest at dawn on the fatal day when Satyavan must die. While the pre-dawn darkness, filled with a mixture of dread and promise, slowly changes into the common light of day, we find her preparing for the coming ordeal. She reviews her life on earth leading up to this day, and finds within herself the spiritual strength that will be needed for her confrontation with Death. For this is not to be a merely human defiance of our inevitable mortality, but a struggle between two cosmic forces that hold the evolutionary fate of the world in balance. Savitri is an emissary from the Divine Mother who has taken human birth to change the prevailing conditions of life on earth (Plate XI). She has come to assert the supremacy of Spirit over Matter in the course of the soul's evolution.

> A flaming warrior from the eternal peaks
> Empowered to force the door denied and closed
> Smote from Death's visage its dumb absolute
> And burst the bounds of consciousness and Time.[33]

According to Sri Aurobindo, the immediate goal of evolution is the transformation of the human into the supramental being. He did not seek this transformation for himself but for the divine soul concealed in all human beings. As we have seen in Chapter VII, evolution can be envisioned as a cosmic process involving the successive descent of higher principles into matter; this leads to the appearance of new forms of being on earth. In the case of humanity, which has reached the level of mind, the next stage will be the emergence of Supermind. Since this is a transcendent principle previously unmanifested in the universe, its appearance would constitute a major event in history. Life on earth would change dramatically, with even the elimination of death becoming possible. A transformation of such magnitude lies far beyond present human capacities and calls for a divine intervention in the normal evolutionary process. Such an intervention, with its enormous potential for the future, must be aspired for by the vanguard of the race.

In Sri Aurobindo's epic, Savitri's father, King Aswapathy, represents this vanguard. He is not petitioning the Divine Mother for a child, but rather for a quickening of the slow advance toward transformation. His concentrated aspiration takes him up through a succession of psychic worlds, symbolized as a cosmic stairway, where he silently observes the different kinds of beings and activities going on in each of them.[34] He passes through increasingly subtle ranges of the universe in search of the secret knowledge that can heal the division between Spirit and Matter. This inner journey includes a brief visit to a pit of horror and deception reminiscent of Dante's Hell, but its comprehensive and upward thrust leads him into the silent spiritual heights above the mind. All that he learns is described in images that evoke vivid impressions of these worlds. We are made to feel them as inner states of our own being. King Aswapathy's quest is to reach the top of the "World-Stair" and commune directly with the Divine Mother. Reaching this height, he is entranced by the sweetness of the aura surrounding her:

> For one was there supreme behind the God.
> A Mother Might brooded upon the world;
> A Consciousness revealed its marvellous front
> Transcending all that is, denying none:
> Imperishable above our fallen heads
> He felt a rapturous and unstumbling Force.
> The undying Truth appeared, the enduring Power
> Of all that here is made and then destroyed,
> The Mother of all godheads and all strengths
> Who, mediatrix, binds earth to the Supreme.[35]

He has come to her from this suffering world to seek a boon for humankind, seemingly doomed to an implacable and incomprehensible fate:

Plate XI. Savitri's Arrival

A Strength he sought that was not yet on earth,
Help from a Power too great for mortal will,
The Light of a Truth now only seen afar,
A sanction from his high omnipotent Source.[36]

At first, she appears to be reluctant to intercede in our destiny, enjoining Aswapathy to return to earth and help humanity where possible, but leave the future in the hands of God: "All things shall change in God's transfiguring hour."[37] After a momentary silence, he recovers his heart's voice and makes an impassioned plea on the earth's behalf urging her to intervene at once in this troubled and imperfect world. The long passages of his appeal are expressed in magnificent rhythms that possess great illuminative power:

How shall I rest content with mortal days
And the dull measure of terrestrial things,
I who have seen behind the cosmic mask
The glory and the beauty of thy face?
Hard is the doom to which thou bindst thy sons!
How long shall our spirits battle with the Night
And bear defeat and the brute yoke of Death,
We who are vessels of a deathless Force
And builders of the godhead of the race?[38]

As he continues his plea, Aswapathy recounts a vision in which he saw a future race of Immortals descending to earth in an irrepressible influx of Spirit:

I saw the Omnipotent's flaming pioneers
Over the heavenly verge which turns towards life
Come crowding down the amber stairs of birth;
Forerunners of a divine multitude
Out of the paths of the morning star they came
Into the little room of mortal life.
I saw them cross the twilight of an age,
The sun-eyed children of a marvelous dawn,
The great creators with wide brows of calm,
The massive barrier-breakers of the world
And wrestlers with destiny in her lists of will,
The laborers in the quarries of the gods,
The messengers of the Incommunicable,
The architects of immortality.
Into the fallen human sphere they came,

Faces that wore the Immortal's glory still,
Voices that communed still with the thoughts of God,
Bodies made beautiful by the Spirit's light,
Carrying the magic word, the mystic fire,
Carrying the Dionysian cup of joy,
Approaching eyes of a diviner man,
Lips chanting an unknown anthem of the soul,
Feet echoing in the corridors of Time.
High priests of wisdom, sweetness, might and bliss,
Discoverers of beauty's sunlit ways
And swimmers of Love's laughing fiery floods
And dancers within rapture's golden doors,
Their tread one day shall change the suffering earth
And justify the light on Nature's face.[39]

Aswapathy concludes with a prayer that she make this vision a reality upon earth:

O Wisdom-Splendour, Mother of the universe,
Creatrix, the Eternal's artist Bride,
Linger not long with thy transmuting hand
Pressed vainly on one golden bar of Time,
As if Time dare not open its heart to God.
O radiant fountain of the world's delight
World-free and unattainable above,
O Bliss who ever dwellst deep hid within
While men seek thee outside and never find,
Mystery and muse with hieratic tongue,
Incarnate the white passion of thy force,
Mission to earth some living form of thee.[40]

The response is immediate and decisive:

A seed shall be sown in Death's tremendous hour,
A branch of heaven transplant to human soil;
Nature shall overleap her mortal step;
Fate shall be changed by an unchanging will.[41]

Hence Savitri was born to contend with Death in the fields of time.

The epic continues with the dramatic events of Savitri's outer life and a description of her unprecedented inner preparation for her husband's death. In the last part of the narrative, Savitri confronts the shadowy figure of Death. She doggedly follows him into an eerie twilight toward the gloomy depths of his abode, constantly demanding that he release the soul of Satyavan from his grasp. Along the way, he cleverly counters all her appeals. In this poem, Death is not merely a symbol of our mortality but a cosmic power representing the negation of being and the antithesis of all evolutionary effort. There are long dialogues in which he tries to undermine Savitri's resolve to reclaim her husband's soul, for Satyavan is the evolving soul in humanity destined to become the immortal supramental being on earth. Death must be defeated on the plane of profound metaphysical debate before the divine force in Savitri finally overcomes him.

At one point, Death, the clever sophist of nihilism, admonishes her:

> O soul misled by the splendour of thy thoughts,
> O earthly creature with thy dream of heaven,
> Obey resigned and still, the earthly law.[42]

A part of her answer is that:

> This universe an old enchantment guards;
> Its objects are carved cups of World-Delight
> Whose charmed wine is some deep soul's rapture-drink:
> The All-Wonderful has packed heaven with his dreams,
> He has made blank ancient Space his marvel-house;
> He spilled his spirit into Matter's signs:
> His fires of grandeur burn in the great sun,
> He glides through heaven shimmering in the moon;
> He is beauty carolling in the fields of sound;
> He chants the stanzas of the odes of Wind;
> He is silence watching in the stars at night;
> He wakes at dawn and calls from every bough,
> Lies stunned in the stone and dreams in flower and tree.[43]

She continues:

> O Death, I have triumphed over thee within;
> I quiver no more with the assault of grief;
> A mighty calmness seated deep within
> Has occupied my body and my sense:
> It takes the world's grief and transmutes to strength,
> It makes the world's joy one with the joy of God.
> . . . .

My will is greater than thy law, O Death;
My love is stronger than the bonds of Fate:
Our love is the heavenly seal of the Supreme.[44]

Near the end of their great debate, Savitri finally declares:

Why dost thou vainly strive with me, O Death,
A mind delivered from all twilight thoughts,
To whom the secrets of the gods are plain?
For now at last I know beyond all doubt
The great stars burn with my unceasing fire
And life and death are both its fuel made.[45]

Death challenges her to reveal her power by showing him the face of "the Mighty Mother"—only then will he give Satyavan back to her. But that demand ends the debate: the dark form of Death is dissolved in the light radiating from Savitri's transfigured body, and he is driven back into the Inconscient from whence he came. Even so, fading remnants of his power are allowed to linger for a while, preventing humanity from becoming too complacent. They are still capable of causing havoc through those who are susceptible to their influence. In the end, Death himself is revealed to be a mask of the Divine. Savitri has removed the major obstacle to the evolution of the soul, and both she and Satyavan return triumphantly to their lives on earth. They are greeted with wonder and amazement by the throngs that gather about them, for all have mysteriously benefited from her inner contest with Death. The epic concludes with Night auspiciously nursing in her bosom the promise of a greater dawn.

Just before the poem closes, a perplexed priest-sage questions Savitri about the vibrant aura of peace she radiates after her decisive struggle with Death to reclaim the life of her deceased husband. She replies that it is enough to feel love and oneness with all beings:

Awakened to the meaning of my heart,
That to feel love and oneness is to live
And this the magic of our golden change
Is all the truth I know or seek, O sage.[46]

These words reveal the essence of the soul and the secret of the cosmos. For they express the creative delight that has entered the world to become a divine being within it. The love she refers to is this delight directed toward a perceived form of divinity. As such, it has little to do with the transitory personal sentiments usually associated with love, though even these may display a trace of it. Love for another soul can widen to include the whole universe and be finally transmuted into the Eternal Love that cradles each being in its close embrace.[47] Savitri, who has fully realized the divinity within herself, is speaking of love in all these senses. They correspond to the three modes of consciousness distinguished in Chapter I. In our reading of the epic, its message is that *Love has already overcome Death,* and that the promise of this tremendous inner victory, which cleared the way for the evolving soul, is destined to be fulfilled outwardly on earth.

EPILOGUE

Scaling a mountain
Sky above and earth beneath
The bright clouds dancing.

Plate XII. Ascent to the Truth

CONCLUDING REMARKS

A question may linger in the minds of some readers, since it was stated earlier that the universe appears to be more like a great poem than a computer. We reviewed four poems, each of which expresses a cosmic vision different from the others. How can they all be true? The key to resolving this dilemma lies in my suggestion in the Prologue that the various types of cosmology are not all on an equal footing. A similar observation can be made concerning the poems we have just examined: they are all true to some extent but vary widely in scope. Poems that present consciousness as an eternal reality underlying the universe are superior to those that do not, because they suggest an opportunity for transcending our mortality. Moreover, if soul possesses cosmic stature, the poem that makes this clearest is more likely to be the truer one.

The measure of the truth of a cosmic poem lies in its capacity to raise us to higher levels of perception, freedom, and delight. More than merely a logical property of certain statements, Truth is a spiritual power that deepens and transforms our view of ourselves and the universe. Sri Aurobindo's *Savitri* offers the most far-reaching vision we yet possess, for it relates the destiny of the soul to the fullest conception of an evolutionary cosmos. The other poems ignore the soul's potential for further evolution. Even the *Bhagavad Gītā,* which introduces the possibility of a higher consciousness attainable by man on earth, stops short of a complete picture of the continuing progress of the soul. Evolution is inescapably historical in character and merely thinking about it cannot give any certainty about the future: evolution is profounder than the mind's capacity to know or measure it.

Although philosophical speculation plays an important role in cosmology, it remains indecisive because of its essentially intellectual nature. It cannot entirely avoid the charge of being an exercise in futility, no matter how firmly grounded in logic or experience. Therefore, we trust in the power of *feeling* wherever possible. This is not as subjective as it may sound, for when our deepest feelings are free of interfering influences from the lower nature, they become a valuable means of penetrating into the cosmic mystery. What might seem like baseless fantasy to the logical mind can then be realized as indubitable fact. Scholarly literature is full of references to intuition, spiritual experience, union with God, and so forth, but feeling is a simple and direct contact with reality known to mystics all over the world.

Many philosophers believe that appeals to intuition are not valid claims to knowledge. But they could be overreacting to excessive claims made on its behalf. Some type of intuition is involved in the pursuit of knowledge. For example, creative insights have led to great discoveries in the arts and sciences. Nevertheless, mental knowledge is subject to an uncertainty that cannot be completely eliminated. There are always presuppositions lurking behind the mind's pretensions to knowledge. These presuppositions are never proved because they are already assumed in every demand for proof. If intuition is only a means to this kind of knowledge, it will be exposed to the same uncertainty. In that case, there is little hope for a final solution to the problem of knowledge, or indeed to any human problem. A way out of this impasse looks for a power of knowledge that lies above the mind, whatever name we may choose to call it.

Mind is inherently a confused mixture of truth and falsehood. With its powers of sense perception, reason, and intuition, mind is only a limited form of consciousness. Consciousness is self-revealing and divine; surely it has modes of knowledge and experience lying beyond the purview of the mind. Rational thought cannot reach higher modes of consciousness. Myth and imaginative vision can help, but they depend upon an uncommon degree of openness. Even what is revealed is insufficient, since there is a strong tendency to pull the original inspiration down to a muddling mental level. Only great mystics and yogis have been able to rise above this tendency. In order to progress still further, what is revealed must descend and gradually transform our limited mental nature into a greater power of knowledge and truth. But this needs a sustained aspiration, which leaves behind the opinions and prejudices of philosophers and theologians. This is necessary because their assertions are already mentalized, thus sharing to some extent the general ignorance of the mind.

Feeling plays an important role in the transition to a new mode of knowledge. We made frequent references to the power of feeling throughout this book, beginning with Sri Aurobindo's mention of the ocean of Bliss from which the world arose. Following this there was a discussion of cosmic consciousness through which we become aware of the unity of the cosmos and learn to love it as our very selves. Cosmic consciousness, rather than intellectual curiosity, was identified as the most effective motivation for the study of cosmology. Through it, an individual feels at one with the infinite extent of being: a sense of harmony with the whole cosmos develops. Beyond this mode of consciousness is the transcendent Divine, which the thinking mind finds impossible to grasp: that transcendence is the ultimate source of all that we know and love here.

Many allusions to the Divine Mother stressed her function as the dynamic force behind manifestation, fostering all our efforts toward spiritual growth. The key to recognizing her presence lies in the soul's capacity to love. For love is the link between soul and the universe—that is, the soul's love of the Divine in its multitudinous manifestation. Love like this plays a vital role in the transition to a new mode of being: it is the driving force in human evolution, revealing aspects of the universe inaccessible to the mind. In this regard, cosmic poetry was acknowledged as an indispensable means of expressing spiritual truths. All of the above themes are related to feeling. They point to inner truths that take precedence over the judgmental intrusions of the mind. As such, they are among those "most precious things" referred to by the Mother, which cannot be seen with physical eyes (Plate 1).[1]

At the heart of things lies the soul, the elusive pearl beyond all price, without which the existence of the universe seems pointless. It is a golden bird singing in the night to herald the coming dawn. Soul knows the universe to be one indivisible whole with everything sharing in the divine delight. In the end this realization will prevail. Realizations like these cannot be forced, but grow quietly like flowers appearing out of the soil in the bloom of time. They call for keen aspiration on our part, based on a firm foundation of inner peace. So we have to exercise great patience and restraint in the pursuit of cosmological knowledge. For there are sure to be many surprises still waiting as we tread the path of the soul's emerging presence in our lives.

Whatever view one takes about the poems we have just discussed, there is one important consideration that deserves our attention. Three of them refer to a spiritual power that acts in the universe in a positive way. In the *Bhagavad Gītā,* the Supreme Person incarnates as Krishna to lead man forward into a new consciousness. Dante, in the *Divine Comedy,* focuses on Divine Grace radiating from the Virgin Mary as the power that draws man to God. For Sri Aurobindo, Savitri herself, representing the Divine Mother on earth, defeats the dark Adversary opposing the evolution of the soul. Only Lucretius' poem lacks any reference to a power of grace at work in the world. Even though he invoked the goddess Venus as a creative principle, she was only a metaphor describing the fertility of atomic interactions that are counteracted by the inevitable decay symbolized by Mars. His gods have no influence on the course of events and care nothing about the fate of man. We are left to our own devices in a world that dooms us to final extinction. Lucretius' cosmology may have some appeal as a straightforward, unsentimentalized view of the human condition: it is, nonetheless, tied to a very limited conception of the nature of the universe.

The larger view subscribed to in the other poems brings into play the power of Divine Grace in a universe that has far greater significance. In the poems before us, grace is not only a saving power compensating for human frailty but a cosmic force that raises aspiring individuals to spiritual heights they could not have reached on their own. There is little room for sentimentality in Dante's vision of a cosmos fraught with unsuspected dangers at every turn, and nothing could be more realistic than Krishna's call to Arjuna to participate in the impending battle looming before him. Similarly, the dangerous course of the soul's evolution in Nature envisioned by Sri Aurobindo is not for the faint-hearted. Its culmination, however, presupposes a universe in which a higher power is at work. For who other than an incarnation of the Divine Mother could successfully challenge Death's hold over the world in order to clear the future for an evolving humanity?[2]

This brings us back once again to the Prologue, where we suggested that cosmology could aid us in recovering the divine delight concealed within the universe. But this delight should not be confused with sense pleasure, or even with the contemplative life considered by many philosophers to be man's highest good. The delight referred to is the essence of cosmic existence. It is always present within the universe supporting the endless procession of forms, though rarely experienced by us in our outer consciousness. The Divine above is also below as the soul aspiring for greater perfection in the universe, which is itself a divine manifestation. All existence is one indivisible whole with everything sharing in the divine delight. As Sri Aurobindo expresses it:

> And what is the end of the whole matter? As if honey could taste itself and all its drops together and all its drops could taste each other and each the whole honeycomb as itself, so should the end be with God and the soul of man and the universe.[3]

The Mother's grace is not meant to help us gain worldly success or to promise a glorious reward in heaven for the faithful.[4] After death, there may be a temporary release from life's burdens, but the primary focus of her grace is to thrust the soul forward in the still incomplete task of evolving toward perfection in this world. No human power or institution can guarantee the success of our efforts in this direction, since there are formidable obstacles yet to be overcome. But if life on earth is viewed as progress toward greater light and truth, we will be well on the way toward a better future. Achievement of a divine life would be the highest goal to be sought in an evolving universe. One way to facilitate this is to see the cosmos as a sublime poem in which the power of grace is drawing us beyond our present "all-too-human" failings. The universe *as a whole*, with all four of its faces, is the grandest poem of all, because it embodies the Delight from which all things arose and out of which new beings continue to appear. Delight manifests as beauty in the object (universe) and love in the beholder (soul). When love unites soul with the universe, we can experience this cosmic delight. *Soul then recognizes the whole universe to be its very Self.* In this sense, we can agree with the English poet John Keats, who wrote:

> "Beauty is truth, truth beauty,"—that is all
> Ye know on earth, and all ye need to know.[5]

There are even further reaches of knowledge to be attained, for Supermind has yet to manifest its splendor. Above it lie still unrevealed heights of pure Delight, Consciousness-Force, and Existence that Sri Aurobindo barely hints at. They too must eventually play a role in evolution and the outpouring of the Mother's grace. Although this grace is available to all, its efficacy is keyed to how open we are to receiving it. Openness to grace is a form of surrender to the Divine, but surrender must be distinguished from mere resignation. True surrender is an alert and receptive participation in the Divine Will, whereas resignation is passive submission to forces that would obstruct our evolution.[6] Meanwhile, we push onward in pursuit of the secret soul, which one day will fully reveal its radiant divinity on earth. In Sri Aurobindo's incomparable words:

> A few shall see what none yet understands;
> God shall grow up while the wise men talk and sleep;
> For man shall not know the coming till its hour
> And belief shall be not till the work is done.[7]

Spiritual freedom is related to the scope of a person's vision of the universe as a whole. Challenges confront any serious attempt to achieve a fully integrated vision. But this is not surprising, given a universe as deep and complex—and ultimately inspiring—as the one in which we live.

NOTES

PROLOGUE

1. Sri Aurobindo, *The Secret of the Veda,* included in the *Sri Aurobindo Birth Centenary Library* (Pondicherry, 1973), Vol. 10, p. 102. All subsequent quotations from Sri Aurobindo's works will be keyed to this edition as SABCL.
2. The Sanskrit word *ānanda* can be translated as either bliss or delight, where "bliss" signifies a more passive state and "delight" a more dynamic one. Sri Aurobindo uses it in both ways, but he usually places the emphasis on delight. Pure *ānanda* has a metaphysical quality that should not be confused with ordinary subjective feeling.
3. In the *Ṛg Veda,* illumined knowledge is symbolized by the cows of the Aryans. The cows have been stolen by the Panis (powers of ignorance) and concealed in the dark cave of subconscient physical being. The task of the Rishis (Vedic Seers) was to recover the knowledge and delight represented by the cows.
4. See the suggestive verse in the tenth Book of the *Ṛg Veda:* "With three-fourths Purusha [the Cosmic Man] went up: one-fourth of him again was here." *Ṛg Veda* 10. 90. 4 (Griffith translation). There are also four states of Brahman mentioned in the Mandukya Upanishad. Note, in addition, the four worlds of the *Kabbalah,* where the physical world (*Asiyyah*) is the last in a series of emanations from the Infinite (*Ein Sof*). In a similar vein, the four angelic faces appearing in Ezekiel's "Vision of the Chariot" have a cosmological significance related to the fixed signs of the zodiac.
5. "Psychic" refers generally to that which lies beyond the physical world and its laws. But it also exists in an individualized form that Sri Aurobindo calls the "psychic being" (or spiritual soul). He uses this term to distinguish it from the mind and vital emotions. Soul *feels,* but it does not "emote." Since "psychic" has other meanings as well, the word "occult"—which simply means "hidden"—could have been used when referring to the psychic face of the universe. Unfortunately, this has acquired sinister connotations best avoided in a cosmological context.
6. In this book, the universe with all four faces is taken to be the universe *as a whole.*
7. This is done, for example, by Fritjof Capra in *The Tao of Physics: An Exploration of the Parallels between Modern Physics and Eastern Mysticism* (Berkeley, 1975).
8. Compare Leibniz's contemporary, Spinoza, who avoided overlapping categories by distinguishing between the different attributes of a single substance, which he called God or Nature. But this was a purely formal solution to a more complex problem.

9. Many scientists would disagree, claiming that the primary motive for science is intellectual curiosity. This is true enough, as far as it goes, but the view taken here is that even the complete satisfaction of curiosity, if it were attainable, would not be sufficient to establish an authentic relationship with the universe.
10. Wordsworth, William. "Lines Composed a Few Miles above Tintern Abbey." *Wordsworth.* Selected, with an introduction and notes, by David Ferry (New York, 1959), pp.35-36.
11. Ibid., p. 36. Sri Aurobindo called Wordsworth and his fellow Romantics "Poets of the Dawn" because he perceived a new spiritual impulse beginning to emerge in their poetry.

CHAPTER I. CONSCIOUSNESS AND THE UNIVERSE

1. Compare this with the Vedic image of two birds on the same tree: one of them flits about in the branches below while the other sits quietly above enjoying the view.
2. The German philosopher Schopenhauer claimed that "the world is my representation" (idea), and concluded that without the ego it is nothing. In contrast, the approach to cosmology being offered here is that each person is a representation (microcosm) of a world that exists independent of the ego. The reality of this world is known by the soul.
3. The point is made succinctly by the Zen Master Sokei-an in an essay titled "Where Bodhisattvas Abide." He maintains that ordinary people live in their own personal worlds, but bodhisattvas abide in a world that has an independent nature of its own. This can be illustrated by an example drawn from everyday life: when a felon sees a policeman he becomes frightened, whereas a law-abiding citizen realizes that there is nothing to fear. See Sokei-An, *Cat's Yawn* (New York, 1947), p. 45. Sokei-an's life is described, mostly in his own words, in *Holding the Lotus to the Rock,* edited by Michael Hotz (New York, 2002).
4. In ancient Egypt, the constellation of Orion was associated with Osiris, the god of death and resurrection, but I was not aware of this at the time.
5. The professor was Milton K. Munitz. He was an excellent teacher, and went on to write numerous books and articles on cosmology.
6. *The Rubaiyat of Omar Khayyam,* XXVII, translated by Edward Fitzgerald (many editions). Although this passage is usually interpreted negatively as a reference to the vanity of intellectual discussions about the universe, Paramhansa Yogananda claims that it is really a profound tribute to Omar's teachers, who taught him how to perceive higher spiritual truth. Omar was a Sufi, and Yogananda's interpretation clarifies many poetic images and allusions that remain opaque in Fitzgerald's hedonistic rendering of the poem. For further details, see Yogananda, Paramhansa, *The Rubaiyat of Omar Khayyam Explained,* pp. 119-121.

7. Philosophers have worked out several compromises with simple materialism, such as naturalism and epiphenomenalism, but physical matter and energy remain the basic realities.
8. The triune quality of divine being is captured in the great Vedantic formula Sat-Chit-Ananda, Existence-Consciousness-Bliss. They are an essential unity (Saccidānanda), for Existence is infinite Consciousness and infinite Consciousness is pure Bliss (because there is nothing outside that could disturb it). For Sri Aurobindo, this formula points beyond the philosophical distinction between Nirguna Brahman (Impersonal God without attributes) and Saguna Brahman (Personal God with attributes) toward a more inclusive total reality. As will be seen later, Consciousness is also a force, or the creative energy that brings forth the universe.
9. For those who are familiar with Indian philosophy, this will be recognized as the position of Advaita Vedanta. Certain schools of Buddhism hold similar views.
10. Some quantum physicists claim that consciousness is active in subatomic processes. But, even if this is true, its extent of operation and level of involvement still need to be clarified.
11. In this context, Consciousness is not to be confused with "mind," which is a limited form of it. The manifestation of mind in the brain is the *physical* mind. This is the only aspect of mind studied by neuroscientists, who ignore its deeper nature.
12. The view taken here is crucial in what follows. There are only a few concerns of this kind that are relevant to cosmology. For example, our answer to the question "What is the nature of ultimate reality?" is *Consciousness*. If one then asks "Is the universe real?" the reply is that it exists but has no inherent reality of its own apart from Consciousness. And the response to "Do we have any real freedom?" will be yes—but only the soul is really free. These answers, and others like them, are based on a comprehensive vision of the world. Visions can be criticized, of course, but not in the same way as causal explanations. Trying to show that a vision is false misses the point, which would be to see it in terms of a larger, more inclusive vision. Comprehensive visions usually possess some truth, no matter how partial they may be.
13. Sri Aurobindo, *The Synthesis of Yoga,* SABCL, Vol. 20, p. 247.
14. Sri Aurobindo, *Letters on Yoga,* SABCL, Vol. 22, p. 315.
15. See Richard M. Bucke, *Cosmic Consciousness: A Study in the Evolution of the Human Mind* (New York, 1959). This book has been in continuous circulation for more than a century.
16. Ibid., p. 10.
17. Walt Whitman, *Leaves of Grass* (New York, 1983), "Passage to India," p. 331.
18. Ibid., pp.334-335.
19. Ibid., "On the Beach at Night Alone," p. 211.
20. Bucke, *Cosmic Consciousness,* p. 5.
21. Ibid., p. 384.

22. This is a special term used by Sri Aurobindo to designate the soul. There is a difference between the vital (or emotional) soul, which is commonly felt as "soul," and a pure manifestation of Consciousness like the *psychic being*.
23. It is also possible that a fully developed psychic being will be united with the Jivātman, which is the central being of each person. We ignore subtle psychological distinctions made by Sri Aurobindo among soul, psyche, psychic entity, and psychic being, as they are not essential to the present discussion. When soul is mentioned in this book it will refer to the *psychic being,* or true personality, not the vital soul.
24. Compare Faust's cringing in the presence of the Spirit of the Earth, in *Goethe's Faust,* the original German and a new translation and introduction by Walter Kaufmann (Garden City, 1961), pp. 101-103.
25. Sri Aurobindo, *Letters on Yoga,* SABCL (vol. 22), pp. 316-317.
26. See especially the section "Spiritual Evolution" in Chapter VII.
27. The noted French historian of science Alexandre Koyré entitled an influential book on the Scientific Revolution in this way. See A. Koyré, *From the Closed World to the Infinite Universe* (New York, 1958). Bruno is discussed in Chapter II.
28. Dorothea Waley Singer, *Giordano Bruno: His Life and Thought, with an Annotated Translation of His Work On the Infinite Universe and Worlds* (New York, 1950), pp. 248-249.
29. There were other influences on Bruno's thought, which we will take up in Chapter VI on "Traditional Cosmology." The historian Francis Yates believed that the Church Inquisitors were more concerned about Bruno's association with Renaissance magic than with his cosmological views.
30. Bruno was put to death in Rome in 1600 AD, a year that was taken by the English philosopher Alfred North Whitehead to mark the inauguration of the new scientific picture of the universe. See his *Science and the Modern World* (New York, 1969), p. 1. Nevertheless, Bruno's cosmology goes far beyond science.
31. There are several biographies of Bruno available in English. Although somewhat outdated, J. Lewis McIntyre, *Giordano Bruno: Mystic Martyr* (Aberdeen, 1903) gives a general overview of his life and philosophy. For a careful study of Bruno's philosophical cosmology, see Paul-Henri Michel, *The Cosmology of Giordano Bruno* (Ithaca, 1962). Bruno's popular dialogues in Italian have been translated into English. They were written in the England of Sydney and Shakespeare, and may have influenced these great Elizabethan poets. A spirited defense of Bruno as a cosmologist has recently appeared in Ramon G. Mendoza, *The Acentric Labyrinth: Giordano Bruno's Prelude to Contemporary Cosmology* (Rockport, MA, 1995). There is much to be commended in this perceptive study of Bruno's vision of the universe.
32. In mythical cosmology, the psychic universe encompasses the physical universe, which is assumed to be dependent on it (see Chapter III).
33. "Mechanism" is derived from the Greek *mēchanē* (a machine). Interpretations of mechanism have varied with the progress of science. In

the nineteenth century, it referred to the doctrine that the universe, like any machine, could be explained entirely by the laws of mechanics. Today, it implies that the universe is governed by the laws of physics as presently understood.

CHAPTER II. MYTHICAL COSMOLOGY

1. See, for example, books by the archaeoastronomer Anthony Aveni, especially *Ancient Astronomers* (Washington, 1993) and *Stairways to the Stars: Skywatching in Three Great Ancient Cultures* (New York, 1997).
2. The bright and dark waters were, presumably, the result of a differentiation that occurred in the primeval ocean.
3. Many scholars have admired Babylonian arithmetical astronomy, but the astronomers were also priests who were presumably committed to their great creation myth, the *Enuma Elish*. It remained for the more philosophical Greeks to introduce geometrical models into cosmology.
4. Giorgio de Santillana and Hertha von Dechend, *Hamlet's Mill: An Essay Investigating the Origins of Human Knowledge and its Transmission through Myth* (Boston, 1977). In their book, the authors proposed a cosmological model similar to that taught by some magical schools in the ancient world. But they were apparently unaware of these esoteric parallels.
5. The literal meaning of the term *universe* is "turned as one."
6. Readers who would like more details about this interpretation can consult the section "Intermezzo: A Guide for the Perplexed," in *Hamlet's Mill*, pp. 56-75.
7. This is a very important point. It is worthwhile to keep in mind the distinction made by Carl Jung between a symbol and a sign. A *sign* designates something that can be known in a straightforward, conventional way, whereas a *symbol* (especially a mythic one) embodies a psychic power that operates in a secret manner known only through its effects. See Carl G. Jung (ed.) *Man and his Symbols* (New York, 1976), pp. 3-4.
8. Some mythologists distinguish between *myths* (sacred narratives) and *folktales* (secular stories). The main difference is that authentic myths possess symbolic truth, whereas folktales are purely fictional. For useful distinctions between myths, folktales, and legends, see Alan Dundes (Ed.), *Sacred Narrative: Readings in the Theory of Myth* (Berkeley, 1984), pp. 1,5, *et passim*.
9. This usage should not be confused with the "psychic being," a term employed by Sri Aurobindo to refer to an aspect of the divine spirit that is evolving in the world.
10. This was the title given to a television documentary about him, later published with the same title. There is a recent biography of Campbell by Stephen and Robin Larsen, *A Fire in the Mind: The Life of Joseph Campbell* (New York, 1991).
11. Joseph Campbell, *Myths to Live By* (New York, 1972), p. 13.

12. Robert A. Segal gives a scholarly critique of Campbell's view of myth in "Joseph Campbell's Theory of Myth," Dundes, *Sacred Narrative,* pp. 256-269. See also Segal's more extended survey of Campbell's work, *Joseph Campbell: An Introduction* (New York, 1990).
13. For a clear statement of Jung's position, see C.G. Jung, "The Psychology of the Child Archetype," in Dundes, *Sacred Narrative*, especially pp. 249-250.
14. Bronislaw Malinowski, *Magic, Science and Religion and Other Essays* (Garden City, 1959).
15. Mircea Eliade, *Cosmos and History: The Myth of the Eternal Return* (New York, 1959).
16. Sri Aurobindo, *The Secret of the Veda,* SABCL, Vol. 10.
17. *The Secret of the Veda,* SABCL, Vol. 10, p. 4.
18. For a recent review of the evidence for this, see Georg Feuerstein, Subhash Kak, and David Frawley, *In Search of the Cradle of Civilization: New Light on Ancient India* (Wheaton., 1995).
19. *The Secret of the Veda,* SABCL, Vol. 10, pp. 5-6.
20. Ibid., p.6.
21. Ibid.
22. Ibid., pp. 225, 235.
23. Ibid., p. 37. Suggestions of cosmic consciousness abound in the *Ṛg Veda.* This is especially evident in references to the god Varuna (a name related to the Greek *Uranus*) who is closely associated with the *Ṛta.* Varuna represents the oceanic wideness of the Divine Consciousness pervading the cosmos. Symbolically, he is correlated with etheric space and the starry heavens. His all-embracing spaciousness and purity support the universe and protect it by upholding the *Ṛta.*
24. A similar idea is found in ancient Egypt, where the goddess Maat represents the correct ordering of the universe. She wears a feather on her head symbolizing Truth and Justice. In the *Book of the Dead,* the heart of a dead person is weighed against the feather. If its sins make it heavier than the feather, it is judged accordingly.
25. As a sample of this literature, we may note two books by David Kinsley: *Hindu Goddesses: Visions of the Divine Feminine in the Hindu Religious Tradition* (Berkeley, 1988) and *The Goddess' Mirror: Visions of the Divine from East to West* (New York, 1989). A convenient collection of essays is Carl Olson (ed.), *The Book of the Goddess Past and Present: An Introduction to Her Religion* (New York, 1990).
26. J.J. Bachofen, *Myth, Religion, and Mother Right: Selected Writings of J. J. Bachofen* (Princeton, 1973).
27. Marija Gimbutas, *The Goddesses and Gods of Old Europe: Myths and Cult Images* (Berkeley, 1982). See also her more comprehensive study, *The Language of the Goddess* (San Francisco, 1991).
28. As will be seen in the next chapter, however, the "Stanzas of Dzyan" suggest that the situation is not altogether hopeless.
29. Genesis 1:1-8 (Revised Standard Version).
30. In *The Mystical Theology,* for example, Dionysius the Areopagite writes: "The Divine Dark is nought else but that inaccessible light wherein the

Lord is said to dwell." Quoted by Evelyn Underhill in *Mysticism: A Study in the Nature and Development of Man's Spiritual Consciousness* (New York, 1955) p. 347.

31. When man is referred to as the "image of God," this would seem to indicate that the Biblical God is *androgynous*. Otherwise, half the human race would be excluded from the divine image.
32. Daniel C. Matt, *The Essential Kabbalah: The Heart of Jewish Mysticism* (San Francisco, 1996), p. 94.
33. For a more detailed examination of the doctrine of creation in Lurianic Kabbalah, see Gershom Scholem, *Kabbalah* (New York, 1978), pp 128-144.
34. *Chhandogya Upanishad,* in Swami Nikhilananda, *The Upanishads*, Volume Four (New York, 1959), pp. 218-219.
35. The meaning of "chaos" in myth should not be confused with scientific chaos theory, where the chaotic behavior of a physical system follows from the laws of physics. Chaos results when tiny differences in the initial conditions of a process grow so large that the results cannot be predicted with absolute accuracy. But the *mythical* chaos precedes the laws of physics.
36. The Upanishads originated in ancient India. They consist of philosophical discourses dealing with a wide variety of spiritual subjects, particularly the identity of Ātman (the Self) with Brahman (the Absolute).
37. Ananda K. Coomaraswamy: *The Dance of Shiva* (New York, 1957), p. 78.
38. For a brief summary of the calculation involved, see Joseph Campbell, *The Mythic Image* (Princeton, 1974), pp. 141-144.
39. The term Brahman should not be confused with Brahmā. Brahmā is the nominative form of Brahman, from which it differs only in gender. Whereas Brahman refers to the impersonal reality underlying the universe, Brahmā is a personal God. Therefore, Brahmā (like Śiva) can appear and disappear in successive cycles.
40. See the discussion of the "Oscillating Universe Model" in Chapter IV.
41. Chapter III, *The Night of the Universe.*
42. *Collected Works of the Mother,* Centenary Edition (Pondicherry, 1985), Vol. 4, p. 23 fn. The Mother, Mirra Alfassa Richard, was born in France but lived more than half her life in India. She originally met Sri Aurobindo in Pondicherry and, after a four-year stay in Japan, returned to India and subsequently became the dynamic center of the Sri Aurobindo Ashram. Her connection with Sri Aurobindo is briefly touched upon in Chapter VII.
43. The traditions she is referring to may have roots in Kabbalistic lore, where it is said that before the creation of this world, God had created and destroyed others that were not satisfactory for his purpose.
44. Physicists employ the second law of thermodynamics (entropy) to define the unique direction of time. Physical systems generally tend to evolve toward states of higher entropy (greater disorder). But this does not really explain it. The second law is only statistical, entropy being theoretically reversible (though this is extremely unlikely). Attempts to account for time asymmetry in terms of physics alone are inconclusive. Therefore, appeal to

a metaphysical basis for time's direction is a reasonable option, unless we wish to do away with time altogether. We will see later (in Chapter VII) that spiritual evolution supersedes entropy. The soul in the universe requires a progressive future for its full development and this, more than entropy, determines the direction of time.

45. Much has been written about *Ākāsha*. It is a subtle state of matter pervading the physical universe, which floats in it. There are several gradations of Akasha, from extremely subtle to more gross, but the details will not be explored here. In this connection, the ancient Stoic conception of *pneuma* is also worth noting. *Pneuma* was thought of as a tenuous material substance filling the whole world. The Stoics considered it to be a living power marked by inner stresses and tensions. The physical universe was embedded in it, and derived its form and coherence from it.

CHAPTER III. THE STANZAS OF DZYAN

1. A recent biography of Madame Blavatsky that is reasonably objective concerning the details of her life and work is Sylvia Cranston, *HPB: The Extraordinary Life and Influence of Helena Blavatsky, Founder of the Modern Theosophical Movement* (New York, 1993). For a scholarly study of the movement she initiated, see Bruce F. Campbell, *Ancient Wisdom Revived: A History of the Theosophical Movement* (Berkeley, 1980).
2. Sri Krishna Prem and Sri Madhava Ashish, *Man, the Measure of All Things in the Stanzas of Dzyan* (Madras, 1966), p. 10. This book is a detailed commentary on the Stanzas of Dzyan from a psychic point of view.
3. H.P. Blavatsky, *The Secret Doctrine: The Synthesis of Science, Religion, and Philosophy* (Pasadena, 1952), Vol. I, p. viii.
4. Ibid., pp. 14-17.
5. Ibid., p. 13.
6. See *Man, the Measure of All Things,* pp. 1-34.
7. Sri Ramana Maharshi, the great sage of Arunachala, called him "a rare combination of a jnani and a bhakta." A memoir is available, written by Dilip Kumar Roy, *Yogi Sri Krishnaprem* (Bombay, 1968).
8. *Man, the Measure of All Things,* p. 34.
9. *The Selected Poetry and Prose of Shelley,* edited by Harold Bloom (New York, 1966), p. 448.
10. See Joseph Campbell, *The Inner Reaches of Outer Space: Metaphor as Myth and as Religion* (New York, 1986), Chapters III-V. In India it is part of the classical *Kundalini Yoga.* A comparable system is suggested by the Kabbalistic tree of the *sefirot.*
11. In *The Secret Doctrine,* the psychic universe is divided into seven levels (including the physical) corresponding to seven similar ones in the constitution of man. But the number of levels may vary in other systems. The important point is that there are different gradations of being in the psychic world.
12. *The Secret Doctrine,* Vol. I, p. 54.

13. Sri Aurobindo, *Savitri,* SABCL, Vol. 28, Book One, Canto One, p.1.
14. *Rig Veda* X. 129. 4-5 (Sri Aurobindo's translation).
15. *Man, the Measure of All Things,* p.31.
16. *The Secret Doctrine,* Vol. I, p. 21.
17. *Man, the Measure of All Things,* p. 32.
18. *The Secret Doctrine,* Vol. I, pp. 27, 28.
19. See the section on "The Importance of Transitional States" in this chapter.
20. *The Secret Doctrine,* Stanza I.8.
21. Physical space is defined by a *metric* that places restrictions on space in general. It specifies the geometry of a space (including its dimensionality) and renders it measurable. Space in general, or "universal space," is equivalent to a dimensionless point: it has no intrinsic metric of its own. The mind cannot exclude this possibility and must resort to stories to make it intelligible. For example, if space is imagined as an extensive medium, we could say that the Divine imposes a metric upon it. If it is viewed as a dimensionless point, the Divine could be said to enter into relations with itself out of which a metric emerges. In physics, this is similar to the alternative approaches of general relativity and quantum mechanics. Which theory is favored depends on its usefulness in dealing with situations that interest scientists.
22. A useful presentation of this controversy is *The Leibniz-Clarke Correspondence,* edited with an introduction and notes by H.G. Alexander (Manchester, 1956).
23. *The Secret Doctrine,* Stanza II.2.
24. Subjectively, this can be compared to what happens when we begin to awaken from sleep. The world has not yet fully appeared, but we are just becoming aware of it.
25. See Stanza III.7, in subsection *The Awakening of Cosmos.*
26. Three stages of realization regarding this distinction can be traced in Indian philosophy. In the first stage, the Sāṁkhya system discriminates between Puruṣa (Soul) and Prakṛti (Nature). They are distinct realities, corresponding roughly to the difference between spirit and matter. Vedanta, on the other hand, recognizes only one reality, Brahman (the Absolute), with Māyā as its inscrutable power to appear as the empirical world. Finally, some systems inspired by Tantra maintain the full equality of Īśvara (the Lord) and Śakti (Creative Force). Although they can be distinguished mentally, both refer to the same reality viewed in alternative modes.
27. See Stanza I.2. To understand this verse, we must distinguish between the passage of time and time as mere extension (here called "duration"). Duration is free of the distinctions between past, present, and future that are parts of our ordinary conception of time. In this sense, it is similar to universal space and is part of the pure extension of Being. The potential for a passage from past to future is inherent in it, just as dimensionality is a potential of universal space (see note 21). In the Stanzas of Dzyan, flowing time is like a living entity that grows by assimilating the past. It sleeps in

pralaya and awakens with a new universe, enriched by the experience of previous ones.

28. There is a recurring problem with the quotations used in this book. Many were written before the feminist revolution took a prominent place in our culture. Hence they often include masculine terms. For the sake of clarity, these are allowed to remain wherever they occur.
29. Ideally, families are bound together by love, which is also *in origin* a cosmic principle. Love is the bond that holds the universe together in perfect unity, as Plato suggested in *Timaeus* 32 c. See Chapter VI, Section 3 on Plato's *Timaeus*. This is not brought out explicitly in the Stanzas of Dzyan.
30. Mystical relationships are not spatial in essence. We conceive them in relative terms of higher and lower, inner and outer, which can be represented visually as a vertical line or concentric circles, respectively. Both are ways the mind uses to understand a universe transcending its limited powers of knowledge.
31. This is a reference to the cosmic powers necessary to manifest the Universal Mind. They have different functions in the universe, but are not its "creators." Rather, they are spiritual principles on higher levels of the cosmos, that in various traditions have been called gods, *devas,* angelic hosts, *dhyān chohans, dhyāni buddhas,* etc.
32. Stanza I.5. The "new wheel" is a cosmic cycle during which Universal Mind unfolds the potentialities of a new universe.
33. *Man, the Measure of All Things,* pp. 50-51.
34. See Stanza III.2.
35. *The Secret Doctrine,* Vol. I, p. 38.
36. Refer to "Beethoven's Ninth Symphony: A Brief Analysis" at the end of the chapter.
37. *The Secret Doctrine,* Vol. I, pp. 28-30.
38. One school of Indian philosophy, *Kashmir Shaivism*, postulates an initial vibration (*spanda*) of consciousness that fills space with pulsations of creative energy. In modern physics, the theory of superstrings reduces the whole universe to microscopic patterns made by vibrating strings. Could this be a convergence of insights from two different approaches to cosmology?
39. Sri Aurobindo, *Savitri,* SABCL, Vol. 28, Book One, Canto One, p. 3.
40. *Man, the Measure of All Things,* pp. 163-164.
41. See Stanza III.7.
42. Cp. Genesis 1: 6-7.
43. Stanza II.2.
44. Karma is usually defined as "the law of *moral* cause and effect," but it can also apply to causality in general.
45. *The Secret Doctrine,* Vol. II, pp. 304-306. In the case of an electrical wire, for example, the immediate cause of a shock is touching the wire. The power of electricity itself, however, is simply what it is by virtue of its place in the cosmic order. Compare the following quote: "Let us then call Karma no longer a Law, but rather the many-sided dynamic truth of all

action and life, the organic movement here of the Infinite." Sri Aurobindo, *The Hour of God,* SABCL, Vol. 17, p. 34.

46. The modern conception of a "mathematical field" is closer to the idea of karma presented here. See "Laws of Nature" in Chapter IV.
47. This is related to the pilgrimage of the Son referred to in Stanza I.5.
48. According to Leibniz, the monads were causally isolated from one another, and thus had no connections at all. In other words, they were "windowless."
49. This is the Hua Yen (Japanese, *Kegon*), or "Flower Garland" School.
50. See Chapter VII on "Evolutionary Cosmology" for further details.
51. This subject is dealt with in *The Secret Doctrine,* Vol. II.
52. *The Secret Doctrine,* Vol. II, p. 170.

CHAPTER IV. MODERN SCIENTIFIC COSMOLOGY

1. With the appearance of mind, soul leaves behind the dreamlike state of the psychic world in which the difference between subject and object is weak and indistinct. Mind perceives the world as a separate object in relation to a subjective self or ego. Although this has some practical advantages, the inner nature of the object remains unknown. The progress of the soul lies not in returning to a lower level but in evolving into something that transcends the divisive tendencies of the mind. What, then, should we call "knowledge"? For it would become a *knowledge by identity* with the object.
2. See Colin A. Ronan, *The Shorter Science and Civilisation in China (Vol. I): An Abridgement of Joseph Needham's Original Text* (Cambridge, 1980), pp. 285-291. Needham discusses the background of the concept of "laws of nature" in Europe and contrasts it with the lack of a similar concept in ancient China.
3. Maxwell's equations of electromagnetism, for example, are sometimes called "laws," but they are actually a concise notation for describing the mathematical properties of the electromagnetic field. See the subsection on *The Awakening of Cosmos* in the previous chapter, especially note 45.
4. Technically, a "field" in physics is a mathematical construct describing a region of space in which forces are present at each point.
5. This subject is discussed again in connection with "singularities" in cosmology (see "The Standard Big Bang Model" in this chapter).
6. For the historical circumstances surrounding the Great Debate and its resolution by Hubble, see Robert W. Smith, "Cosmology 1900-1931," in Norriss S. Hetherington (ed.) *Cosmology: Historical, Literary, Philosophical, Religious, and Scientific Perspectives* (New York, 1993), pp. 329-345. More detail is given in R. W. Smith, *The Expanding Universe: Astronomy's "Great Debate" 1900-1931* (Cambridge, 1982).
7. Hubble's law is expressed as follows:
   (Radial velocity of a galaxy) =
   (Hubble's constant) x (Distance to the galaxy)
   or more concisely, $v = H \times d$.

8. Among the countless books on relativity, Einstein's original attempt at a popular exposition of his ideas is matchless for its clarity and charm. Written shortly after he completed his general theory, it lacks many essential details, but remains a classic in its field. Einstein was the first to realize that the general theory had important things to say about the whole universe, thus opening the subject of cosmology to further scientific exploration. See Albert Einstein, *Relativity: The Special and General Theory* (New York, 1961). There have been many editions of this book since its appearance in German in 1917. I read the book initially when I was sixteen years old, but understood very little of it at that time. Still, I was particularly struck by Part 3 concerning the "universe as a whole." Having recently discovered that the stars were organized into galaxies, the idea that the universe could be grasped *in toto* as a finite yet unbounded hypersphere was fascinating. Cosmology has progressed far beyond this today, yet the insight remains priceless. I am now convinced that Einstein had a brief but intense experience of cosmic consciousness. It shaped the course of his later research and led him to an increased emphasis on mathematics as the key to understanding the physical world.
9. This statement can be expressed mathematically as a relation between two masses, m and m', and the distance between them: $F = G\ (m \times m' / r^2)$, where G is the gravitational constant that represents the strength of gravity in our universe. The force of attraction, F, acts along the line connecting the masses.
10. Mendel Sachs, *Relativity in Our Time: From Physics to Human Relations* (London, 1993), p. 2.
11. Light rays follow the shortest distance between two points. This is called a *geodesic* in non-Euclidean geometry.
12. There have been different explanations of a falling body. When Aristotle saw a stone fall, he assumed that it was the natural tendency of a heavy body to move toward the center of the world. Newton, on the other hand, attributed the fall of an apple to a force attracting it to the earth. Einstein was impressed by the statement of a man who had fallen from a building. The man said he did not feel a force pulling him down, but that the ground seemed to rise up to meet him.
13. Newton believed that space was the medium in which God directly perceived material bodies in motion. A careful critique of his ideas on space, time, and the divine sensorium is given in E. A. Burtt, *The Metaphysical Foundations of Modern Physical Science* (London, 1949), pp. 243-263; see also *The Leibniz-Clarke Correspondence,* edited with an introduction and notes by H. G. Alexander (Manchester, 1956).
14. Amir D. Aczel, *God's Equation: Einstein, Relativity, and the Expanding Universe* (New York, 1999).
15. It was inscribed in the original German above the fireplace of the faculty lounge at Princeton University. Although its meaning is open to several interpretations, the remark seems to convey Einstein's belief that the secrets of the universe are not concealed to deceive us but follow from its profound sublimity. If the cosmos were not so mysterious, it would not

hold our interest for very long. A detailed examination of Einstein's religious views can be found in Max Jammer, *Einstein and Religion* (Princeton, 1998).

16. Albert Einstein, Foreword to Dagobert D. Runes (Editor), *Spinoza Dictionary* (New York, 1951).
17. Spinoza, *Ethics,* Part Two, Proposition XLIV, Corollary 2.
18. Albert Einstein, *Ideas and Opinions* (New York, 1954), p. 38.
19. In tensor form, the equation is written: $R_{ij} - 1/2\ g_{ij}\ R = -8\pi G\ T_{ij}$, where R_{ij} is the *Ricci Curvature Tensor* (a complicated function of the metric tensor and its derivatives), g_{ij} the *Metric Tensor*, R the *Ricci Curvature Scalar*, T_{ij} the *Mass-Energy Tensor*, and G the *Gravitational Constant.* This is the same G that appears in the equation expressing Newton's law of gravitation. The expression on the left represents the curvature of spacetime, while that on the right depends on the distribution of matter and energy.
20. Note the discussion of "universal space" in Chapter III, subsection *The Night of the Universe.*
21. See E. R. Harrison, *Cosmology: The Science of the Universe* (Cambridge, 1981), Chapter 5, "Containment and the Cosmic Edge."
22. Brian Greene, *The Elegant Universe: Superstrings, Hidden Dimensions, and the Quest for the Ultimate Theory* (New York, 1999), is an excellent introduction to string theory.
23. "Universe at large" is more appropriate than "universe as a whole," since the latter term (as used in this book) includes more than the physical universe.
24. This is discussed in Chapter V, section on "A Runaway Universe?".
25. See the description of de Sitter's universe below.
26. Harrison discusses the historical background of Mach's Principle, including Mach's influence on Einstein, in *Cosmology,* pp. 176-179. One formulation of the principle is the following: "[It] states that local inertial forces are determined by the distribution and quantity of matter in the universe."(Ibid., p. 178).
27. For a description of scientific developments in this period, see Sir Arthur Eddington, *The Expanding Universe* (Ann Arbor, 1958), Chapter I.
28. Recent observations of the cosmic background radiation using the Wilkinson Microwave Anisotropy Probe (WMAP) provide strong evidence that the universe is *flat.* This corresponds well with the prediction of the Inflationary Universe model to be discussed in Chapter V.
29. For a popular exposition of this model, see George Gamow, *The Creation of the Universe* (New York, 1970).
30. The historical background of Olbers' Paradox is discussed in Harrison, *Cosmology,* pp. 249-251. Also see his more extended treatment of the subject in E. R. Harrison, *Darkness at Night: A Riddle of the Universe* (Cambridge, 1987).
31. For more detail, consult Steven Weinberg, *The First Three Minutes: A Modern View of the Origin of the Universe* (New York, 1977).

32. Compare the analogy of a soap bubble, where it is the skin that stretches as the bubble expands.
33. For example, Tolman states that "a continued succession of irreversible expansions and contractions . . . would seem very strange from the point of view of classical thermodynamics, which would predict an ultimate state of maximum entropy and rest as the result of continued irreversible processes in an isolated system." Richard C. Tolman, *Relativity, Thermodynamics, and Cosmology* (New York, 1987), pp. 439-440; also see his diagram (Figure 10) on p. 443.
34. The historical background is reviewed by Helge Kragh, "Steady State Theory," in Hetherington, *Cosmology,* pp. 391-403. For a more extensive treatment, see Helge Kragh, *Cosmology and Controversy: The Historical Development of Two Theories of the Universe* (Princeton, 1996).

CHAPTER V. THE BIG BANG AND BEYOND

1. An interesting formulation of the relationship between harmony and variety was given by Leibniz. During a discussion of his theory of monads, he states: "And this is the way to obtain as great a variety as possible, but with the greatest possible order [harmony]; that is, it is the way to obtain as much perfection as possible." *Monadology,* article 58, Philip P. Weiner (ed.), *Leibniz: Selections* (New York, 1951), p. 544. His point seems to be that too much order, or harmony, without an adequate amount of variety would impoverish the universe, while too much variety without harmony would be an indiscriminate chaos.
2. Einstein once said that what he really wanted to know was whether God had a choice in creating the universe. In an *absolute* sense, of course, the divine consciousness is free from all needs and limitations, but it is also free to limit itself for some purpose. If a final theory is found, it might be so restrictive that only one universe would be possible. In any case, one could say (in a *relative* sense) that once the divine choice is made, everything that follows will be necessary for fulfilling its purpose.
3. A word of caution is perhaps warranted at this point. It is nicely stated by Goethe:

   Gray, my dear friend, is every theory,
   And green alone life's golden tree.

   Goethe's Faust, op.cit., p. 207. But this is asserted by Mephisto, and should not be taken as the last word on the subject.
4. Albert Einstein and Leopold Infeld, *The Evolution of Physics: From Early Concepts to Relativity and Quanta* (New York, 1938), p. 297.
5. For the *wave function* ψ of a particle with mass m moving in a potential V, the Schrödinger equation may be written:
   $-\hbar^2/2m \{ \partial^2\psi/\partial x^2 + \partial^2\psi/\partial y^2 + \partial^2\psi/\partial z^2 \} + V\psi = i\hbar\partial\psi/\partial t,$
   where $\hbar$ is Planck's constant, which appears in the equation as an imaginary number (i = the square root of -1). This partial differential equation governs the orderly development of a quantum system. In this

sense, quantum mechanics is fully deterministic, but the wave function itself is interpreted in a probabilistic way.

6. He drew this idea from the philosophy of Aristotle, who introduced the term *potentia* to describe the tendency of a latent form to become actualized. It is also reminiscent, we may add, of the conception of "chaos" in mythical cosmology.
7. See, for example, David Bohm, *Wholeness and the Implicate Order* (London, 1983). The notion of an implicate order suggests the view of the ancient Greek philosopher Anaxagoras that everything is contained in everything.
8. Another place that physics appears to touch a boundary concerns the inner nature of a particle. Physicists speak of "point-like" particles, but points are abstract geometrical entities without discernible physical properties. Recent experiments indicate that a fundamental particle like the proton has a complex internal structure made up of quarks and gluons. But these may themselves be made up of even smaller entities. See Robert Kunzig, "The Glue That Holds the World Together," *Discover,* July 2000 (Volume 21, Number 7), pp. 64-69.
9. For example, if the position x is exactly known (i.e., $\Delta x = 0$), the momentum must be unknown (since Δp becomes infinite), and vice versa.
10. Edward P. Tryon, "Is the Universe a Vacuum Fluctuation," in John Leslie (ed.), *Physical Cosmology and Philosophy* (New York, 1990), pp. 216-219.
11. The idea of multidimensional spaces has become scientifically manageable in some of the recent versions of string theory.
12. In mathematics, "imaginary" does not imply "nonexistent," but has a well-defined numerical sense. So-called "complex numbers" have both real and imaginary components, and these play an important role in Hawking's analysis.
13. A good summary of recent scientific cosmology, which includes a discussion of these topics, can be found in Martin Rees, *Before the Beginning: Our Universe and Others* (Reading, 1997).
14. For an exhaustive treatment of different varieties of the anthropic principle, see J. D. Barrow and F. J. Tipler, *The Anthropic Cosmological Principle* (New York, 1986).
15. This is the Inflationary Universe model discussed in the next section.
16. Edgar Allan Poe, *Eureka: An Essay on the Material and Spiritual Universe* (New York, 1848). A convenient place to find it is in Harold Beaver (ed.), *The Science Fiction of Edgar Allan Poe* (New York, 1976), pp. 211-309. Poe's work is dedicated to the nineteenth century naturalist Alexander von Humboldt whose multivolumed book *Kosmos* was just beginning to appear in English translation.
17. *Eureka,* in Beaver, *The Science Fiction of Edgar Allan Poe,* p. 306.
18. Ibid.
19. Ibid., pp. 306-307.
20. Ibid., p. 262.
21. Scalar fields, like the temperature at each point in a room, are purely numerical. Unlike gravitational and electrical fields, they do not point in a

given direction. A constant scalar field is indistinguishable from a vacuum; it could only be noticed if variations occur within it. The presence of scalar fields in space is thought to give elementary particles like electrons their masses. In the context of inflationary models, they generate a repulsive force that can overcome gravity.

22. An early account of this model is Andrei Linde, "The Universe: Inflation out of Chaos" in Leslie (ed.), *Physical Cosmology and Philosophy.* Also, see John Leslie, "Creation Stories, Religious and Atheistic," in Clifford N. Matthews and Roy A Varghese (Eds.), *Cosmic Beginnings and Human Ends: Where Science and Religion Meet* (Chicago, 1995), pp. 339-340.
23. The structure of the quantum vacuum is exceedingly complex. Disturbances in the scalar field cause density perturbations required for the formation of galaxies. They would appear as slight temperature differences in the cosmic background radiation. These were discovered in 1992 by the Cosmic Background Explorer (COBE).
24. *The Selected Poetry and Prose of Shelley,* edited by Harold Bloom (New York, 1966), p. 343. The whole stanza is:

    Worlds on worlds are rolling ever
    From creation to decay,
    Like the bubbles on a river
    Sparkling, bursting, borne away.

25. Delight is the third aspect of the One Reality that we have taken to be the ultimate source of all things (note the Vedantic conception of Sat-Chit-Ananda, which was discussed in Chapter I).
26. For a full examination of this issue, see Sri Aurobindo, *The Life Divine,* Book One, Chapter 11 ("Delight of Existence: The Problem") and Chapter 12 ("Delight of Existence: The Solution"), SABCL, Vol. 18, pp. 91-111. A modernized version of theodicy can be found in John Leslie, *Universes* (London, 1989), Chapter 8. Leslie offers a modified Neoplatonic interpretation in which God is viewed as an abstract ethical requirement rather than an almighty being.
27. Further details can be found in Chapters VII and VIII of the present book.
28. More background on this topic can be found in Donald Goldsmith, *The Runaway Universe: The Race to Find the Future of the Cosmos* (Cambridge, 2000).

CHAPTER VI. TRADITIONAL COSMOLOGY

1. A key figure in the seventeenth century transition to a modern scientific outlook was the French monk Marin Mersenne, Catholic apologist and enthusiast of mechanistic science, who detested magic in all its forms. He regarded proponents of the magical universe as "atheists, animists, and deists"—all subject to what he considered a peculiar kind of madness. But aside from the interesting historical issues this raises, it should be obvious

that nothing was really proven one way or the other regarding the nature of the universe *as a whole.*

2. Titus Burckhardt, *Mirror of the Intellect: Essays on Traditional Science and Sacred Art,* translated and edited by William Stoddart (Albany, 1987), p. 17.
3. Illustrations of this sort can be seen in the numerous astrological pictures that connect the organs of the human body with the stars and planets.
4. The Universal Intellect is sometimes thought of as the macrocosm embracing the whole universe within itself. The universe would in that case be regarded as the microcosm, since these terms are very flexible.
5. Kurt Seligmann, *The History of Magic* (New York, 1948), pp. 128-129.
6. A classic study of the intellectual history of this idea is Arthur O. Lovejoy, *The Great Chain of Being* (New York, 1960).
7. This view of Nature should be compared with the idea in mythical cosmology of the Great Mother as the cosmic creatrix. Also, see the conception of the Divine Mother in Chapters VII and VIII of the present book.
8. Recent attempts like the "Gaia hypothesis" of James Lovelock fail to capture the full-blooded traditional image of the Great Mother. They amount to little more than metaphors applied to supposedly self-regulating natural processes. An excellent portrayal of the vicissitudes that the concept of Nature has undergone since the inception of the Scientific Revolution is Carolyn Merchant, *The Death of Nature: Women, Ecology and the Scientific Revolution* (San Francisco, 1980).
9. The two preeminent modern commentaries on the *Timaeus* in English are A.E. Taylor, *A Commentary on Plato's Timaeus* (London, 1928) and F. M. Cornford, *Plato's Cosmology* (New York, 1952). Cornford's work, which includes a translation and running commentary, is the later of the two and presumably the more reliable.
10. The Greek word *demiourgos* means "public servant," or "craftsman." Plato applied it to the maker of the universe, who constructs the world out of preexisting chaotic materials. A craftsman transforms disorganized things into an ordered and beautiful whole. This idea is comparable, in some ways, with the Universal Mind mentioned in the Stanzas of Dzyan.
11. There was an ancient story told in the Babylonian creation epic, *Enuma Elish,* of the god Marduk shaping the heavens and assigning places to the planetary gods after he had destroyed Tiamat, the embodiment of primordial chaos. Plato may have had access to some version of this story.
12. Although Plato does not say so, it is tempting to see in this Form the universal Archetype of Man, the intelligent creature par excellence.
13. Cornford suggests that Plato may have had access to a visual model of these circles, such as an armillary sphere. This is a plausible assumption, but the instrument was probably not as sophisticated as the later ones we are familiar with.
14. Cornford, *Plato's Cosmology,* p. 97 (*Timaeus* 37 c).
15. Ibid., p. 44 (*Timaeus* 32 c).

16. A presentation of the scientific details in the *Timaeus* can be found in Gregory Vlastos, *Plato's Universe* (Seattle, 1975).
17. Cornford, p. 359 (*Timaeus* 92 c).
18. The English historian, Frances Yates, stressed the historical significance of arguments offered by Isaac Casaubon in 1614, based upon his new dating of the *Corpus Hermeticum,* that the Hermetic writings were late Christian forgeries. But this ignores the possibility that they may contain traces of a more ancient Egyptian cosmological doctrine.
19. See Frances A. Yates, *Giordano Bruno and the Hermetic Tradition* (Chicago, 1964). An example of Bruno's cosmological speculations is his 1584 dialogue *De l'infinito universo e mondi*. An English translation of it can be found in Dorothea Waley Singer, *Giordano Bruno: His Life and Thought* (London, 1950), pp. 225 ff.
20. *Fama Fraternitatis,* in Frances A. Yates, *The Rosicrucian Enlightenment* (London, 1972), p. 238.
21. Frances A. Yates, "The Hermetic Tradition in Renaissance Science," in Charles S. Singleton, *Art, Science, and History in the Renaissance* (Baltimore, 1967), pp. 263-264.
22. See Chapter III, "The Stanzas of Dzyan."
23. Robert Fludd, *The Origin and Structure of the Cosmos,* tr. Patricia Tahil, Magnum Opus Hermetic Sourceworks No. 13 (Edinburgh, 1982). The diagram in the text has been reproduced countless times. Selections from Fludd's writings can be found in William H. Huffman, *Robert Fludd: Essential Readings* (London, 1992).
24. In Tibetan Buddhism, circular diagrams like this are called "mandalas." They are useful devices for visualizing the powers of the psychic world, enabling practitioners to interact safely with them. Similar techniques were used in Europe during the Renaissance. Cosmic diagrams functioned as magical talismans for imprinting an image of the universe in the mind. Giordano Bruno, for example, employed them as a means of opening doors into cosmic consciousness. See Frances A. Yates, *The Art of Memory* (Chicago, 1966).
25. In this representation, man's capacity to participate in the Intellect is not indicated because Fludd is giving prominence to the practical arts that promise a better life on earth. But in other diagrams, he depicts the presence of the Intellect in human beings. See, for example, S. K. Heninger, Jr., *The Cosmographical Glass: Renaissance Diagrams of the Universe* (San Marino, 1977), p. 144 (Figure 84).
26. Seligmann, *A History of Magic,* p. 72.
27. Although Fludd's diagram is probably not the one referred to in *Goethe's Faust* as the "Symbol of the Macrocosm," the feeling it must have inspired is well expressed by Faust's reaction to it:

    What jubilation bursts out of this sight
    Into my senses—now I feel it flowing,
    Youthful, a sacred fountain of delight,
    Through every nerve, my veins are glowing,

Was it a god that made these symbols be
That soothe my feverish unrest,
Filling with joy my anxious breast,
And with mysterious potency
Make nature's hidden powers around me, manifest?

Am I a god? Light grows this page —
In these pure lines my eye can see
Creative nature spread in front of me. . . .
All weaves itself into the whole,
Each living in the other's soul.

Goethe's Faust (translated by Walter Kaufman), op.cit., pp. 97, 99. Eventually, Goethe came to recognize the energizing influence of the "Eternal-Feminine" in all human aspiration (Ibid., p. 503).

28. Creative imagination plays an important role in this process. Man approaches the One by imprinting in his mind magical images associated with the stars and planets. In so doing, he is able to regain his true dignity as the microcosm. This is possible because the celestial spheres are derived from Ideas in the Intelligible World and function as governors of the visible cosmos.
29. A good summary of this interpretation of the model can be found in Titus Burckhardt, *Alchemy: Science of the Cosmos, Science of the Soul* (Baltimore, 1971), Chapter III.
30. Note the famous statement of Pascal's *"libertin,"* which describes the purposeless world of modern scientific cosmology: "The eternal silence of these infinite spaces frightens me." *Pascal's Pensées* (New York, 1958), p. 61.
31. This appeared in the pseudo-Hermetic *Book of the XXIV Philosophers,* which was compiled anonymously in the twelfth century. It was applied to the universe by Renaissance philosophers like Nicholas of Cusa and Giordano Bruno.
32. A traditional reference to evolution may be implicit in the Hindu myth of the ten Avatars, or Incarnations, of Vishnu. They seem to represent an evolutionary progression from a fish through various types of animals, up to the god-men Rama and Krishna, and the future Avatar, Kalki. Note Sri Aurobindo's comments in SABCL, Vol. 22, *Letters on Yoga*, pp. 402-404.
33. The original version of the *I Ching* has been attributed to King Wên of the early Chou dynasty (about 1050 B.C.E.), but no one knows how far back the underlying cosmological outlook goes.
34. See Joseph Needham and Colin Ronan, "Chinese Cosmology," in Hetherington (Ed.), *Cosmology,* pp. 25-32.
35. A widely used edition of this book is Richard Wilhelm (tr.), *The I Ching or Book of Changes* (New York, 1971).
36. Ibid., p. 127.
37. See Ronan, *The Shorter Science and Civilization in China,* pp. 142-150.
38. *Tao Te Ching,* translated by Gia-Fu Feng and Jane English (New York, 1972), Chapter l. There are countless translations of the *Tao Te Ching*. This

one has been chosen because it reflects an intimate feeling for Tao that many others seem to lack.

39. Ibid., Chapter 25.
40. Ibid., Chapter 6.
41. Ibid., Chapter 40.
42. Ibid., Chapter 34.
43. For another version of this story, see Laurence Binyon, *The Flight of the Dragon* (London, 1959), pp. 85-86.

CHAPTER VII. EVOLUTIONARY COSMOLOGY

1. The general historical background is covered in John C. Greene, *Science, Ideology, and World View: Essays in the History of Evolutionary Ideas* (Berkeley, 1981). See especially Chapter 6, "Darwinism as a World View," in which Greene clearly distinguishes between Darwinism as a scientific theory and as a worldview.
2. See Stephen Jay Gould, *Wonderful Life: The Burgess Shale and the Nature of History* (New York, 1989).
3. *Nominalism* is the theory that only particular things exist, whereas universal terms like "humanity" are merely names having no objective existence outside the human mind. For a clear statement of the significance of population thinking, see Ernst Mayr, *The Growth of Biological Thought: Diversity, Evolution, and Inheritance* (Cambridge, 1982), pp. 45-47.
4. Some evolutionary biologists prefer the image of a branching bush to that of a tree. They claim it is a more adequate representation of the idea that evolution is not a goal-directed process. Where the bush is very thick, it means that many related species have radiated as a group in various directions. In this case, none of them can be considered higher or lower in the evolutionary scale.
5. One scientific definition of life is "a self-sustained chemical system that is capable of undergoing Darwinian evolution." But this does not tell us *why* it is capable of doing so.
6. A useful summary of what is known and not known about the origin of life is Robert Shapiro, *Origins: A Skeptic's Guide to the Creation of Life on Earth* (New York, 1986).
7. See the discussion in Chapter I, Section 5, "Worldviews and Cosmology."
8. This phrase is part of the title of a monumental, though somewhat outdated, treatment of the subject by Andrew D. White, *A History of the Warfare of Science with Theology in Christendom* (New York, 1955).
9. Mechanism implies that everything can be explained exclusively in terms of cause and effect.
10. Greene, *Science, Ideology, and World View,* pp. 133 ff.
11. Herbert Spencer, *First Principles* (London, 1946), p. 358.
12. See Plato, *The Sophist,* 246A.

13. Charles Darwin, *On the Origin of Species by Means of Natural Selection: Or the Preservation of Favoured Races in the Struggle for Life* (London, 1947), p. 462.
14. Sri Aurobindo, *Evolution* (SABCL, Vol. 16), p. 230.
15. Ibid., pp. 230-231.
16. There is an English translation by Joseph McCabe (New York and London, 1900).
17. See our previous discussion of fine-tuning and the anthropic principle in Chapter V.
18. Henri Bergson, *Creative Evolution*. Tr. Arthur Mitchell (New York, 1911).
19. Samuel Alexander, *Space, Time and Deity: The Gifford Lectures at Glasgow 1916-1918* (New York, 1966).
20. The fundamental exposition of his ideas is *The Phenomenon of Man* (New York, 1959). Other writings, such as *The Divine Milieu* (New York, 1957) and *The Future of Man* (New York, 1964), fill out his evolutionary vision.
21. Jean Gebser, *The Ever-Present Origin* (Athens: Ohio University Press, 1985).
22. Philosophers sometimes argue that it is logically impossible for eternal being to change. This presupposes that the Infinite is limited by the terms of our mental logic. It may be that in the Infinite, apparent contradictories are really complementary. From this perspective, it could not only change but also evolve without losing its eternal nature. Evolution could be the result of an inherent power of self-concealment and rediscovery.
23. The Mother undertook the practical fulfilment of Sri Aurobindo's vision for the future of mankind. Her writings throw light on every aspect of life and yoga. See the *Collected Works of the Mother.* 17 Volumes. (Pondicherry: Sri Aurobindo Ashram Trust, 1985).
24. This was before Gandhi arrived to lead India to freedom from British domination. Gandhi became immersed in the political struggle, but did not foresee the larger implications of Indian independence for the spiritual destiny of the world.
25. A convenient short biography that presents the salient features of his life is Peter Heehs, *Sri Aurobindo: A Brief Biography* (Delhi, 1989). For an authentic appreciation of his work by a leading sadhak, see M.P. Pandit, *Sri Aurobindo* (The Builders of Indian Philosophy Series), Pondicherry, 1998.
26. In particular, see *The Secret of the Veda* and *Hymns to the Mystic Fire* (SABCL, Volumes 10 and 11).
27. Sri Aurobindo, *The Life Divine,* SABCL, Vol. 18, p. 1.
28. Ibid., p. 3.
29. Ibid., p. 4.
30. Ibid., p. 5. This is especially the case for *vijñāna,* a concept mentioned but not fully developed in Vedantic texts. Sri Aurobindo often equates it with Supermind (see below).
31. For example, see the doctrine of the five sheaths in the *Taittirīya Upaniṣad* (Swami Nikhilananda, *The Upanishads,* Vol. IV, pp. 39-50). This culminates in the upanishadic identification of Ātman and Brahman.
32. Ibid., pp. 67-74.

33. The relation between light and consciousness is not arbitrary, for both are *self*-revealing. This suggests their underlying connection.
34. Compare the story of Zeus and Semele in Greek mythology.
35. Alfred, Lord Tennyson, *In Memoriam,* Section 56. *The Selected Poetry of Tennyson,* edited, with an introduction, by Douglas Bush (New York, 1951), p. 182.
36. Ibid., p. 183. The "veil" is most likely a reference to the Saitic Isis, who is alluded to several times in Tennyson's writings. See Chapter VI on traditional cosmology.
37. Sri Aurobindo, *The Life Divine,* SABCL, Vol. 18, p. 295.
38. Sri Aurobindo, *The Life Divine,* SABCL, Vol. 19, pp. 662, 663.
39. "The face of Truth is covered with a brilliant golden lid [*hiraṇyamaya pātra*]." "Isha Upanishad," *The Upanishads,* SABCL, Vol. 12, p. 67.
40. References to Supermind are scattered throughout *The Life Divine.* See especially Chapters XIV-XVI, SABCL, Vol. 18, pp. 122-149.
41. There is a related story told by the Mother about four great Beings who were emanated at the beginning of creation. The sense of possessing tremendous power led each to act independently, thus introducing division and disorder into the universe. This mistake was the original cause of ignorance and hostility in the material world. To overcome it, a greater consciousness and love had to descend through the intervention of the Divine Mother to help bring the world back to its supreme origin in Freedom and Delight (*Collected Works of the Mother,* Vol. 9, pp. 205-207). Although her story resembles the Kabbalistic myth about Adam Kadmon and the breaking of the vessels that necessitated the work of divine restoration, it probes more deeply into the roots of the world mystery. See Chapter II, Section 7, "Types of Creation Myths".
42. According to Sri Aurobindo, there are various mental regions above the ordinary mind but beneath Supermind; in ascending order they are Higher Mind, Illumined Mind, Intuition, and Overmind. In addition, there is a "subliminal" nature surrounding our surface consciousness that is in close contact with the universal typal levels. None of these powers is fully operative in our lives at present, though they can act upon us in subtle ways. But this topic belongs more to spiritual psychology than to cosmology.
43. Sri Aurobindo, *The Life Divine,* SABCL, Vol. 18, pp. 264-265.
44. A question arises as to whether evolution can occur on planets other than our own. Astronomers continue to discover new planets beyond the solar system, and the chances are that some of them might harbor life. Where there is life, mechanisms like natural selection will no doubt operate to bring about the transformation of species. But *spiritual* evolution is a different matter, since it requires the presence of the psychic being that comes from the Divine itself. According to Sri Aurobindo, *this* kind of evolution is only taking place on earth. Hence the earth still retains a unique status in the cosmos.
45. There is an inscription on a golden tablet found in an Orphic grave in Petelia, South Italy (fourth/third century B.C.E.). The soul is being given

instructions about how to proceed on its after-death path in the underworld. When it reaches the holy spring outside Elysium, it is advised to tell the guardians of the spring:

> Say, "I am a child of Earth and starry Heaven;
> But my race is of Heaven (alone)."

W.K.C. Guthrie, *Orpheus and Greek Religion: A Study of the Orphic Movement* (New York, 1966), p. 173.

46. An interesting parallel to this can be found in the Hermetic treatise, *Poimandres*, where the cosmic Man (*Anthropos*) saw his Divine Form reflected in Nature and, falling in love with it, willed to dwell therein as the soul (*Hermetica,* edited and translated into English by Walter Scott, pp. 121-122). In the Hermetica, the object is to release the soul so that it can return to the Heavenly Realm from which it fell. For Sri Aurobindo, on the other hand, the Divine has come into the universe as the soul in order to establish itself here through evolution.
47. Spinoza, in an entirely different context, had an inkling of the nature of this love. In the *Ethics,* near the end of a long philosophical exposition on the universe as a single substance, he arrived at what he called "the intellectual love of God." He states: *"The intellectual love of the mind toward God is the very love with which He loves Himself, not in so far as He is infinite, but in so far as He can be manifested through the essence of the human mind, considered under the form of eternity; that is to say, the intellectual love of the mind toward God is part of the infinite love with which God loves Himself."* Benedict de Spinoza, *Ethics and On the Improvement of the Understanding* (New York, 1955), Part Five, Proposition XXXVI, p. 274.
48. Sri Aurobindo, *The Life Divine,* SABCL, Vol. 19, pp. 1069-1070.

CHAPTER VIII. COSMIC POETRY

1. Sri Aurobindo, *Essays on the Gita* (SABCL, Vol. 13).
2. Sri Krishna Prem, *The Yoga of the Bhagavat Gita* (Baltimore, 1973).
3. This is a title in the UNESCO Indian translation series. The book is a thirteenth century Marathi commentary on the Gita. There is also an earlier translation by Manu Subeda, *Gita Explained* by Dynaneshwar Maharaj (Palli Hill, Bandra, 1932).
4. The Gita accepts the Vedantic view of spiritual liberation (*mokṣa*) as the ultimate goal of life, but supplements it with a many-sided yoga of knowledge, works, and devotion. Stress is placed on the performance of desireless action (*niṣkāma karma*) in the world.
5. *Bhagavad Gita and Its Message* (With Text, Translation and Sri Aurobindo's Commentary), edited by Anilbaran Roy (Pondicherry, 1995), I. 46.
6. Ibid., VII. 6-7.
7. Ibid., XV.7.
8. Ibid., XI. This inner vision is granted to Arjuna through Krishna's mysterious power (*yogamāyā*) to reveal his cosmic form. It is the same

power by which the Godhead manifests itself in the process of cosmic creation (see *Bhagavad Gita and Its Message,* IV. 6, VII. 25).

9. Ibid., XI. 9-14.
10. Ibid., XI. 32.
11. Ibid., XI. 33.
12. Ibid., IX. 33.
13. Joseph Needham claims that Lucretius did not have in mind the later concept of a "law of nature." Lucretius advocated natural and causal explanations of natural phenomena, but generally talked of "principles" rather than "laws." Needham attributes this to the Epicurean denial that the gods had created the world or took an interest in it. They did not rule the universe and so did not establish "laws" for it. See Ronan, *The Shorter Science and Civilization in China:* Vol.1, pp. 286-287.
14. Lucretius, *The Nature of the Universe,* translated with an introduction by Ronald Latham (Baltimore, 1962), p. 128.
15. Ibid., pp. 128-129.
16. Ibid., p. 28. The Greek word *atomos* means uncuttable; hence an "atom" is literally indestructible. This is contrary to modern usage, in which atoms are visualized as systems of particles. Lucretius does not actually use this word but speaks rather of seeds, first bodies, etc.; his "atoms" would correspond better to what are now called elementary particles.
17. Although Lucretius' view of the universe is basically mechanistic, he follows the Greek philosopher Epicurus in allowing a spontaneous swerve (*clinamen*) of the atoms from the downward motion caused by their weight. But this is not the result of conscious choice, so his general outlook does not deviate altogether from blind mechanism.
18. *The Nature of the Universe,* p. 31.
19. Ibid., p. 33.
20. The earliest Greek atomists on record are Leucippus and Democritus, who belong to the fifth century B.C.E.
21. *The Nature of the Universe,* p. 31.
22. *The Divine Comedy of Dante Alighieri,* a verse translation by Allen Mandelbaum. 3 volumes (New York, 1984), Vol. I, *Inferno,* Canto I, p. 9.
23. *Inferno,* Canto XXXIV, p. 317.
24. *The Divine Comedy of Dante Alighieri,* Vol. II, *Purgatorio,* Canto I, p. 3.
25. *Purgatorio,* Canto XXXIII, p. 313.
26. At one point in his ascent through the heavens, Dante looks down through the starry spheres at the earth far below and marvels at its insignificance in the cosmos. He refers to it as "the little threshing floor that so incites our savagery." (*The Divine Comedy of Dante Alighieri,* Vol. III, *Paradiso,* Canto XXII, p. 203.) This is a common perception in the early stages of cosmic consciousness. A comparable experience is described in Cicero's cosmological fragment known as *The Dream of Scipio.*
27. The symbolism of the rose appears everywhere in medieval art and literature, particularly in the stained glass windows of the great Gothic cathedrals. The magnificent thirteenth century rose window in the north transept of Notre Dame de Paris is an outstanding example. The

multicolored panes radiating from the center represent the universe in all its glory. At the center, the Virgin Mary with the Christ-child in her lap is depicted as the focus of all creation. When divested of its theological trappings, this window has deep cosmological significance. Mary can be seen as a symbol of the Divine Mother holding in her bosom the newly born soul (psychic being), the child of the Mother, who is destined to evolve into a divine being on earth.

28. *The Divine Comedy,* Vol. III, *Paradiso,* Canto XXXIII, p. 297.
29. Ibid., pp. 301-303, *et passim.* Although the three circles are usually interpreted as the Christian Trinity, they are also suggestive of the three modes of consciousness distinguished by Sri Aurobindo. The second circle would then represent cosmic consciousness.
30. As the Mother once said, "He has crammed the whole universe in a single book." *Sweet Mother: Harmonies of Light,* Words recollected by Mona Sarkar (Pondicherry, 1978), p. 22.
31. Tales of a Goddess reclaiming someone from the dead can be found in many cultures. The Egyptians tell of Isis seeking the body of Osiris, and the Babylonians of Ishtar descending into the underworld to rescue Tammuz. This theme is repeated, with variations, in other myths. But these myths are only concerned with her pursuit of a lost lover. A larger vision of cosmic evolution does not play a role in them.
32. Compare the Hindu myth of the Boar Avatar (Varāha), who rescued the Earth-Goddess from a great flood by diving into the sea and raising her up on his tusks.
33. Sri Aurobindo, *Savitri,* Book One, Canto Two, "The Issue." SABCL, Vol. 28, p. 21.
34. His inner journey is described in great detail in Book Two, "The Book of the Traveller of the Worlds," Cantos One to Fifteen.
35. Book Three, Canto Two, p. 313.
36. Book Three, Canto Three, p. 317.
37. Book Three, Canto Four, p. 341.
38. Ibid.
39. Ibid., pp. 343-344.
40. Ibid., p. 345.
41. Ibid., p. 346.
42. Book Ten, Canto Two, p. 619.
43. Book Ten, Canto Three, p. 630.
44. Ibid., p. 633.
45. Ibid., p. 638.
46. Book Twelve, Epilogue, p. 724.
47. It is worth recalling Walt Whitman's haunting poem, "Out of the Cradle Endlessly Rocking," where the rising and falling of the Mother-sea suggests a rocking cradle.

CONCLUDING REMARKS

1. The reader will recall that the number *four* has an inner significance that goes far beyond its usefulness as a convenient peg on which to hang concepts. It represents *integrality;* this is reflected in the "four faces" of the universe, which are inseparable aspects of a unified whole.
2. The world-saving power of the Divine Mother is a major theme of the Hindu myth of Durgā slaying the Buffalo Demon Mahiṣa. Her autumn festival, Durgā Pūjā, is still celebrated throughout India.
3. Sri Aurobindo, *Thoughts and Glimpses,* SABCL, Vol. 16, p. 384. Honey (*madhu*) is an upanishadic term for *ānanda*, the divine delight of existence.
4. It is worth noting that the Divine appeared to Sri Ramakrishna in the form of Kālī as the Mother of the Universe to remind him of the divine nature of the world. This was a powerful inner realization for him and he gave himself entirely to her. Yet she did not move him to attempt transformation on the physical plane.
5. "Ode on a Grecian Urn" Stanza V, *The Selected Poetry of Keats,* edited by Paul de Man (New York, 1966), p. 253. Also see *Endymion,* Book I, Lines 1-33, pp. 92-93.
6. It has been said that the winds of grace are always blowing, but that we must hoist our sails before they can move us. Once a life has been genuinely offered to the Divine, its course is set and one does not think much about it any longer. We simply do the best we can in what is given us to be accomplished.
7. Sri Aurobindo, *Savitri,* SABCL, Vol. 28, p. 55.

BIBLIOGRAPHY

The literature relating to the four types of cosmology discussed in this book is far too extensive to be adequately represented here. Most of the titles listed have been cited in the endnotes. Many works by Sri Aurobindo that are included in the SABCL are also available separately. His major writings are published in handsome volumes by Lotus Light Publications, Box 325, Twin Lakes, WI 53181 U.S.A. Lotus Press also offers a CD ROM with substantial selections from Sri Aurobindo's writings: *Sri Aurobindo: Selected Writings* (Software CD ROM version for Macintosh and Windows).

Aczel, Amir D. *God's Equation: Einstein, Relativity, and the Expanding Universe.* New York: Four Walls Eight Windows, 1999.

Alexander, H. G. (ed.). *The Leibniz-Clark Correspondence*. Manchester: Manchester University Press, 1956.

Alexander, Samuel. *Space, Time, and Deity: The Gifford Lectures at Glasgow, 1916-1918.* 2 volumes. 1920. Reprint. New York: Dover, 1966.

Aveni, Anthony. *Ancient Astronomers.* Washington: St. Remy Press, 1993.

———. *Stairways to the Stars: Skywatching in Three Great Cultures.* New York: John Wiley & Sons, 1997.

Aurobindo, Sri. Sri Aurobindo Birth Centenary Library (SABCL). 30 volumes. Pondicherry: Sri Aurobindo Ashram Trust, 1973.

Vol. 9: *The Future Poetry* (1917-20).

Vol. 10: *The Secret of the Veda* (1914-16).

Vol. 11: *Hymns to the Mystic Fire* (1946, 1952).

Vol. 12: *The Upanishads* (1909-20).

Vol. 13: *Essays on the Gita* (1916-20).

Vol. 16: *The Supramental Manifestation and Other Writings* (1949-50).

Vols. 18, 19: *The Life Divine,* rev. ed. (1943-44; first published 1914-19).

Vols. 20, 21: *The Synthesis of Yoga,* rev. ed. (1959; first published 1914-21).

Vol. 22: *Letters on Yoga* (1947+).

Vols. 28, 29: *Savitri: A Legend and a Symbol* (1950-51).

Bachofen, J. J. *Myth, Religion, & Mother Right: Selected Writings of J. J. Bachofen.* 1967. Reprint. Princeton: Princeton University Press, 1973.

Barrow, J. D. and F. J. Tipler. *The Anthropic Cosmological Principle.* New York: Oxford University Press, 1986.

Beaver, Harold (ed.). *The Science Fiction of Edgar Allan Poe*. New York: Penguin, 1976.

Bergson, Henri. *Creative Evolution.* Tr. Arthur Mitchell. New York: Random House, 1911.

Binyon, Laurence. *The Flight of the Dragon: An Essay on the Theory and Practice of Art in China and Japan.* 1911. Reprint. London: John Murray, 1959.

Blavatsky, H. P. *The Secret Doctrine: The Synthesis of Science, Religion, and Philosophy.* 1888. Reprint. 2 volumes. Pasadena: Theosophical Press, 1952.

Bohm, David. *Wholeness and the Implicate Order.* 1980. Reprint. London: Ark Paperbacks, 1983.

Breuer, Reinhard. *The Anthropic Principle: Man as the Focal Point of Nature.* Translated by Harry Newman and Mark Lowery. Cambridge: Birkhäuser Boston, 1991.

Bucke, Richard M. *Cosmic Consciousness: A Study in the Evolution of the Human Mind.* 1901. Reprint. New York: E. P. Dutton, 1959.

Burckhardt, Titus. *Alchemy: Science of the Cosmos, Science of the Soul.* Tr. William Stoddart. 1962. Reprint. Baltimore: Penguin, 1971.

———. *Mirror of the Intellect: Essays on Traditional Science and Sacred Art.* Tr. William Stoddart. Albany: SUNY Press, 1987.

Burtt, E. A. *The Metaphysical Foundations of Modern Physical Science.* London: Routledge and Kegan Paul Ltd., 1949.

Campbell, Bruce F. *Ancient Wisdom Revived: A History of the Theosophical Movement.* Berkeley: University of California Press, 1980.

Campbell, Joseph. *Myths to Live By.* New York: Viking Press, 1973.

———. *The Mythic Image.* Princeton: Princeton University Press, 1974.

———. *The Inner Reaches of Outer Space: Metaphor as Myth and as Religion.* New York: Harper and Row, 1988.

Capra, Fritjof. *The Tao of Physics: An Exploration of the Parallels between Modern Physics and Eastern Mysticism.* Berkeley: Shambala, 1975.

Coomaraswamy, Ananda K. *The Dance of Shiva: On Indian Art and Culture.* New York: The Noonday Press, 1957.

Cornford, F. M. *Plato's Cosmology: The* Timaeus *of Plato translated with a running commentary.* 1937. Reprint. New York: The Humanities Press, 1952.

Cranston, Sylvia. *H.P.B.: The Extraordinary Life and Influence of Helena Blavatsky, Founder of the Modern Theosophical Movement.* New York: G. P. Putnam's Sons, 1993.

Darwin, Charles. *On the Origin of Species by Means of Natural Selection: Or the Preservation of Favoured Races in the Struggle for Life.* 1859. Reprint. London: J. M. Dent & Sons, 1947.

De Santillana, Georgio and Hertha von Dechend. *Hamlet's Mill: An Essay Investigating the Origins of Human Knowledge and its Transmission Through Myth.* Boston: David R. Godine, 1977.

Dnyaneshwar Maharaj. *Gita Explained.* Tr. Manu Subeda. Palli Hill, Bandra, 1932.

Dundes, Alan (ed.). *Sacred Narrative: Readings in the Theory of Myth.* Berkeley: University of California Press, 1984.

Eddington, Arthur. *The Expanding Universe.* 1933. Reprint. Ann Arbor: University of Michigan Press, 1958.

Einstein, Albert. *Relativity: The Special and General Theory: A Popular Exposition.* Authorized translation by Robert W. Lawson, 1921. Reprint. New York: Crown, 1961.

———."Foreword" *to Spinoza Dictionary.* Ed. Dagobert D. Runes. New York: Philosophical Library, 1951

———. *Ideas and Opinions.* Tr. Sonja Bargmann. New York: Crown, 1954.

Einstein, Albert and Infeld, Leopold. *The Evolution of Physics: From Early Concepts to Relativity and Quanta*. New York: Simon & Schuster, 1938.

Eliade, Mircea. *Cosmos and History: The Myth of the Eternal Return*. Tr. Willard R. Trask. New York: Harper & Row, 1959.

Fludd, Robert. *The Origin and Structure of the Cosmos*. Translated by Patricia Tahil. Introduction by Adam McLean. Edinburgh: Magnum Opus Hermetic Sourceworks No. 13, 1982.

Feuerstein, George, Subhash Kak, and David Frawley. *In Search of the Cradle of Civilization: New Light on Ancient India*. Wheaton: Quest Books (Theosophical Publishing House), 1995.

Gamow, George. *The Creation of the Universe*. 1952. Reprint. New York: Bantam, 1970.

Gia-Fu Feng and Jane English. *Tao Te Ching*. New York: Vintage Books,1972.

Gebser, Jean. *The Ever-Present Origin*. Authorized Translation by Noel Barstad with Algis Mickunas. Athens: Ohio University Press, 1985.

Gimbutas, Marija. *The Goddesses and Gods of Old Europe 6500-3500 BC: Myths and Cult Images*. 1974. Reprint. Berkeley: University of California Press, 1982.

———. *The Language of the Goddess*. San Francisco: Harper Collins, 1991.

Goethe, J.W., *Goethe's Faust*. The original German and a new translation and introduction by Walter Kaufmann. Garden City: Anchor Books, 1961.

Goldsmith, Donald. *The Runaway Universe: The Race to Find the Future of the Cosmos*. Cambridge: Perseus Books, 1999.

Gould, Stephen Jay. *Wonderful Life: The Burgess Shale and the Nature of History*. New York: W.W. Norton, 1989.

Greene, Brian. *The Elegant Universe: Superstrings, Hidden Dimensions, and the Quest for the Ultimate Theory*. New York: W.W. Norton, 1999.

———. *The Fabric of the Cosmos: Space, Time, and the Texture of Reality*. New York: Alfred A. Knopf, 2004.

Greene, John C. *Science, Ideology, and World View: Essays in the History of Evolutionary Ideas*. Berkeley: University of California Press, 1981.

Griffith, Ralph T.H. (tr.). *The Hymns of the Rig Veda*. 1889. Reprint. 2 volumes. Varanasi: The Chowkhamba Sanskrit Series Office, 1963.

Guthrie, W. K. C. *Orpheus and Greek Religion: A Study of the Orphic Movement*. New York: W.W. Norton, 1966.

Haeckel, Ernst. *The Riddle of the Universe*. Tr. Joseph McCabe. New York: Harper & Brothers, 1900.

Hallyn, Fernand. *The Poetic Structure of the World: Copernicus and Kepler*. Translated by Donald M. Leslie. New York: Zone Books, 1993.

Hamilton, Edith and Huntington Cairns (eds.). *Plato: Collected Dialogues*. Princeton: Princeton University Press, 1961.

Harrison, Edward R. *Cosmology: The Science of the Universe*. Cambridge: Cambridge University Press, 1981.

———. *Darkness at Night: A Riddle of the Universe*. Cambridge: Harvard University Press, 1987.

Heehs, Peter. *Sri Aurobindo: A Brief Biography*. Delhi: Oxford University Press, 1989.

Heninger, S.K., Jr. *Touches of Sweet Harmony: Pythagorean Cosmology and Renaissance Poetics*. San Marino: The Huntington Library, 1974.

———. *The Cosmographical Glass: Renaissance Diagrams of the Universe*. San Marino: The Huntington Library, 1977.

Hetherington, Norris S. (ed.). *Cosmology: Historical, Literary, Philosophical, Religious and Scientific Perspectives*. New York: Garland Publishing, 1993.

Hoffman, Banesh. *Albert Einstein: Creator and Rebel* (with the collaboration of Helen Dukas). New York: Viking Press, 1972.

Holy Bible (containing the Old and New Testaments). Revised Standard Version. Teaneck: Cokesbury, 1946.

Hotz, Michael (ed.) *Holding the Lotus to the Rock: The Autobiography of Sokei-an, America's First Zen Master*. New York: Four Walls Eight Windows, 2002.

Huffman, William H. (ed.). *Robert Fludd: Essential Readings*. London: The Aquarian Press, 1992.

Jammer, Max. *Einstein and Religion: Physics and Theology*. Princeton: Princeton University Press, 1999.

Jnaneshvar, Shri. *Jnaneshvari*. Translated from the Marathi by V.G. Pradhan and edited with an Introduction by H.M. Lambert. Albany: SUNY Press, 1987.

Jung, Carl G. *Man and His Symbols*. 1964. Reprint. New York: Dell Publishing, 1976.

Keats, John. *The Selected Poetry of Keats*. Edited by Paul de Man (The Signet Classic Poetry Series). New York: New American Library, 1966.

Kinsley, David. *Visions of the Divine Feminine in the Hindu Religious Tradition*. Berkeley: University of California Press, 1988.

———. *The Goddesses' Mirror: Visions of the Divine From East and West*. New York: SUNY Press, 1989.

Koyré, Alexandre. *From the Closed World to the Infinite Universe*. 1957. Reprint. New York: Harper & Brothers, 1958.

Kragh, Helge. *Cosmology and Controversy: The Historical Development of the Two Theories of the Universe*. Princeton: Princeton University Press, 1995.

Krishna Prem, Sri. *The Yoga of the Bhagavat Gita*. 1938. Reprint. Baltimore: Penguin, 1973.

Krishna Prem, Sri and Sri Madhava Ashish. *Man the Measure of All Things in the Stanzas of Dzyan*. Madras: Theosophical Publishing House, 1966.

Larsen, Stephen and Robin Larsen. *A Fire in the Mind: The Life of Joseph Campbell*. New York: Doubleday, 1991.

Leslie, John. *Universes*. New York: Routledge, 1989.

———. *Physical Cosmology and Philosophy*. Edited, with introduction and annotated bibliography. New York: Macmillan, 1990.

Lovejoy, Arthur O. *The Great Chain of Being: A Study of the History of an Idea*. 1936. Reprint. New York: Harper & Brothers, 1960.

Lucretius. *The Nature of the Universe*. Translated with an introduction by R. E. Latham. 1951. Reprint. Baltimore: Penguin, 1962.

Malinowski, Bronislaw. *Magic, Science and Religion and Other Essays*. Garden City: Doubleday, 1954.

Mandelbaum, Allen (tr.). *The Divine Comedy of Dante Alighieri*. 3 vols. New York: Bantam Books, 1984.

Matt, Daniel C. *The Essential Kabbalah: The Heart of Jewish Mysticism.* San Francisco: HarperCollins, 1996.

Matthew, Clifford N. and Roy A Varghese. (eds.). *Cosmic Beginnings and Human Ends: Where Science and Religion Meet.* Chicago: Open Court, 1995.

Mayr, Ernst. *The Growth of Biological Thought: Diversity, Evolution, and Inheritance.* Cambridge: Harvard University Press, 1982.

McIntyre, J. Lewis. *Giordano Bruno: Mystic Martyr 1548-1600.* London: Macmillan & Co., Ltd., 1903.

Mendoza, Ramon G. *The Acentric Labyrinth: Giordano Bruno's Prelude to Contemporary Cosmology.* Rockport, MA: Element Books, Inc., 1995.

Merchant, Carolyn. *The Death of Nature: Women, Ecology and the Scientific Revolution.* San Francisco: Harper & Row, 1980.

Michel, Paul-Henri. *The Cosmology of Giordano Bruno.* Tr. R.E.W. Maddison. London: Methuen, 1973.

Mother, The. *Collected Works of the Mother* (Centenary edition, Vol. 4). Pondicherry: Sri Aurobindo Ashram, 1984.

Munitz, Milton K. (ed.) *Theories of the Universe: From Babylonian Myth to Modern Science.* New York: The Free Press, 1957.

Nikhilananda, Swami (tr.). *The Upanishads.* 4 volumes. New York: Bonanza Books, 1949.

Olsen, Carl (ed.). *The Book of the Goddess Past and Present: An Introduction to Her Religion.* New York: Crossroad, 1990.

Pandit, M. P. *Sri Aurobindo* (The Builders of Indian Philosophy Series). Pondicherry: Dipti Trust, Sri Aurobindo Ashram, 1998.

Pascal, Blaise. *Pascal's Pensées.* Tr. W. F. Trotter. New York: E. P. Dutton, 1958.

Poe, Edgar Allan. *Eureka: An Essay on the Material and Spiritual Universe.* New York: Funk & Wagnalls, 1848.

Rees, Martin. *Before the Beginning: Our Universe and Others.* Reading: Helix, 1998.

Ronan, Colin A. *The Shorter Science and Civilisation in China (Vol I): An Abridgement of Joseph Needham's Original Text.* 1978. Reprint. Cambridge: Cambridge University Press, 1980.

Roy, Anilbaran (ed.). *Bhagavad Gita and Its Message* (With Text, Translation and Sri Aurobindo's Commentary). Pondicherry: Sri Aurobindo Ashram Trust, 1995.

Roy, Dilip Kumar. *Yogi Sri Krishnaprem.* Bombay: Bharatiya Vidya Bhavan, 1968.

Sachs, Mendel. *Relativity in Our Time: From Physics to Human Relations.* London: Taylor & Francis, 1993.

Scholem, Gershom. *Kabbalah.* New York: Penguin, 1978.

Scott, Walter, (tr.). *Hermetica: The Ancient Greek and Latin Writings Which Contain Religious or Philosophic Teachings Ascribed to Hermes Trismegistus.* 1924-36. Reprint. Boulder: Hermes House-Great Eastern, 1982.

Segal, Robert A. *Joseph Campbell, An Introduction.* New York: Penguin, 1989.

Seligmann, Kurt. *The History of Magic.* New York: Pantheon, 1948.

Shapiro, Robert. *Origins: A Skeptic's Guide to the Creation of Life on Earth*. New York: Bantam, 1987.

Shelley, Percy Bysshe. *The Selected Poetry and Prose of Shelley*. Edited by Harold Bloom (The Signet Classic Poetry Series). New York: New American Library, 1966.

Singer, Dorothea Waley. *Giordano Bruno: His Life and Thought, with an Annotated Translation of His Work On the Infinite Universe and Worlds*. New York: Henry Schuman, 1950.

Singleton, Charles S. (ed.). *Art, Science, and History in the Renaissance*. Baltimore, MD: John Hopkins Press, 1967.

Smith, Robert. *The Expanding Universe: Astronomy's 'Great Debate' 1900-1931*. Cambridge: Cambridge University Press, 1982.

Sokei-An. *Cat's Yawn*. New York: The First Zen Institute of America, 1947.

Sonnert, Gerhard. *Einstein and Culture*. New York: Humanity Books, an imprint of Prometheus Books, 2005.

Spencer, Herbert. *First Principles*. 1862. Reprint. London: Watts & Co., 1946.

Spinoza, Benedict. *Ethics and On the Improvement of the Understanding*. New York: Hafner, 1955.

Taylor, A. E. *A Commentary on Plato's Timaeus*. 1928. Reprint. Oxford: Clarendon Press, 1962.

Teilhard de Chardin, Pierre. *The Divine Milieu*. New York: Harper & Row, 1960.

———. *The Phenomenon of Man*. New York: Harper & Row, 1965.

———. *The Future of Man*. London: Harper & Row, 1969.

Tennyson, Alfred, Lord. *The Selected Poetry of Tennyson*. Edited, with an introduction, by Douglas Bush (Modern Library College Edition). New York: Random House, Inc., 1951.

Tolman, Richard C. *Relativity, Thermodynamics, and Cosmology*. 1934. Reprint. New York: Dover, 1987.

Underhill, Evelyn. *Mysticism: A Study in the Nature and Development of Man's Spiritual Consciousness*. New York: The Noonday Press, 1955.

Vlastos, Gregory. *Plato's Universe*. Seattle: University of Washington Press, 1975.

Weinberg, Steven. *The First Three Minutes: A Modern View of the Universe*. New York: Basic Books, 1977.

———. *Dreams of a Final Theory: The Scientist's Search for the Ultimate Laws of Nature*. New York: Vintage, 1994.

Weiner, Philip P. (ed.). *Leibniz: Selections*. New York: Charles Scribner's Sons, 1951.

White, Andrew D. *A History of the Warfare of Science with Theology in Christendom*. 1896. Reprint. New York: George Braziller, 1955.

Whitehead, Alfred North. *Science and the Modern World*. 1925. Reprint. New York: The Free Press, 1969.

Whitman, Walt. *Leaves of Grass*. 1892. Reprint. New York: Bantam, 1983.

Wilhelm, Richard (tr.). *The I Ching or Book of Changes*. 1950. Reprint. Bollingen Series XIX. Princeton: Princeton University Press, 1971.

Wordsworth, William. *Wordsworth.* Selected, with an introduction and notes, by David Ferry (The Laurel Poetry Series). New York: Dell Publishing Co., 1959.

Yates, Frances A. *Giordano Bruno and the Hermetic Tradition.* Chicago: The University of Chicago Press, 1964.

———. *The Art of Memory.* Chicago: The University of Chicago Press, 1966.

———. *The Rosicrucian Enlightenment.* London: Routledge & Kegan Paul, 1972.

Yogananda, Paramhansa. *The Rubaiyat of Omar Khayyam Explained.* Nevada City, California: Crystal Clarity Publishers, 1994.

INDEX

D

E

F

G

H

I

J

K

L

M

U

V

W

Y

Z